The Protest of
A Troubled Protestant

HAROLD O. J. BROWN

THE PROTEST OF

A TROUBLED

PROTESTANT

ARLINGTON HOUSE   *New Rochelle, New York*

SBN 87000-046-2

Library of Congress Catalog Card Number 68-57437

MANUFACTURED IN THE UNITED STATES OF AMERICA

To my parents

· Contents ·

· Acknowledgments ·

Among the many teachers, colleagues, and friends who by their instruction, advice, criticism and example have contributed greatly to my Christian and theological education, and thus directly or indirectly to the writing of this book, I would like to mention the following by name: Harvard Divinity School professors and ex-professors George H. Williams, Georges Florovsky, and James Luther Adams, who will not necessarily agree with what I have written, but each of whom has set an outstanding example of fidelity, personal integrity, and scholarship; to my senior colleagues and teachers in the ministry, Harold John Ockenga, Otto Rodenberg, and Francis A. Schaeffer, each being a courageous and distinctive defender of the truth and the validity of the historic Christian faith; and to philosopher Herman Dooyeweerd of Amsterdam, who together with Francis Schaeffer has done so much to forge the intellectual, critical, and spiritual weapons with which to meet the secular attack on eternal truths.

There is little virtue and great danger for a theologian in trying to be original. For what is of value in this book, I am most often indebted to one or more of the men named above, and to other colleagues and friends, many of them different in religious affiliation or theological conviction, but exemplary in fairness of criticism, scholarly integrity, and personal loyalty. The faults are my own.

I wish to express my thanks to the many publishers who have given permission to quote from works under copyright, who are acknowledged by name in the text. Finally I want to discharge a tiny fraction of my obligation to my wife Grace for her share in this book by acknowledging her typing and reading of the manuscript and reading of the proofs.

· Author's Preface ·

Protest is very much in the air today, even more so now than when the present work was first conceived and begun late in 1966. This book is certainly a protest. In large measure it is a reaction, vehement if not violent, to conditions with which the author has been faced as a minister, university chaplain, and just as a Christian trying to bear witness to a message which is "the power of God unto salvation," but of which so much of the church seems ashamed.

Like all protests, it takes its shape in large measure from those particular abuses which have impressed its author. They are not the only problems within Christendom; they may not even be the most significant ones. But they exist, and they are evils. Therefore they must be exposed, explained, and fought.

There is personal invective in this book, more perhaps than there should be. Yet in a sense that ought to be understandable, even if not commendable. Treachery within one's own ranks always produces bitterer antagonism than honest opposition from outside, and what Christendom is facing is treachery on a grand scale.

Yet, having begun as a protest in the modern sense, this book would be a disservice to the cause of Christianity if it were not also a protest in the older sense (*protestari*, Latin: to testify *for*), a positive testimony. Because, in the smoke of battle, the positive side may come too short, let me say this clearly: Christians can and must indeed protest *against* theological error and moral evil, especially within their own ranks. They must be willing to be negative about doctrinal errors, for false teachings poison and destroy those who are looking for truth. Fundamentally, however, the Christian faith is a positive thing. The Gospel of Jesus Christ is God's answer to man's lostness, in the twentieth century as in the first. Therefore, the Christian must have the courage to attest the truth and the greatness of God's plan, and to say with St. Paul, "I am not ashamed of the Gospel of Christ, for it is the power of God unto salvation, to everyone who believes, to the Jew first, and also to the Greek" (Romans 1:16).

Lausanne, Switzerland
January 6, 1969. The Feast of the
Manifestations of Christ to the Nations.

The Protest of
A Troubled Protestant

CHAPTER I

· FACT AND FOLLY ·

Let no man deceive himself. If any man among you appears to be wise in this world, let him become a fool, that he may become wise.

ST. PAUL, I CORINTHIANS 3:18

---

1. Is Theology a Science?

Theology is called the science of the knowledge of God. It is an ambiguous, difficult kind of science, because God is not readily available for investigation and analysis. In a sense, the more of a science theology is, the less useful it is as a tool to expand one's knowledge of God.

The "scientific," academic, scholarly aspect of Christian theology involves subjecting the "data" to careful analysis. The data of theology are the biblical documents themselves and the experience of the church through the ages. They are in themselves limited, selective, and impossible to reproduce under experimental conditions. Every attempt to create a complete theological system on the basis of these limited data is going to involve at least *some* extrapolation and speculation. The most interesting, exciting, or "radical" theologies are those which involve the most speculation—and they are precisely the ones most apt to be unreliable when it comes to understanding what God is really like.

The God of the Bible and of historic Christianity is a living, personal God. It is difficult if not impossible to get to know another human being by mere objective study and analysis of his characteristics. The typical human who is subjected to a long period of analysis and study by people who are not interested in him as a person does not like it, and will try to escape it as rapidly as possible. Under most circumstances, a personal relationship is indispensable for the knowledge of another human being. For this reason, we cannot really *know* Julius Caesar—or even Martin Luther, about whom literally thousands of different books have been written, and who left us over sixty volumes of collected works.

If we cannot be very sure of our knowledge of a man whom we have studied objectively but never met, we certainly can have no confidence in a knowledge of God which is based only on study. With him as with another human being a personal relationship is indispensable. But a personal relationship with God must either be one of unconditional obedience, or one of unqualified rebellion. Neither of these is neutral, and therefore both of them are detrimental to the objectivity and disinterestedness required of a true science.

In a very real sense, then, *scientific* theology is an impossibility. St. Paul himself wrote, ". . . a natural man does not accept the things of the Spirit of God; for they are foolishness to him, and he cannot understand them, because they are spiritually appraised" (I Corinthians 2:14, N.A.S.B.[1]). As soon as a science begins to require literal *inspiration,* i.e. the work of the Holy Spirit, *Spiritus Sanctus,* it has obviously ceased to be an objective science comparable to other objective sciences. Unless theology *does* have this particular kind of inspiration, it remains the work of the "natural man."[2] By this expression, St. Paul means precisely the man who is not guided by the Holy Spirit, but who is thrown entirely upon his own intellectual resources. Such a man cannot help but misunderstand the things of the Spirit of God and find them foolishness.

This is a drastic limitation which stands at the beginning of any theological enterprise. Man, particularly sophisticated, self-confident *homo academicus,* resents any suggestion that his capacity to understand what he studies is subject to any barrier at all. It is an assumption of most scientific study that the handicap of man's finitude, of his infinitesimal smallness and shortness of life in this universe, will slowly but surely be overcome with the passage of time and the careful accumulation of knowledge. Indisputably the natural sciences make progress in understanding the universe, although occasionally even they take a wrong turn in investigation and get bogged down for an embarrassingly long time. But can we speak of "progress" in theology? Admittedly modern scientists like Albert Einstein and Werner Heisenberg have added much more to our accurate knowledge of the real universe than have ancient philosophers like Aristotle. But do we really think that modern theologians, because they are more recent, know more of God than St. Paul, or Augustine or Luther or John Wesley? That is a different matter.

Questions of this type imply that there is something fundamentally wrong with *scientific* theology. Anyone who makes such an implication can expect to be criticized as unscientific, obscurantist, fundamentalist, or, to use a term of reproach peculiar to professional theologians, "pietistic." In fact, the shoe is on the other foot. In any science, it is unscientific to neglect the basic requirement for obtaining knowledge. In studying the cells of the human body, it would be ridiculous to neglect to use the instrument which makes it possible to see them, the microscope. Is it less ridiculous to neglect the basic requirement for a true science of theology, which is a personal relationship of obedience to God, and dependence on his Holy Spirit? To attempt to do without the Holy Spirit is even more foolish than to attempt to do without the microscope in the study of cells: it is rather as though one were to try to do without light itself.

It is paradoxical that the expression "pietistic" should be a term of reproach in academic theological circles. Can there be a knowledge of God which does not lead to true piety, to the fear and the love of God? John Calvin, in his famous *Institutes of the Christian Religion*,[3] a very significant and influential work of Reformation theology, writes, ". . . we shall not say that, properly speaking, God is known where there is no religion or piety" (Book I:ii:1). In other words, where there is not an active trust of God and reverence for him, there is no true knowledge of him. Academic theology shies away from expressions of trust and reverence. This results partly from the common academic tendency to exalt detachment and to decry enthusiasm. But what hope is there for theology without *enthusiasm*, which is actually the whole point of it? (From the Greek *en*, meaning in, and *théos*, god; enthusiasm is the state of having God indwell one, and this is precisely what the New Testament promises the Christian, e.g. I John 4:15 and many other NT passages.)

The reluctance of many academic theologians to express trust of and reverence for the God about whom they allegedly can teach is not due only to this lamentable diffidence. In many cases they do not express it precisely because they lack it. It is not our place to judge another person's faith and obedience: God himself will do that (Romans 14:4). Unfortunately, in many cases we do not need to investigate and judge. The facts speak for themselves. Academic theologians so often speak superciliously and irreverently not only of the church, the Bible, and the saints of the past, but also of Christ and of God himself, that such language has virtually lost its power to shock all but the most pious and uninitiated. We have come to expect it of theologians. If a theologian were to speak of God in words and a tone of voice which betrayed awe, reverence, and love, we would think him a bit odd, and certainly unscientific. In reality, he might be the only real scientist of God among all his colleagues.

Modern theology presents us with a bewildering variety of trends, schools, and theories, about which it is difficult to generalize, but one thing we can say: it certainly is not characterized by promoting trust of and reverence for God. Can we then say that it is really theology, that it really involves the knowledge of God? According to Calvin's definition of the knowledge of God, the answer is no. But this is not entirely adequate. The Bible also speaks of a different kind of knowledge of God: the knowledge of the rebellious spirits, which involves both terror and hatred (James 2:19). A British theologian once said, "Theology without personal commitment to Christ[4] is the recrucifixion of Christ." The contemptuous treatment of Christ and God in the works of many of our most fashionable theologians offers a terribly clear illustration of the truth of this observation. In the nineteenth century it was philosophers like Nietzsche who liked to shock with statements verging on blasphemy. Today theologians do it.[5]

Blasphemous and semi-blasphemous references to God, whether they are merely an attempt to be witty and sophisticated, or involve a deliberate attempt to misrepresent Christian doctrine and to deceive the reader, are always irresponsible. They show a contempt for the people who so easily misunderstand them, as well as for God. They are at best unworthy of men who are supposed to be pastors and Christian brothers. At worst they come under the condemnation of God, who said, "The Lord will not hold him guiltless who takes his name in vain" (from the Decalogue, Exodus 20:7).

The situation in contemporary theology has reached the point where we virtually expect irreverence and blasphemy from theological professors if not from preachers. Of course some of it may be excused as an attempt to wake people out of their lethargy and to get them to pay attention to what is being said. This can never excuse literal blasphemy (indignity offered to God in word or writing); the desire to attract attention, even for an ostensibly good purpose, can never override a clear and literal commandment of God. It must further be said, to the shame of many of our modern theological shock troops, that often they give no evidence that they even have anything particularly valuable to say once they have aroused our pained attention.

2. The Justification of Theological Science

The attempts—one should almost say the pretensions—of theologians to be objective scholars and scientists result in part from an understandable if somewhat vain desire to meet the standards of the academic world in which they live. They have some justification in one very important fact: the Christian faith is based on an objective, *historical* revelation. The Bible does not claim to give man a vision of the being of God, nor does it promise mystical experience. Such things are not *excluded* from the Bible. They have been granted to individuals from time to time in the history of Israel and the church, but they are not the standard. Instead, the Bible purports to be the account of God at work in *real space* and in *real time,* in human history, creating a chosen people to do his will and to be his children: first the people of Israel, then the "New Israel," the Christian church.

The Bible is not *primarily* a revelation of doctrine, although there is doctrine in it and we legitimately derive doctrines from it. It is primarily a record of God's action, together with some explanation and interpretation. Israel owed its very existence, as well as its faith, to events which actually took place in history and which formed their experience as a people. One example will serve to illustrate them all: the crossing of the Red Sea during the Exodus from Egypt. In giving the Law at Mt. Sinai, God asserted his right to command and instruct Israel with the words, "I am the Lord thy God, which brought thee out of the land of Egypt, out of the house of bondage" (Exodus 20:2).

We recognize that the crossing of the Red Sea would have been far less meaningful to the Jews without the explanation of God's purpose which he gave to Moses and which Moses transmitted to the people. No doubt the Egyptians who survived the disaster interpreted it differently; at any rate it is not recorded that Egyptians began to convert to the religion of Israel. Nevertheless, without the actual *fact* of the passage of the Red Sea by the Jews and the catastrophic fate of the pursuing Egyptians, not only would the *explanation*, i.e. the Old Testament, be unreliable, but the commandments based on the fact of God's action, which we know as the Ten Commandments, would have no claim to authority. It is not necessary to visualize the crossing of the Red Sea in the way Cecil B. DeMille did in his spectacular, *The Ten Commandments*, as a supernaturally-powered marvel of hydraulic engineering; it is perfectly possible to accept Moses' somewhat more naturalistic description (". . . and the Lord caused the sea to go back by a strong east wind all that night, and made the sea dry land" (Exodus 14:21). The important point is that something tangible happened, and that it was correctly recognized and interpreted by those directly involved as the action of God in history.

The origin of the church is similar to the beginning of Israel. The disciples were despondent and beaten men after the death of their leader on Good Friday. Three days later the Resurrection gave them an undreamed-of new certainty and joy. The events of Pentecost fifty days later gave them the assurance and self-confidence to proclaim it boldly, and "turn the world upside down" (Acts 17:6). We may not agree with theologian Wolfhart Pannenberg that these things are sufficiently clear and tangible in the historical record so that no one can fail to see them unless he is deliberately ill-willed. We must admit that the effect which they have on us is achieved only through the way the Apostles and the early church reacted to them: in short, through their faith, which they have transmitted to us. But we cannot, as reasonable men (quite apart from being believing Christians) accept the claims of modern theologians that what is *most* important is the *message* preached by the Apostles (Rudolf Bultmann) or the *idea* of the Christ (Paul Tillich) rather than the events which make them possible and worthy of belief. Without the facts the message would be a fraud (I Corinthians 15:14-15).

By stating that both Israel and the church owe their origin to events which actually happened in history, the Bible points to an area in which history and faith overlap. Sometimes it seems that some modern theologians are trying to shift all the emphasis from the events to their interpretation, i.e. the message (Gr. *kérugma*) or the idea, in order to guard against the possibility that the Christian faith could be refuted by future historical discoveries. As a matter of fact, there is so little non-biblical evidence available for the events surrounding the Resurrection and the Exodus that it is extremely unlikely that serious historical scholarship will ever claim to disprove them. But if it were to happen, precisely what the church should not do is to take refuge in the "message" or the "idea."

If the historical events were to be disproved, the Ten Commandments *should* lose their authority, and Christ *should* be seen as a tragic charlatan rather than as the Light of the World. Christians who either openly or implicitly adopt the attitude: "We don't care whether it's true, we want to believe it anyway," discredit themselves in the sight of everyone of normal intelligence. To the extent that they are taken as representative of Christianity, they discredit the Christian faith as well, instead of making it more acceptable. Would-be benefactors of mankind like Professor Gordon Allport and Sir Julian Huxley may sincerely think that men are happier with a religious faith or a "mythology," and may prescribe one myth or another to meet their needs, but twentieth-century men will have none of it. Even if a religious orientation is supposed to be conducive to psychological health and well-being, a thinking man cannot really accept one unless he can believe that it is true.

Modern apologists who endeavor to protect the Christian faith from the question of fact actually make it *incredible*, whether they do so by stressing only its meaning (some theologians) or its psychological value (some pastors and psychologists). Many of its would-be exponents are making Christianity difficult to believe by their assertions that it is really very easy to do so. This is one of the causes for the present ridiculous situation in Christian evangelism and apologetics.[6] People are being converted to the most fanciful cults from the very parishes in which the clergy are unwilling to preach historic Christian doctrine. They fear being thought out-of-date and therefore incredible. Their people listen to those who have a message.

Whatever else may be said for or against Mormonism, for example, it is clear that its doctrines are not intrinsically more reasonable or easier to believe than those of orthodox Christianity; rather, the opposite is true. Nevertheless, Mormon missionaries equipped with little more than a knowledge of their own teachings and a zeal for their propagation, but without all the professional training and urbane intellectuality which Christian theologians feel they need, are proclaiming Mormon doctrines throughout the world, and are making converts. The converts they are making are twentieth-century men and women—or do they manage to find a ready supply of nineteenth-century people in today's world?

Christianity is based on certain events which are supposed to have happened here on this earth in real space and in real time, and to have meant something that we can understand (as well as much that we cannot understand). There is a considerable amount of historical evidence for the factuality of these events, just as for the factuality of the events of Roman history. The evidence available is not enough to compel a person to believe against his will, but it is certainly enough to render orthodox Christianity plausible and intellectually respectable. It is a well-known fact in British and American Inter-Varsity[7] circles that when university scientists stand up for religion at all, it is usually for the doctrines of historic Christian orthodoxy— whether in its Protestant or Roman Catholic form. The tangible and factual claims of Christianity appeal to scientists precisely because they *are* tangible and based on facts. Experimental scientists tend to find the vague aspirations of supposedly modern theology meaningless,[8] whereas orthodox theology, whatever it is, is not meaningless. If it is true, it is the most meaningful knowledge we can have; if false, it is dangerous, but not meaningless.[9]

The essential connection of the Christian faith with certain real events does then permit a limited amount of legitimate objective, historical inquiry, and does justify a certain claim on the part of Christian theology to be a science. Nevertheless the fact, or the account of the facts, if you will, quickly confronts even the most "objective" and "neutral" researcher with the claims of the God of Israel—and of the Christ who says that he will return to judge the living and the dead. Once this contact has been made, neutrality is no longer possible: there is only faith and obedience, or disbelief and disobedience.

There may be a thousand different reasons for unbelief. One can disbelieve for sincere and adequate-sounding reasons. One may have been so wronged and hurt by Christians that submission to their Lord is a practical impossibility. Whatever the reason, and no matter how understandable or even justifiable they are, disbelief and disobedience are not neutrality. A neutrally and objectively scientific theology is just as impossible for the unbeliever as for the believer. We should never forget this fact as we try to understand and to evaluate the claims and counter-claims of rival theological fashions. On the other hand we must not let the necessity of commitment and the impossibility of objectivity and neutrality blind us. What is at stake in the statement and defense of the historic Christian faith is not an opinion or a message, not an idea or even a commitment, but truth itself.[10]

3. The Foolishness of Christianity

Theology is a subject which Christians have in common with the devils, not with the angels. The angels stand in God's presence and continually do his bidding. They have a face-to-face knowledge which is not clouded by rebellion nor rendered fantastic by speculation. Milton imagined that when the fallen angels began to try to make the best of their lot in hell, they erected a theological academy (to discuss predestination and other subtle problems).[11] Whether or not there are such seminaries in hell, Milton was absolutely right in his insight that rebellion against God does not dampen speculation about him. One does well to remind oneself of this before, during, and after the reading of any theologian, and especially the modish ones.

There *are* intellectual arguments against Christianity, and some of them are quite weighty. No one is obliged to familiarize himself with all the endless discussions *pro* and *contra* the historic Christian faith before he himself believes, but every man ought to know enough of the positive evidence in favor of it in order to believe honestly, without a sacrifice of his intellect. There is certainly a point when one does not know enough to believe honestly, and at that point an act of submission, or "commitment to Christ," would be dishonest. But there is also a point at which there is enough evidence at hand, at which further inquiry is just postponement, and ultimately disobedience—and the theology of a disobedient man is not a knowledge of God. The Christian must admit that there are intellectual problems in the historic Christian position, and must respect those for whom they are difficult or insuperable. It is difficult, if not impossible, to judge individual cases, but it is accurate enough to generalize and say that many if not most supposedly *intellectual* conflicts which prevent people from accepting the faith are in the last analysis not intellectual but conflicts of *obedience*.

"No man can serve two masters," Jesus Christ told his disciples (Matthew 6:24). But he left his followers in the world, to coexist with their former masters and to find some way of meeting their continuing obligations. For the early Christians, the most serious rival to Christ was Caesar. The Roman Emperor demanded honors which they could give only to God. Eventually the Emperor Constantine capitulated to Christ. After his conversion, the people who had been kept away from the church by the fear of imperial persecution flocked to it in the hope of imperial favor. Thus began a new phase in the rivalry between the Master and the other masters. When Christianity was persecuted, only those who were genuinely convinced of its truth would undertake the risk and the burdens of being within the church. When it was first promoted by the Emperors and then established by law, the unconvinced flocked to be baptized. They have remained within the churches ever since, and in many cases make up the majority of the membership.

To the great shame of the church, it must be said that there is virtually as much need for conversion within the church as outside it. There is not *exactly* as much need, for at least *some* of those nominally within the churches are also convinced and committed believers, and no real believers should remain outside the church. Most nominal church members, however, have never come to grips with the conflicting claims of the two masters. In the realms of religious behavior, and perhaps even of conduct, they try to please God, but in other realms they try to satisfy the standards of the world. This sort of thing has been going on for a very long time, but recently it has achieved a special degree of sophistication. Early and medieval Christianity abounded with examples of hypocrisy, but it remained for our century to baptize hypocrisy and claim that pleasing the world is the way to please God.

The Christian church has never been tremendously successful in its attempt to convert the world. Christian missions in the ancient world did not go much farther than what had been the limits of the old Roman Empire, and the wave of Moslem conquest swept away a considerable part of the ancient church.[12] After Christianity became established as the official religion of the Roman Empire, the church had to begin its long, arduous, and still unfinished fight against unbelief in its own ranks. Christians have found various rationalizations for their failure to evangelize effectively, but it is only recently that the church has begun to take pleasure in its failures. The new trend is to give up the task of converting the world to Christ, and to set about the task of conforming the church to the world. Bishop John Robinson undertook his venture in rewriting Christianity (*Honest to God* and subsequent writings) in the hope of making Christianity more easily palatable to skeptical modern men; his colleague Paul van Buren (*The Secular Meaning of the Gospel*) is trying to make happily skeptical modern men out of Christians.

The simple fact is that *there is no way to overcome the enmity between the church and the world, between Christian faith and unbelief.* There is no way short of the absolute victory of one side or the other. We Christians know that the true church can never be overcome, neither by the world, nor by hell (John 16:33, Matthew 16:18); we also know that there has been treachery and apostasy in the church from the earliest days (Revelation 2:4, 2:14). But for the Christian to accept conformity to the world, either for himself as an individual or for his church as a whole, in an ostensible effort to help the world, is not only to betray Christ: it is ultimately to betray the world as a whole. Christ has sent his church into the world for the healing of the world. He has given his disciples the rank of ambassadors (II Corinthians 5:20). Their task can only be fulfilled by representing *Him.* For a Christian to allow himself to become conformed to the world is ultimately to deprive the world of precisely the friction which is intended to make it aware of the meaning of Christ: "You are the salt of the earth; but if the salt has become tasteless, how will it be made salty again? It is good for nothing any more, except to be thrown out and trampled under foot by men" (Matthew 5:13).

As long as Christians preserve their character as followers of Christ, they will have to face the antagonism of the world. Even if they remove every possible obstacle, and succeed in being gentle, kind, loving, and wise, they will not be able to earn general acceptance or fit smoothly into the machinery of society. There is a place for serious theology, and it is a high one. But all too much of our theology is the effort to win the intellectual admiration of people who ultimately reject Christ. We are in effect saying, "Perhaps you cannot believe in Christ. But surely you must admit that my way of presenting him is sensible, attractive, and balanced, and that I am not a fool for believing in him." That is precisely what the non-Christian, in the last analysis, cannot admit. To do so would be to admit that he himself is a fool (literally, a damned fool) for not believing. The man who preserves his ultimate loyalty to Christ must remain, in the eyes of the world, a fool, because he has placed himself alongside the one who was—and is—"despised and rejected of men" (Isaiah 53:3). All the updating in the world cannot free a truly Christian theology from that scorn and rejection. But the scorn and rejection are easily overcome as soon as Christ is abandoned. The real danger to the church and to the Christian is not that his theology may appear foolish and weak to men, but that it may be popular—like the Beatles—and attract general attention and approval. "The foolishness of God is wiser than men, and the weakness of God is stronger than men" (I Corinthians 1:25).

Notes

[1]N.A.S.B. = *The New American Standard Bible, New Testament* (Cleveland and New York: The World Publishing Company, 1960). Copyright, The Lockman Foundation, La Habra, California. This and subsequent quotations from this translation are used by permission.

[2]"In [verse] 14, the natural man is the unregenerate man whose wisdom is only that to which he is able to attain by the use of his natural faculties. He has no power of examining truth which is revealed and interpreted only through the [Holy] Spirit." *A New Commentary on Holy Scripture,* eds. Charles Gore, Henry Leighton Goudge and Alfred Guillaume (London: S.P.C.K., 1955; 1st ed., 1928), p. 489.

[3]Calvin's *Institutes of the Christian Religion* are available in many editions.

The most modern is in *The Library of Christian Classics,* Vol. XX (2 volumes), edited by John T. McNeill and translated by Ford Lewis Battles (Philadelphia: The Westminster Press, 1960). Used by permission.

[4]Fifty years ago the term "personal commitment to Christ" would have been understood by everyone as meaning commitment to him as Saviour and as Lord, as true God and true man. Today the term "commitment" has been so abused that it is necessary to say that it involves believing acceptance of Christ's divinity and submission to his authority, as he himself required of his disciples in John 13:13. The absurd modern perversion of the meaning of the word "commitment" is seen in Alan Ansen's description of writer William S. Burroughs as "a deeply committed personality." Burroughs, author of *Junkie, Queer,* and *Naked Lunch,* is a drug addict, a self-confessed homosexual, promiscuous, and an alcoholic. Ansen writes, "This commitment he finds in addiction to narcotics. . . . To use drugs without losing consciousness or articulateness, to love boys without turning into a mindless drab is a form of heroism." Comments Harry Blamires on this use of commitment and expressions like it: "This is only a further development of that perversion of language and concepts which is well begun in England already in the regular write-up of films, plays, and books, lowbrow and highbrow alike, in our daily and weekly journals." *The Christian Mind* (London: S.P.C.K., 1963), pp. 101f. Used by permission.

[5]Let one well-known example suffice: "It [the doctrine of the Incarnation of Jesus Christ] conjures up the idea of a divine substance being plunged in flesh and coated with it like chocolate or silver plating." John A. T. Robinson, *Honest To God* (London: S.C.M. Press, 1963), pp. 66f. Used by permission. Quite aside from the fact that this language irresponsibly misinterprets the meaning of the historic Christian creeds, it certainly makes it unnecessary to wonder whether Robinson is trying to demonstrate trust and reverence.

[6]By evangelism I mean the proclamation of the Christian faith with a view to winning people to a personal faith in Christ. Apologetics is the defense of the truth of Christian doctrine. Naturally effective apologetics will have an evangelistic impact.

[7]The Inter-Varsity Fellowships in Britain, America, and elsewhere originated with the revivals sparked in English universities by Dwight L. Moody. They number among their graduate members many university professors in the natural sciences and medicine.

[8]This fact is attested by chemist Walter R. Thorson of the University of Alberta in "The Concept of Truth in the Natural Sciences," *Themelios* (Lausanne, Switzerland), Vol. V, No. 2 (1968), pp. 27-39.

[9]I pass over the arguments of those logical positivist philosophers who claim that all religious language is meaningless. Those who wish to familiarize themselves with this rather unappealing and artificial theory may consult Eric L. Mascall, *The Secularisation of Christianity* (London: Darton, Longman, and Todd, 1965, and New York: Holt, 1966), pp. 40-150, and the references given there.

[10]See the book by Harry Blamires (n. 4 above), pp. 106-131, for a valuable discussion of the Christian conception of truth.

[11] "Others apart sat on a Hill retir'd
In thoughts more elevate, and reasond high
of Providence, Foreknowledge, Will, and Fate,
Fixt Fate, free Will, Foreknowledge absolute,
And found no end, in wandring mazes lost."

Paradise Lost, Book II, lines 557ff.

[12]Via Persia some missionaries did reach the Far East, and Christianity also existed in India and Ethiopia, but its influence was concentrated chiefly in the part of Europe that had been Roman, in Asia Minor, and in the lands of the Slavic and Germanic peoples.

Chapter 2

· TRUTH IN WORSHIP ·

But when the people of Ashdod went into the house of Dagon on the following morning, they saw Dagon lying with his face upon the earth before the ark of the Lord. Then they lifted him up again and put him in his proper place. On the next morning, however, Dagon again lay on his face before the ark of the Lord . . .

I Samuel 5:3-5

The Philistines have a bad reputation. If the average adult remembers anything from his Sunday School days, he probably remembers that the Philistines were no good. Actually—considering what they had to contend with—the picture the Old Testament paints of them is not so bad. Circumstances forced them to deal with the bellicose and self-confident Hebrews, who had caused some spectacular disasters to the Egyptians, a much more powerful nation than the Philistines. The Hebrews were reputed to have a real God on their side, and events tended to bear them out. Of course, each of the peoples of the ancient Near East had one or more deites to which it could appeal, but the God of the Hebrews gave some evidence of being in a different league.

In I Samuel 4 the Hebrews and the Philistines are facing one another for one of their frequent battles, this time for a real showdown. The Hebrews apparently had uneasy consciences. Their conduct in the period preceding the battle had not been all that one could expect of a chosen people with a special relationship to God, and they wondered whether they could count on him to pull them through. The hostilities, in fact, began unfavorably enough: on the first day Israel suffered severely.

Thereupon the Hebrews decided to make sure that God would

help them. They sent to Shiloh for the Ark of the Covenant, and had it brought to their camp. When it arrived, such a shout went up from Israel's army that the Philistines were filled with dread. They knew what the God of Israel had done to the Egyptians. Did they know enough about him to realize that it might not be so easy for his chosen people to manipulate him by the expedient of carrying his Ark around with them? Perhaps their intelligence service was not that well developed. At any rate, they decided to put a brave face on the situation and make the best of it. "Philistines," the word went out, "take courage and be men, so you will not be slaves to the Hebrews, as they have been to you" (I Samuel 4:9). With those words, they set out to fight. They devastated the Israelite army, which lost the battle, thirty thousand men, and the Ark.

Having defeated the Hebrew army, the Philistines saw no reason to court trouble by insulting the God of Israel. Perhaps they owed their victory to his favor—at least he had not effectively helped their enemies. It would not hurt to give him some recognition for his benevolent neutrality. They therefore brought his Ark back to their capital of Ashdod, and gave it a place of honor in the Temple of Dagon, alongside the statue of Dagon itself. It was a reasonable thing to do, and very human—rather like what a modern political leader does when he calls upon all the religious groups in his country to pray for him. It is better to be safe than sorry, and a gesture in God's direction—or in the direction of all the gods—couldn't hurt, could it?

Unfortunately the Philistines' reasoning resulted in a fiasco. The God of Israel did not want a reasonable share of their reverence. The first morning after the Ark was put alongside the statue of Dagon, the statue was found on its face. The second morning it was broken into pieces. The Philistines eventually got the point. They sent the Ark back to the defeated Hebrews, together with an atonement-offering to the God of Israel. Presumably after that they were able to repair or replace Dagon's statue and put it back up again.

The conduct of the Philistines is a crystal-clear example of one of the two major trends in Christian worship today: *syncretism*.[1] To divide one's religious observance, giving a bit of attention here and a bit there, seems like a plausible thing to do. It relieves one of the necessity of careful investigation to discover which religion is actually

right, and leaves one covered against all eventualities. The only difficulty—as the Philistines discovered—is that God evidently does not
operate on the basis of human reason. If there is one thing that comes
through clearly in the whole of the Old Testament, it is that the
God of Israel has very exclusive tendencies. He is not willing to
share divine honors with anyone.

From the human point of view, especially in our tolerant twentieth
century, such conduct seems a bit unreasonable. It hardly seems
worthy of a being endowed with all the qualities of magnanimity
and loving gentleness which we like to ascribe to God whenever it
suits us to do so. After all, one might reason, if he really *is* God, he
doesn't need to be so jealous of his prerogatives—he has all the glory
anyway. But perhaps that is precisely what it means to be God, the
God of Truth: that he is neither willing nor able to share the honor
which belongs to him with those to whom it does not belong.

Jesus taught his disciples that God wants to be worshipped in spirit
and in truth (John 4:23). A great deal can be said about the *spirit*
of modern Christian worship, and we shall turn to it later. But here
truth is at stake. It ought to be clear that we cannot have both *syncretism* and *truth* in our worship. The two are mutually exclusive.
Syncretism is part of the twentieth-century mood, but truth is part
of the nature of God. If we want our worship, or attempts at worship,
to mean anything, we have to strive to conform it to the nature and
will of God, and not to the mood or taste of the twentieth century.

In twentieth-century America, with its millions of well intentioned
but fuzzy-minded "good Christian people," we rejoice—in certain
circles, anyway—when church attendance rises, and are concerned
when it declines. This is a mistake. Throughout our fair land, a good
many of our churches are in the position of the Philistines' temple
at Ashdod. They are trying to worship two or more deities, which are
not mutually compatible. The God of the Bible cannot coexist peace-
fully in the temple with a Dagon—either Dagon will wind up in
pieces, or God will leave, or both.

It is all too easy to take a supercilious attitude towards the actual,
day-to-day life and Sunday-to-Sunday worship of our churches. Every
Christian editor and many non-Christian ones have a quiverful of
editorials against hypocrisy in the churches. We are all familiar, even
ad nauseam, with the pontifications of the type of would-be religious

revolutionary who thinks that he has finally discovered what the Gospel really means after two thousand years of confusion and uncertainty. It is not our task to tabulate and evaluate all the major and minor inconsistencies found within each church, and thereby to imply that we are not like the rest of men. The fundamental biblical principle is worth repeating: in the last analysis, it is God who will judge the performance of the church and of its individual members (Romans 14:4). Nevertheless, when this has been said, we still have some facts to face: first, we cannot have two or more Gods, if one of them is to be the God of the Bible; second, syncretism *is* a prominent factor in Christian worship in America today.

1. Syncretism in the House of God:
Ecumenical Philistinism

If twentieth-century Christian worship is syncretistic, it is not fulfilling its purpose. As syncretism, it can neither please God, nor help man. It is not a question of religious purism or Puritanism. It is simply a matter of fact. If the God of the Bible is really God, we cannot serve him each in our own way: we have to serve him each in *his* way. The spread of unrecognized syncretism is attacking the vitals of the church. Intellectually, it is a problem in the theological seminaries and in the whole field of religious literature and art; on the level of day-to-day encounter, it is a tremendous and growing problem in worship.

The most obvious intrusion of syncretism in worship is on the conscious level, as ecumenism. Strictly speaking, *ecumenism* is a phenomenon *within* Christianity. Non-Christians are not part of the ecumenical movement. Dialogue, cooperation, and interaction between Christians and adherents of non-Christian religions such as Judaism, Islam, and Buddhism, is designated by the term *inter-faith*. It ought therefore to come as somewhat of a shock that an *ecumenical* commemoration service scheduled for St. Paul's Cathedral (Church of England) in London on Commonwealth Day was to have included *Moslem, Hindu,* and *Buddhist* elements. Pressure from conservative groups in the Church of England, evangelicals and Anglo-Catholics,

spurred the Archbishop of Canterbury to forbid the scheduled ceremony. The Church of England may have come a long way since the
days when archbishops and bishops needed to be willing to die for
their faith, but it has not yet come all the way. Some things are still
out of the question, and for the time being an amalgamation of Christianity with Islam, Hinduism, and Buddhism seems to be one of them.

Ecumenism properly speaking does not yet include the non-
Christian religions, at least not if they are represented by their own
leaders. Hinduism can in fact be preached from an Anglican pulpit
(and has been) but only by an Anglican. But that is another matter.
A clue to the way the religious health of Christianity has deterior-
ated is given by the fact that many Christians felt relieved when they
learned that Archbishop Ramsey had actually banned the multi-faith
service. There are more than a few affinities between Christianity and
Islam, so that it is not absolutely out of the question for adherents
of the two religions to find some way to address themselves to the
same God. (Ultimately, it is impossible, for they *are* different religions, but it is a more plausible undertaking than some of the others.)
If we consider Hinduism and Buddhism, however, the case is crystal
clear. Fundamental to Christianity (as to Judaism and Islam) is the
statement that God is *one* and that he is *personal*. How can a common ground, short of madness, be found with Hinduism, with its
myriad personal divinities and great impersonal spirit, or with Buddhism, which has no god at all? "Surely each of us believes in some
kind of something," a bored Lord said during the 1928 English
Prayer Book discussions. It is very important in what kind of what,
or to put the matter in more clearly Christian terms, in whom one
believes.

It is not sufficient for the Archbishop of Canterbury to have foiled
one year's attempt at a pan-religious service. It may be years before
such a thing is seriously proposed again, but the fact that it *was proposed at all* gives staggering evidence of the fact that within a
major Christian church there is little concern for truth in worship.

Much more common than inter-faith or pan-religious services are
ecumenical ones. The several Christian confessions admittedly have
infinitely more in common with each other than Christianity does
with Buddhism or Hinduism. The basic doctrines of the ancient ecumenical Creeds[2] are shared by all major Christian churches—to the

extent that they have not yet succumbed to intellectual relativism or theological syncretism. There is certainly enough in common between Christians of the major groups to allow joint prayer. As soon as one goes much beyond that, problems arise. The Roman Catholic is accustomed to pray to the Virgin Mary; in fact, apart from the Mass itself, it seems that prayer is made more often to Mary than to God.[3] The Roman Catholic who wants to pray with a Protestant must forego the intercession of the Virgin Mary, and this doubtless puts a burden on the project.

At the level of more formal worship, the situation becomes intolerable: for a Roman Catholic the Mass is a sacrifice, made possible by the miraculous transformation of bread and wine into the body and blood of Christ. For a Protestant, both of these concepts are abominable. There are many prayers connected with the Mass which the Protestant could say with a whole heart, but if he realizes what is supposed to be happening, he cannot easily join in it. If I do not believe that my own Protestant minister can or would even seek to transform bread and wine into the body and blood of Christ, can I believe that a Roman Catholic priest is doing it when I attend Mass with a Catholic friend? And if I do not believe that he can do it, how must I look upon his claim that he is doing it? It is not a question of finding differences between our beliefs, or of scoring debating points; it is a question of truth. Neither Protestantism nor Roman Catholicism is a completely closed system. Each overlaps with the other to some extent. But as a Protestant I cannot simply take over parts of Roman Catholicism without destroying my own Protestant Christianity. That is a dangerous procedure, if I believe that through my present faith I have access to Christ.

In a real sense, *ecumenical prayer ought to be more difficult for the believing Christian, of whatever denomination, than for the unbeliever, or the merely nominal believer.* It sounds paradoxical, but is absolutely true. If I, as an unbeliever, attend a Christian service, I can afford to let it grow on me, to accept parts of it. Not having a definite faith, I have nothing to lose. But if I, as a convinced, evangelical Protestant, begin to admit that the Roman Catholic priest at Mass is actually doing what he (or at least the Council of Trent) says he is doing, then I endanger my own relationship with Christ. Either he is right, in which case my own evangelical conversion and faith are at best lamentably incomplete, or he is wrong, in which case by my credulity I am in danger of apostasy from my true faith. A similar problem confronts the believing Catholic who attends Protestant services.

There is a sense in which conversion is far more plausible than Protestant-Catholic ecumenical worship. Of course, there are things that unite the great confessions. There is much that they have in common, and it is most important. But in order to *have* what is most important, one must have it with some clarity of understanding— and that is precisely what one cannot have in the ecumenical service, once it progresses beyond a certain point, it becomes self-contradictory and unclear. Even if both Roman Catholicism and Calvinism, shall we say, were acceptable alternate ways of worshipping the God of the Bible, one would have to approach him by one or the other, and not by some blend of the two. It is rather like the number system. A given quantity may be expressed by the digits 64, 100, or 144: 64 represents it in the decimal system, which we normally use, 100 in a system with the number 8 as base, and 144 in a system with the number 6 as base. Any of these systems will function perfectly well, once one gets used to it, and any quantity can be expressed in any of them. But one cannot mix them up, or chaos results, in which nothing means anything at all. The decimal system will work, and so will any other system, as long as it is agreed upon to stick with it.

Ecumenical Philistinism, the desire to make a "Hall of Christian Heroes" with Thomas Aquinas, Martin Luther, and John Calvin, is not quite as senseless as the conduct of that Roman Emperor who had images of Orpheus, Appolonius, Christ, and Abraham in his private chapel.[4] It is possible to honor all three, and to recognize in each of them a striking passion for the glory of God. But it is not possible to follow the three as a crowd, for they say different things and point in different directions.

The only way to bring the different Christian traditions together in worship is to tone down doctrine and emphasize ceremony and ritual. This is precisely what is taking place. But every ritual is supposed to have a reason, in other words, a doctrine behind it. Religious ritual without doctrine ultimately becomes contentless self-mystification, and points in the same direction as the "religious" use of L.S.D.: toward feeling and "experience" which cannot be interpreted or communicated. While it is true that there is much in the historic Christian faith which cannot be communicated, it is absolutely essential to it that there are very important things which *can* be: "Everything that I have heard from My Father I have made known to you" (Christ to his disciples in John 15:15).

In the Netherlands, which is fairly evenly divided between Roman Catholics and Calvinists, there are frequent reports of unauthorized intercommunion services taking place between members of the two major churches. We should not discount the motives behind these intercommunions: they are trying to express the real unity which all Christians have through Christ. Instead of talking and preaching about it, which might involve them in a discussion of their doctrinal differences, they prefer to worship together. But in so doing, both sides imply that their doctrinal commitments mean nothing important. As soon as this kind of thing is established, it means ultimately that both sides are cutting themselves off from Christ, and will have only each other, in a kind of Christian togetherness—without Christ.

There is a major difference between ecumenism within Christianity and inter-faith contacts which embrace other great religions. But to the extent that ecumenism minimizes the importance of doctrine and the content of religious ceremonies, as is currently being done in ecumenical worship, it is laying the necessary groundwork for inter-faith worship, which is religion without doctrine, without meaning, and ultimately without God. The so-called "radical theologians" who want to dispense with God in their theology are only the intellectual expression of something which is very widespread on the level of everyday Christian life and worship.

Contentless Form

If the desire to be ecumenical is producing a syncretistic melange which blends contradictory theories as though no conflict existed between them, it is not the only or necessarily the major threat to truth in worship. The chief area of syncretism is not amalgamation of Reformed and Roman Catholic doctrines, nor of Christian and non-Christian, but of theology and non-theology, doctrine and non-doctrine, belief and non-belief.

How can a worship service be a syncretistic fusion of doctrine and non-doctrine? In order to explain this, it is necessary to remind ourselves what *doctrine* is. Derived from the Latin *docere,* meaning to teach, it means simply "teaching" or "body of teachings." The fact that both *doctrine* and its derivative *doctrinaire,* as well as the synonym *dogma* and its derivative *dogmatic* (from Greek *dokein,* to think) have acquired a generally derogatory significance in common usage is an important symptom of the intellectual malaise of our day. It is nowhere more disastrous than in the Christian church, which exists *in order to teach.* (See Christ's "Great Commission" to his disciples, Matthew 28:18-20.) Christians are properly alarmed by the abandonment of certain historic Christian doctrines by their churches (e.g. the Virgin Birth, the Second Coming of Christ, even the physical Resurrection of Christ, all of which are under attack in several major confessions, not excluding Roman Catholicism itself). They should be more alarmed by the fact that *doctrine* itself is being abandoned.

The current activism of large segments of the major churches is in part a responsible and necessary recognition of the fact that the church lives in the world with the rest of mankind and has obligations to the world. In large part, however, it is a *substitute* for the church's primary commitment, which is to God and to his truth.

The fusion of doctrine and non-doctrine takes place when a service of worship involves the pronouncing of words which are negated by the actions surrounding them, whether those words be embodied in a time-honored liturgical formula, or in the free prayer or preaching of a minister. The typical Protestant service contains a vast number of pronouncements and statements which are negated during the service itself.

We all know that the instruction one receives in church is often neglected outside it. A certain amount of hypocrisy characterizes each of us, and it is our task to fight against it. But in Protestant services we are often dealing with something more than mere inconsistency: we are dealing with evident contradictions. No one is perfect, and Christian performance always lags lamentably behind the teaching of Christ. However, when we encounter an obvious disjunction between the words spoken and the actions appended to them, something serious is taking place. We are losing our ability to understand words, or we have come to the point where we do not care for meanings.

Many Presbyterian services begin with words taken from Psalm 95,

"O come, let us worship and bow down, let us kneel before the Lord our Maker . . ." Have we ever seen Presbyterians bow down, much less kneel, on hearing those words? The example may seem trivial. There are some practical and some theological reasons for not bowing or kneeling, and perhaps they are adequate. But then why begin the service with an invitation which is immediately and obviously disregarded? There is much more that is, in a more serious sense, an invitation to hypocrisy. The invitation to the Holy Communion in the Episcopal services invites "all you who . . . are in love and charity with your neighbor" to receive the sacrament. Anyone with any knowledge of the course of human life and of human nature (his own will suffice) would expect that invitation to result in a certain weeding out among the worshippers before they approach the communion table. In the United States it seldom does. When a conscientious worshipper does heed the words and stays away from the table, it should indicate to the minister that something is wrong, and prompt him to a pastoral visit. But in fact, in the vast majority of cases, it does not. No minister would dare to suggest to a parishioner that something is not right between him and God! Of course there are exceptions. Some Christian congregations are consistent enough and serious enough to expect the minister to inquire when he receives so obvious a tip. But most modern Protestants would regard it as pietistic fanaticism for either the minister or the church-member even to think of such a thing, far from actually doing it.

The social life of the church is often regarded as a breeding-ground for hypocrisy. This is bad enough. But when worship itself involves the statement of the most serious proposals, commandments, and invitations in clear language, and their equally clear disregard by all involved, it goes far beyond any inconsistencies in social life.

A great deal has been said pro and contra the clergy who will speak out on contemporary issues from the pulpit. The secular press is particularly fond of the "courage" of those men whose speaking out takes the form of some political cause of which their church is not expected to approve. There are many such examples, and often they are worthy of honor. Many white ministers in the South were subjected to harassment and indignity, and some ultimately lost their positions, for speaking in favor of social and political justice for the Negro. On the other hand, we must judge critically. For a white min-

ister in a segregationist-minded church in the South to speak in favor
of integration *does* demand courage, but a great deal of the "courage"
shown by politically active or doctrinally radical modern ministers
simply involves making a grandstand play—speaking over the heads
of a shocked or puzzled congregation to their fellow clergy, to the
political establishment, or to the press. The acclaim they receive from
such outsiders protects them from any indignation from their congregations.[5]

Where are the clergy who have the courage to speak clearly from
the pulpit of the things which are their duty to discuss? Has the
ecumenical movement been discussed? Have its participants been
challenged to adhere to biblical principles, and not just to follow the
syncretistic trend of the times? How many clergy have the courage
to expound biblical principles clearly, when it means telling a political leader that he is clearly violating a divine law? (John the Baptist
told Herod that his marriage was contrary to God's law. There was a
rather sensational case of adultery and remarriage on the part of a
high state official some years ago, but the courage of the numerous
clergy who had contact with him stopped short of John the Baptist's.)
How many clergy will rebuke or denounce an important parishioner
for an immoral act—unless they know beforehand that they will be
supported from the grandstand?

We must be realistic. The fact of the matter is that the "courage"
of a man like the former Episcopal bishop of California in repudiating the doctrine he had sworn to defend did not get him persecution,
but fame and popularity. For a man with the views he professes to
conduct services of worship and recite the Apostles' or Nicene Creeds
is solemnly and publicly to lie, but it is done. And uncritical worshippers allow themselves to be "led in worship" by such solemn and
public lying. Of course, the more spectacular cases do encounter resistance. But in most cases the congregation, not wishing to appear
"fanatical," goes along with the farce.

Churches—and individual Christians—show in their worship as
clearly as anywhere else that they care little whether words and
deeds correspond to one another. The ritual goes on, but its content
is gone. This is not unprecedented in our history. There were times
and places in the Middle Ages when the situation may have been as
bad. But in the Middle Ages there were reforming movements, both

within and outside of the Roman obedience. Today the "reforming" spirits in both Roman Catholicism and Protestantism are not moving in the direction of internal consistency and fidelity to their statements of faith, but away from it. What is taking place today is not a new *reformation,* as a certain Anglican writer has pompously called his own work,[6] but a *deformation*—a deformation which makes itself felt not least in worship.

2. The Fool at the Eleven o'Clock Service

Nowhere is the divorce between word and meaning, between statement and action, more evident in the church than at eleven o'clock on Sunday morning, when Protestants traditionally hold their major worship service of the week. Protestant worship, we know, traditionally has two poles: praise, thanksgiving and petition offered to God; and proclamation, instruction, encouragement, and edification for the worshippers. The man who goes to the typical Protestant Sunday morning service expecting to find these things is a fool.

The eleven o'clock service in Protestantism represents a deliberate reduction from the varied feasts, observances, ceremonies, and rituals of pre-Reformation Catholicism. Both Calvin and Luther stressed the truly biblical principle that the Christian can and should do his worldly work to the glory of God. There was no need for a special time set apart *only* for fulfillment of one's religious duties, for all of life was a religious duty. The services of preaching and the observances of the sacraments were not seen as oases of "religion" in an otherwise completely secular life: they were rather points of concentration, at which time the purpose and direction present in the whole of Christians' lives was to be confirmed, developed, and given symbolic expression.

If a Sunday church service is the *only* expression of religion in one's life, it is almost worse than no expression. The person who is totally irreligious may well realize that he is, and he may even worry about it. This is why Jesus said that the tax-gatherers and harlots would enter the kingdom of God before the religious leaders of his day (Matthew 21:31). The structure of Protestant worship is meaningful only if Sunday worship is the culmination (or commencement, if you prefer) of a week the whole of which is devoted to the service of God.

In Protestantism we have developed a kind of counterfeit religious experience. If on a Sunday a sermon is preached on love, the congregation may have a kind of second-hand encounter with love. They hear of the evils of lovelessness, and as the preacher cites examples, their hearts are filled with a sense of how they should react in the cases described. If he preaches on the need for repentance and a changed life, they may have a moving experience of the need for repentance and mentally live out the changes which God would have them make in their lives. But they mistake hearing about the thing, or consideration of the thing, for the thing itself. The sermon may be invaluable as an analysis of what has happened in one's Christian life in the light of God's Word; it can also serve as instruction about how to shape that life in the future. But it cannot be a substitute for it. Yet that is precisely what it is, for in all too many cases, the things preached about, and mentally accepted by the congregations, never get beyond the point of verbalization.

If there is one serious criticism that can be made of evangelical or orthodox Protestantism, it is that it understands the theory of Christianity but not the practice. Evangelical Protestantism distinguishes itself from Roman Catholicism on the ground that Catholicism has a false view of good works, and makes them a means of earning salvation.[7] A biblically-based Protestant sermon may clearly demonstrate that we are saved through grace, not works, and that the works are but the grateful response of the redeemed heart. *But then the works do not follow.*

Evangelical Protestantism criticizes "liberal" Protestantism for its humanistic man-centeredness, for its willingness to take its orders from the social sciences rather than from God. In contrast, we evangelicals listen very carefully to the voice of God, so that we will hear and admire his orders—which we then fail to follow.

In one way, the most radical modern theology, including the "death-of-God" school, is in the tradition of evangelical Protestantism, rather than of extreme Protestant liberalism. Evangelical Protestants, through their acquaintance with biblical doctrine, could point out the flaws in everyone else's theology, and there they left it. Theology and worship became a purely academic or intellectual exercise. There were admittedly practical consequences to be drawn, and the ordinary evangelical Protestant believer usually drew them, but the theologians were satisfied with pointing to them, rather than with accepting them. Radical modern theology has virtually gone insane in this direction, carrying the criticism of everyone's theology to absurd extremes. The concern for doctrinal purity has carried them past the point of mere sterility, which characterized much Protestant orthodoxy, to complete non-being. It is a radical aggravation of the dangers inherent in evangelical Protestantism's theological acuteness. It is basically different, in that it rejects the Lord to whom historic Protestantism holds. But we must recognize that this so-called radical theology is stimulated, at least in part, by a typically Protestant theological divorce between doctrine and life.

The eleven o'clock service has become the primary teaching opportunity in Protestantism (as indeed it is the primary opportunity for *every* expression of a religious sort). The actual time available for teaching, with the abandonment of mid-week and Sunday evening services, and with the average sermon length not exceeding half an hour, is reduced to *twenty-six hours yearly*. Quite aside from the fact that many services necessarily have a function other than teaching—whether it be evangelism, the commemoration of a special event, or a festival so traditional, such as Christmas, that no one listens to the "message" about it—can twenty-six hours yearly fulfil Christ's injunction to teach all nations "to observe all that I commanded you" (Matthew 28:19)?

When challenged to produce a genuine miracle in the twentieth century, a preacher remarked, "I don't need to. The church itself is a miracle." What he meant was that the church would not exist without the wonderful acts of God at Easter and Pentecost, and without the work of the Holy Spirit in calling new people into its fellowship. But in another sense, it is really a remarkable, if not miraculous thing, that an organization like the church can continue to exist for so long in conflict with its own expressed principles and purposes.

The "death-of-God" phenomenon[8] and similar aberrations are distressing to many Christians, who wonder if the church can survive such self-destructive teaching in its midst. Perhaps we can take comfort from the fact that somehow it continues to rumble, Sunday after

Sunday, through a phenomenon billed as worship which can be neither pleasing to God nor to man. Actually we should be distressed at the ability of services without meaning to survive, because each one that is conducted is another advertisement for the cause of those who contend that the Christian religion is in fact meaningless. When all is said and done, the Christian church really is a miracle. It is hard to make ourselves believe that an ordinary institution could continue to survive, and in some respects to grow, on such a disorderly basis and with so much self-contradiction within itself.

Most of what is said above is particularly applicable to main-line Protestantism, which at least formally subscribes to the great and basic doctrines of historic Christianity. It does not apply to "liberal" or radical groups which have deliberately cut themselves off from the central truths of the faith—except in as much as they too are discovering how hard it is to relate theology, even their reduced and sub-Christian theology, to life in our modern world. There are individual congregations and perhaps whole denominations which are laudable exceptions. The vast Roman Catholic Church represents a different kind of a problem, both as it was before it began to change, and as it is becoming under the influence of pressure from its own radicals, Christian and post-Christian. We shall consider it in a later chapter. Throughout the Christian church a major, basic problem is this dichotomy between doctrine and life. It is as evident in worship as anywhere, and in worship it is particularly harmful, for that is the only contact which countless millions of "Christians" have with their church.

It is often warned that the doctrinal foundations of Christianity are under severe and prolonged attack, and that we must rally to their protection. That is true. The neglect of doctrine is fatal. But even sound doctrine must be put into practice—that is its whole purpose—and from the nature of Christianity it must be put into practice in the worship of God. Until we recognize and act upon the principle of truth in worship, we are in danger of creating a new Ashdod instead of the New Jerusalem.

Notes

[1]Syncretism is defined as the combining or attempting to combine of mutually opposed opinions, doctrines, or practices, particularly in religion.

[2]There are three principal creeds or confessions of faith which are called ecumenical because of their acceptance by the universal church: The Apostles' Creed (cate circa 135?), the Nicene Creed (written at the Council of Nicaea in 325, expanded at the Council of Constantinople in 381), and the Creed of the Council of Chalcedon (451). There creeds are shared by Eastern Orthodoxy, Roman Catholicism, and the Protestant denominations which arose out of the Reformation, or *were shared*, until theological liberalism began its work of revising them.

[3]It is recognized that this statement may be offensive to Roman Catholics. The author is aware that it does not represent Roman Catholic *doctrine* at its best, but it does seem to be a fair statement of *practice* as it can be witnessed in countless parishes throughout the United States.

[4]The Emperor Severus Alexander (222-235), who was a capable administrator.

[5]In his important study, *The Noise of Solemn Assemblies,* Professor Peter Berger of Hartford Seminary has pointed out how often churches of *all* kinds (from liberal to fundamentalist) have the courage to take precisely the stance on social issues that one would expect from looking at their constituency—Negro churches in favor of integration, white churches in regions of tension opposed to it. What seems "revolutionary" behavior on the part of ministers engaged in the support of radical causes is often precisely what is needed to win them approval from the groups from which they most want it. This is human enough, but it does not prove that the stands they take are dictated by a sense of religious obligation (New York: Doubleday, 1961).

[6]Bishop John A. T. Robinson, author of *The New Reformation?* (London: S.C.M., and Philadelphia: Westminster, 1965).

[7]This is not the place to discuss whether Roman Catholic theology at its best actually teaches salvation by works (it does not). It is sufficient to say that it often gives that impression, which is what matters for our purposes. Neither did Luther teach that if one had faith, one could act as one pleased—but his followers still have to fight against the widespread impression that that is what he stood for.

[8]Two good books on this topic, both by John Warwick Montgomery, are *The "Is God Dead?" Controversy* (Grand Rapids: Zondervan, 1966), and *The Altizer-Montgomery Dialogue* (Chicago: Inter-Varsity, 1967), which is the text of a debate between Montgomery and Thomas Altizer.

CHAPTER 3

· THE QUESTION OF TRUTH: A SECOND FALL? ·

Now the serpent was more subtil than any beast of the field that the Lord God had made. And he said unto the woman, Yea, hath God said, Ye shall not eat of every tree of the garden?

GENESIS 3:1

The Fall of man began with a doubt about the existence of truth. Satan succeeded in making God's rather simple and clear words to Adam and Eve seem implausible, self-serving, and ultimately incredible. That was his real victory. After that it was only a matter of time before Eve reached out for

> "the Fruit
> Of that Forbidd'n Tree, whose mortal tast
> Brought Death into the World, and all our woe."
> (*Paradise Lost*, Book I, lines 1-3)

In the case of our first parents, the disobedience which resulted from distrust had prompt and disastrous consequences. Expelled from Paradise, they began to trust God again. They could not recover Eden, but even as their punishment was being declared, they were given the promise of a Saviour (the so-called *Proto-evangelium,* Genesis 3:15). Since that time, man has had the hope of life (real life, in the biblical sense, i.e. life with God, eternal life) not in the bread which he can raise and bake with his own hands, but in the words which come from the mouth of God.

Biblical religion, both Jewish and Christian, has always been clear about the fact that the worst threat to man comes not from those who can take away his physical food, nor even from those who can kill him, but from those who can deny him access to truth, and thereby cut him off from all final reality and meaning, from the God who is the source both of truth and of life.[1] We recognize that truth, in biblical thought, is not an abstract system of definitions or propositions: it is communication from God to man, reliable because God is its author, and supremely meaningful because, as commandment, prophecy, and gospel, it establishes a valid and viable relationship between man and God. On the other hand, the fact that truth is *personal,* i.e. related to and grounded in the person of God, does not mean that it is not *propositional.* It consists, at least in part, in statements which have a definite, factual content, and which can be understood. There are examples in the Bible where it is not clear whether a text is meant literally or symbolically, and there are some passages which are clearly symbolic, but this does not exclude the vital fact that a very great portion of what the Bible says is presented as literally true according to its simplest and most obvious sense.[2]

Satan's tactic was to question the reliability of what God had said and to impugn his motives. Criticisms and doubts of this kind have been raised over and over again in the history of ancient Israel and of the Christian church. In fact, their history is a catalogue of the myriad plausible and implausible ways man can devise to question the Word or the words of God. An awareness of the long history of false teaching and doctrinal disorder in Israel and the church, and of the confusion and destruction they have caused, may help to put the present theological situation into perspective. In one sense it is neither new nor unusual. Moses had to contend with doubt, syncretism, disobedience, and idolatry even as he was leading the Jews out of slavery in Egypt. A considerable part of the New Testament is the result of the Apostle Paul's struggle with doctrinal error and moral disorder in his infant churches. Christianity has faced some serious crises in the past, and so far has survived them. But in the mid-twentieth century, as the culmination of a development which began at least as long ago as Hegel and Kierkegaard, the devil has improved his tactics. Instead of challenging the truth of a particular doctrine, he challenges the very concept of truth; instead of disguising himself as a serpent and impugning the motives of God, he wears the robes of academic theology and claims to be speaking for God.

This is the cardinal challenge to the life of the Christian church today. The church may conceivably exist without this or that doctrine, but it cannot exist without truth. That is to say, it cannot exist as a *Christian* church. What we are facing today is an attempt to insure the survival of the church as an institution *even at the cost of the principles it is supposed to embody*. Some theologians, prelates, and church officials are completely sincere in their attempts to preserve "the church" in this limited and un-Christian sense; having lost the sense of what truth is and means, they are trying to save the structure which seems to have so many secondary values and cherished associations. If they succeed, they will have destroyed the church as a true *church* or *ekklesía* (*church, kirk, kirche*, from Gk. *kuriakós*, pertaining to the Lord, especially, pertaining to the Lord Christ,[3] and Lat. *ecclesia*, Gk. *ekklesía*, the group that has been called out or gathered [i.e. by the voice of God]). They will also have destroyed the individual Christian's possibility of existence as a Christian, for without truth he has no access to the God of truth.

1. *Pilate's Question: What is Truth?*

When Pilate asked Jesus at his trial, "What is truth?" (John 18:38) it was not an attempt to find an answer. The cynical Roman aristocrat was implying that there is no such thing as truth: that "it's all in how you look at it." This is the spirit of modern thought, but it is definitely not the spirit of Christianity, which claims to bring man authoritative, reliable, and intelligible truth. There is, indeed, a dimension of *mystery* to the truth contained in Christian revelation. The Bible makes no claim to be a *complete* revelation of God. Man, as a finite creature, cannot fully know God. It does claim to be a true revelation, one which is worthy of belief not merely as an expression of commitment to an ideal, but as an acceptance of truth.

We should not make the error of looking at the instrument of Christian revelation, the Bible, as a complete source of all knowledge, from the details of Creation to the street plan of heaven. There is much in it that is incomplete, figurative, or symbolic—and deliberately so. We must not try to present the Bible as though it were some kind of abstractly perfect and complete book. It is claimed that the Book of Mormon was sent down from heaven engraved on golden plates, but no such claim is made for the Bible, which is the work of men. They were, it is true, "men moved by the Holy Spirit [who] spoke from God" (II Peter 1:21), and the Scripture they produced is "inspired by God and profitable for teaching, for reproof, for correction, for training in righteousness" (II Timothy 3:16). That the Bible has a human side is quite consistent with the whole principle of God's revelation to man, which involves his accommodation of his revelation to human capacity. The meaning of accommodation is that there is in fact in God's self-discourse something that we can understand, that it *is* authoritative and reliable, and constitutes an adequate guide to God's nature and will—as the Westminster Confession puts it, "the only perfect rule of faith and practice."⁴

The modern mind, which is represented as much within the church as outside it, rebels against the concept of any objective truth of an ultimate, binding nature. Objective truth carries with it the implied obligation to act in accordance with it. It puts a severe limitation on man's freedom of opinion. It is true that this limitation is one which in the last analysis is fundamental to *sanity*; it is also true that there are major portions of mankind who seem to be willing to surrender sanity itself if they must do so in order to have complete freedom from limitation.

The modern mind objects to authority as authority. We need only reflect for a moment on the fact that the word *authority* itself shares some of the odium associated with its derivatives *authoritarian* and *authoritarianism*. The idea of authority is basic to the concept of a personal God. One of the reasons for the spread of pantheistic ideas, among people as different in their way of thinking as the late Paul Tillich and Sir Julian Huxley, is the fact that the impersonal All-god makes no attempt to exercise authority over men, as does the God of biblical revelation.

If the personal God of biblical revelation is real, he is in fact *the* Author. It makes no difference to his authority whether we approve of it, or of him, although ultimately it makes a great deal of difference to us. It is part of the subjectivism and relativism so characteristic of the mid-twentieth century that the widespread attitude of rebellion against all authority, including God's, is given—and often accepted—as a reason for the church to tone down, or even abandon, its claim to speak with authority. There is nothing new about human rebellion, and the fact that it is more or less widespread in a particular age proves nothing.

A significant and widespread phenomenon, never more common in human history than today, is that rebelliousness against authority in the good sense of that word is often accompanied or followed by submission to tyranny. Let us define the two terms. Inherent in the concept of authority is that of origin, and therefore of the rights of the author. In human experience, a man or an institution which has legitimate authority can use it wrongly: hence we can speak of abuse of authority. The idea of tyranny involves the unjustified acquisition or usurpation of power. A flight from or rebellion against just authority often involves subjugation by a far more restrictive tyranny; sometimes the tyranny is imposed by force, but often the rebels meekly submit to it or even invite it. The most flagrant example in our generation is given by the anarchistic group called the New Left. They oppose every legitimate expression of justly constituted authority, whether it be government, the university, or the church. By so doing they contribute to the chances of Communist tyranny to step in and establish itself.

Many observers feel that the New Left and related groups are simply abysmally short-sighted, i.e. that they do not realize that by attacking the comparatively mild restraints of a democratic society, they are paving the way for the absolutist tyranny of Communism, against which, it is reasoned, they would object even more strenuously "if only they knew what it is really like." The if-only-they-knew argument has been used often in history to defend the motives of people who in fact had plenty of opportunity to know the realities behind what they supported. Luther at first felt that if only the Pope knew the truth about the abuses to which he was objecting, he would suppress them. During World War II, many Germans felt that if only the Fuhrer knew what the S.S. was doing, he would put a stop to it. Although the abuses of the medieval church are not to be compared to the crimes of Nazism, there is this similarity in the reactions of Leo X and Hitler to the failings of their respective subordinates: even if they did not actually approve of them, their willingness to ignore them cannot really be excused on grounds of ignorance.

Undoubtedly there are idealistic Communists who become terribly disillusioned when the system is actually established in their own country, or when they go to live in a "People's Democracy." The 1930's and 1940's furnished numerous examples, including people as distinguished as Arthur Koestler and William Henry Chamberlin. But today the intellectual and pseudo-intellectual supporters of Communistic intrigue cannot reasonably claim ignorance. Some, undoubtedly, are still ignorant. Even the worst system has its naïvely idealistic supporters. The majority, however, which objects to limited, constitutional authority even though its actions may lead to an absolute tyranny, really knows what it is doing. Lawful authority demands from man the *moral* response of willing, chosen obedience. Tyranny makes much greater *physical* demands on those under its power, but no moral ones. It takes all the responsibility for *moral* decision.

The flight from authority characteristic of our period is also a flight from moral responsibility, from the need to be responsible for making decisions which have consequences. Even more typical of the anarchistic New Left than willing submission to Communist tyranny is the acceptance of the still less rational and more pervasive tyranny of L.S.D. and the habit-forming drugs. It seems inconsistent that the same people who will demand freedom from every legal restraint of a more-or-less libertarian society will voluntarily take drugs which they know will enchain them in a mind-destroying slavery. It is not inconsistent. The mild restraints of a free society bring with them moral responsibility and accountability; drugs, like Communism, bring slavery but take away responsibility. The religious use of L.S.D. is a crystal-clear illustration: it makes no moral demands. The so-called religious experience it provides demands no discipline, no examination of conscience, no self-purification. All it requires is the price of the L.S.D.-saturated sugar-cube.[5]

The people who revolt against authority, properly so called, despite the fact that by doing so they will promote tyranny, know exactly what they are doing. It is a reflection of the craving for freedom from the authority of *the Author*. The Bible is the long, long story of God's long, long love for man, but it is not always love as we like to imagine it: "You only have I known of all the families of the earth," God said to his chosen people, "therefore I will punish you for all your iniquities" (Amos 3:2). One cannot know the love of God without an intimation of the terror of the Lord (II Corinthians 5:11). People flee the terror of a responsible relationship with the personal, almighty God of Israel, although he is the God of love, and prefer the impersonal and thankfully blind terror of a thousand human and inhuman tyrannies. "This is the judgment," said Christ—in modern parlance, he could have said: This is the tragedy—"that the light is come into the world, and men loved the darkness rather than the light, for their deeds were evil" (John 3:19).

Pilate's question, and its implicit denial, is the mood of modern thought. Theology is not independent of the modern world: it is an expression of our age and of its spirit. It too is prone to ask Pilate's question, with Pilate's supercilious smile. Adam and Eve refused to believe a specific, clear warning, seduced by the Tempter's ingratiating, "Yea, hath God said . . .?" The question of our age and mentality is that of Pilate. There are only three human beings mentioned by name in the great creeds, the Apostles' Creed and the Nicene Creed. They are Jesus, the Son of Man who was also Son of God,[6] St. Mary the Virgin, who said, "Behold, the handmaiden of the Lord" (Luke 1:38), and Pontius Pilate the imperial governor, who said, "What is truth?" In Adam we have failure and death; in Christ, the Second Adam, we have God's love, and our own life. Do we, in our "mature" modern world, as we echo Pilate's question, have our Third Adam, and Second Fall?

2. The Second Fall

The Fall came when man doubted the truth of a particular statement, a warning given to him by God. The recovery, a long and costly process, began when fallen man realized that the warning had in fact been objectively true. We can be grateful that Adam was simple enough, or that the evidence was compelling enough, that he did not take refuge in some concept such as "symbolic truth" or "religious truth." As long as we refuse to accept the possibility of objective truth, of what one theologian calls *true truth*,[7] we cannot recover from the effects of the Fall. If disbelief in particular words of God formed the basis for the historic Fall, disbelief in the possibility of objective truth is the basis for a kind of Second Fall.

That is the tremendous burden of human freedom: that we can fall. And we can fall not only individually, but we can fall for others, for future generations, perhaps for all our race. It has been suggested that with thermonuclear power, man now has the capacity to blast his whole world, and finally frustrate the prophecy "that the creation itself also will be set free from its slavery to corruption into the freedom of the glory of the children of God" (Romans 8:21). That is a possibility. In *Paradise Lost,* God the Father, speaking to the Son, says of man:

> I formd them free, and free they must remain,
> Till they enthrall themselves: I else must change
> Thir nature . . .
>
> Book III, lines 124-126

That is freedom. The right to use it involves the chance to lose it, and not only in the political realm, but in the intellectual, and perhaps even—if we too arrogantly misread God's promises and too confidently presume upon his patience—in the realm of the spirit.[8] From the first Fall, man was raised by grace. If through a second Fall he convinces himself that there is no truth, then there is therefore no real grace, and who will raise him then?

The nineteenth and early twentieth centuries were dominated by the work of the *reductionists* in theology: men who attacked doctrine after doctrine, discarding the heritage of faith. Their battle-cry was, "It is not really necessary to believe the traditional doctrine of . . ." The fault of such men was serious, but at least they still believed in truth. The unbelief of the nineteenth century was un-belief in something, namely, historic Christianity, and at least it reflected the distinct character and form of what it rejected. The unbelief of the twentieth century is false belief, whether it be in the thousand idols of modern, "scientific," twentieth-century man, or in the great *Panurge* shared by modern Communism and "modern" or "radical" theology, in which God is the universe, the movement of history, process —anything but the God of Israel and the Father of Jesus Christ.

Idolatry is always more dangerous than mere unbelief. If the nineteenth century was an age of confident rationalism, and scepticism, the twentieth is the century of frantic irrationality—and idolatry.

One twentieth-century man of every five lives in the land of Mao Tse-tung. A clearer example of twentieth-century idolatry is scarcely needed. But we need not turn to China for our idols. Let the reader cast his eyes about him. He will not need to look far.

Idolatry is not a fiction. The idols may be unreal, but the thralldom is all too real. It is characteristic of thralldom that one can get oneself into it easily, but getting out is a different question. The half-scientific, mid-twentieth century is the time of the flight from truth, and without truth there is no freedom.

> . . . free they must remain,
> Till they enthrall themselves.

Notes

[1]There are many passages in both the Old and the New Testaments which emphasize the close relationship between truth and the person of God or Jesus Christ, e.g.: Deuteronomy 32:4, "[He is] a God of truth"; He recognizes the man who "speaks the truth in his heart" (Psalm 15:2); He "desires truth in the inmost parts" (Psalm 51:6); Christ is "full of grace and truth" (John 1:14); he is "the way, the truth, and the life" (John 14:6).

[2]Since we have chosen the story of the Fall of Man in Genesis 3 to illustrate our major proposition, we may do well to say that this is an example of a biblical passage which most people reject as a true account of something that actually happened. Liberal Protestant scholars abandoned the idea that there was a first pair and a literal fall long ago; today, even leading Roman Catholic scholars, such as Roland DeVaux, speak of the early chapters of Genesis as "the Creation myths." The difficulty lies in the fact that there is nothing in the way the story of the Fall is told in Genesis 3 to confirm the impression that it was meant to be taken symbolically rather than literally, and in the fact that St. Paul makes a very important comparison between Adam and Christ, the "Second Adam," in Romans 5:12-19. Genesis 3 presents us with many problems, but it is not wise to reject it as a description of something which really happened because we have accepted a doctrinaire *evolutionism* with regard either to the origins of man, or of the Bible, or both. Pure naturalistic evolution as an explanation of the origins of man would rule out the possibility that Genesis 3 is in any sense literally true, *but* naturalistic evolution is itself full of unresolved problems (summarized by John C. Greene, *Darwin and the Modern World View*, Baton Rouge: Louisiana State University Press, 1961,

reprinted as a Mentor Book, New York: The New American Library, 1961). The uncritical and sweeping acceptance of naturalistic evolution which characterizes liberal Protestantism and is coming to dominate Roman Catholic thought in the wake of Teilhard de Chardin is illustrated by the recent article by William T. Keeton in *Christian Century*: "Evolution: Basic to Biology," Vol. LXXXIV, No. 3 (Jan. 18, 1967), pp. 71-76. The shallowness and inadequacy of this approach is challenged by A. E. Wilder Smith, "Darwinism and Contemporary Thought," *Christianity Today*, Vol. XI, No. 17 (May 26, 1967), pp. 843-846, as well as in his more extensive treatment *Man's Origin, Man's Destiny* (Wheaton, Illinois: Harold Shaw, 1968). The impact of the doctrine of naturalistic evolution on other intellectual disciplines is analyzed by Raymond F. Surburg, "The Influence of Darwinism," in Paul A. Zimmermann, ed., *Darwin, Evolution, and Creation* (St. Louis: Concordia, 1959). A clear if somewhat extreme statement of the conservative Protestant rejection of evolutionary doctrine is given by Henry M. Morris, *The Twilight of Evolution* (Grand Rapids: Baker, 1964). Bernard Ramm, in *The Christian View of Science and Scripture* (Grand Rapids: Eerdmans, 1955) attempts to harmonize a kind of creative evolution with Genesis 3 by means of the theory that God placed a *representative pair* in a specially-prepared garden to give them the test by which mankind would stand or fall.

The tremendous impact of the evolutionary philosophy of history and religion on the interpretation of the Bible is examined in Kenneth A. Kitchen, *Ancient Orient and Old Testament* (Chicago: Inter-Varsity, 1967). In effect the Old Testament was remade by 19th-century critics to suit their philosophy of continuous evolution, and their conclusions are still held today, even though their reasoning has lost in credibility with the advance of our knowledge about the ancient Near East.

[3]The Greek *kuriakós* is "assumed to be the original of the Teutonic . . . but how this Greek name came to be adopted by the Northern nations, rather than the Roman name *ecclesia,* has not been satisfactorily explained." Liddell and Scott's *Intermediate Greek-English Lexicon* (Oxford: Oxford University Press, 1955), p. 458.

[4]A concise summary of the church's concept of inspiration is given by Geoffrey W. Bromiley, "The Church Doctrine of Inspiration," in Carl F. H. Henry, ed., *Revelation and the Bible* (Grand Rapids: Baker, 1958), pp. 203-217. The extent and limitations of the Bible's claims to be truth have received an excellent analysis of Prof. Henri Blocher of Vaux-sur-Seine, "La notion de verité dans la Bible," in *Themelios* (Lausanne), Vol. IV, No. 2 (1967), pp. 8-20.

[5]The "religious" use of drugs is categorically rejected by the present writer. The content of Christian revelation and experience transcends our complete understanding, but it always has a content which can be understood and communicated and which has a moral dimension. A new book praising the religious use of drugs, William Braden's *The Private Sea: LSD and the Search for God* (Chicago: Quadrangle, 1967) was not available at the time of

this writing. It is reviewed in *Christian Century*, Vol. LXXXIV, No. 19 (May 10, 1967), p. 626. A short and very gripping account by a Christian physicist who sought to intensify his experience of God through L.S.D. is Lambert Dolphin, Jr., "A Trip with LSD," *His,* Vol. XXVII, No. 6 (March, 1967), pp. 5-7, 23.

[6]Orthodox theology has allowed itself to be stampeded by theological liberalism with its stress on the *mere* humanity of Jesus, to the point where it emphasizes his divinity and neglects his humanity. Jesus is, in the New Testament, the eternal Son of God, "the radiance of His glory and the exact representation of His nature," and he is also the one who is "not ashamed to call [us] brethren" (Hebrews 1:3, 2:11).

[7]Dr. Francis A. Schaeffer of Huémoz, Switzerland, some of whose insights into the place of Christian faith in the twentieth century are given in his two 1968 books, *Escape from Reason* (London: Inter-Varsity) and *The God Who Is There* (London: Hodder and Stoughton, and Chicago: Inter-Varsity), has had a marked influence on the Christian development of many students and younger ministers and theologians, including the present writer.

[8]The orthodox Christian will immediately object that to suggest the possibility of an ultimate victory of evil in the world is Manichaean and not Christian. That is true. On the other hand, we must remember that only a small fraction of the universal church is alive now. The vast majority of its members are, in Harry Blamire's words, already "safe home." The possibility that we could defeat ourselves, and ring down the curtain of history on man's drama, is not excluded. There can be such a thing as a defeated rear guard in a victorious army.

CHAPTER 4

· THE BIG SUBSTITUTION ·

Or do you think that I cannot appeal to My Father, and He will at once put at My disposal more than twelve legions of angels?

MATTHEW 26:53

Suppose that the mid-twentieth-century church in general, and the great Protestant denominations in particular, are guilty of the charges, allegations, and implications made in the first three chapters. It is not serious enough about the factual basis of faith, but instead tends to discount it if not to reject it. It promotes so-called "worship" which is boring to man and an affront to God. There is no evidence of any concern for objective truth. All these charges are negative in nature: the church is forgetting, the church is no longer concerned, the church is failing . . . But the church goes on. Surely it must be doing something positive. Surely it has a vision greater than the manifold *abdication of responsibility* with which it has been charged. What is it? What new thing has appeared to call the church away from her first love?

In the preceding chapter it was admitted that there are men who honestly and sincerely love the church and want to keep it alive, although they reject the church's Founder and deny him his title of Lord. It would be inconsistent for such men of the church to spend their lives and energies in worship, in evangelism, in being shepherds of souls. Where do they find their vocation? Often they are idealistic, unselfish, vigorous men, with a desire to accomplish something worthwhile. In a sense, they probably do not belong in the church at all— not from their point of view, if the church is nothing more than they think it to be, and not from the church's point of view, if it is in fact

what the Bible calls it. But they are there, and they are workers, not
shirkers. Where do they find an outlet for their often creative, often
altruistic, generally sincerely benevolent energy?

The answer is simple. A considerable portion of the church, a segment which has influence and power far beyond its numerical
strength, has replaced the City of God with the City of Man. Social
concerns—in themselves good, perhaps, often worthy—have replaced
the Gospel of Christ. This is not a momentary blindness, a regrettable
inconsistency. It is becoming, in ever wider sections of the Christian
church, deliberate policy. Social and political action is being substituted for the Gospel of God's saving act in Christ.

1. The Substitution

The crucial word in this accusation is *substitute*. If we had said,
"social action is being *added* to the Gospel," the accusation would
not have merely been weaker, it would have been nonsense. The
historic Gospel, the historic church, has always had social action.
Sometimes it has even had too much of it, as most people would
admit happened in the Crusades, and in Prohibition. Of course
Christians, their denominations, and the church in general have
often failed to produce the social actions which are consistent with
the Gospel. Orthodoxy in doctrine is no defense against such inconsistency: often those who are doctrinally above reproach have been
the most serious offenders. Recognizing this, we must not admit too
much. The orthodox elements in the church, those which are traditionally most concerned with saving souls, also do have a tremendous
record of works of charity[1] and benevolence. Where Christian faith
became widespread—and historically Christian faith, when it is
spreading, is always close to orthodoxy—it changed the face of society, and it changed it for the better. Historic Christianity should not
attempt to whitewash its failures and inconsistencies, but it does not
need to beat its breast as though it had done nothing by comparison
with the rest of the world.

No, it is not necessary to *add* social content to the Gospel. It was
always there, although it has too frequently been ignored or at least
neglected. But it is a question of priorities. The Gospel without *any*

social consequences is a fraud and a sham, as St. James warns (James 2:20-26), and cannot save those who merely profess it without practicing it. The Gospel without *enough* social consequences is a weakened and diminished thing, and is not all it should be. But if the priorities are reversed, and the social *consequences* are made the prerequisites, or even the end in themselves, then the Gospel is destroyed.

"Politics is the vehicle through which the will of God is done in the world today," said Robert McAfee Brown, Protestant educator, Stanford professor, and a leading spokesman for ecumenism. As chairman of the Standing Committee on Church and Society of the United Presbyterian Church in the U.S.A., he was addressing that church's 179th General Assembly.[2] Of course politics has always been recognized as *a* vehicle through which God works: St. Paul wrote, "Rulers are servants of God" (Romans 13:6), and Calvin taught that civil government is ordained by God and is a good gift.[3] Something very, very strange has happened to the church when it can be claimed to be *the* vehicle.

Jesus Christ told his disciples, "Seek ye first the kingdom of God and his righteousness; and all these things [food, drink, clothing, i.e., all that the body needs] shall be added unto you" (Matthew 6:33, A.V.).[4] The ex-dictator and self-styled savior of Ghana, Kwame Nkrumah, revised the New Testament text to read, "Seek ye first the political kingdom." It is not a question of an exclusive preoccupation with one or the other, but of priorities. We know on whose authority Nkrumah reversed Christ's priorities: his own. Have our contemporary theologians and church leaders a better and more adequate authority for making the same reversal themselves?

The sweeping charge that the modern church, not only in its liberalized Protestant branches, but also in Roman Catholicism, is making this reversal is easy to document. Robert McAfee Brown's statement does not speak merely for one committee of one American denomination: he is, after all, the leading spokesman for ecumenism among the U.S.A. Presbyterians,[5] if we except their former Stated Clerk, Eugene Carson Blake, now the general secretary of the World Council of Churches in Geneva. From July 12-26, 1966, the World Council's department *Church and Society* held a world conference in Geneva. It was dominated by the theme "revolution." The task of the church was seen as being the handmaiden or water-boy of the world revolution, if it is too presumptuous to be its architect. A vigorous controversy has broken out about this Geneva conference, as to what it said and did not say, and as to whether or to what extent it represents the voice of the organized ecumenical movement. The conclusions of the Geneva Conference do not by any means represent the feelings of the majority of Christians represented in the World Council, but they definitely show the direction that the leadership is taking.[6] As to the Roman Catholic Church, the Easter, 1967 encyclical of Pope Paul VI, *Populorum Progressio,* could easily have been written by one of the W.C.C. sociologists—or even by an optimistic humanist like Sir Julian Huxley, aside from an occasional reference to God and to Jesus Christ. The Roman pontiff's "benediction" in this Easter message is a strange thing:

> Magnanimously We bless you, and call upon all men of good will to unite themselves fraternally with you. For, if *development is the new name of peace,* who would not wish to cooperate with all his powers? Yes, all of you: We invite you to respond to our cry of anguish, in the Name of the Lord.[7]

That the message of Easter is revolutionary, we will not dispute, but when an Easter message from the Pope himself deals with political revolution, replaces the peace of God with economic development, and gives instead of a blessing from God, his own "cry of anguish," it is unnecessary to offer further documentation of the claim that the dangerous substitution is under way in the church of Rome.

Since the preceding lines were written, early in 1967, Pope Paul VI has issued two dramatic documents, the first being his creed of June 30, 1968, the second the encyclical *Humanae vitae.* Is it possible that the Pope has decided to try to stem the doctrinal and ethical changes he formerly seemed willing to tolerate if not to approve? It is too early to be sure what the real meaning and impact of these striking declarations will be, but it is certainly possible that our earlier evaluation of him as an ecclesiastical manager rather than a crusader will be proved inaccurate. Whether even the Pope, humanly speaking, will be able to check the headlong plunge of the Roman Catholic Church into the maelstrom of twentieth-century relativism, remains to be seen.

2. Why This Substitution: The Flight from Responsibility

It is legitimate to ask why the church is turning to political action, especially now. In past centuries, when the papacy had a tremendous and virtually unchallenged influence throughout Europe, many attempts were made by the church to direct the development of government and society. After the Reformation, some leading Protestants took advantage of their position to attempt to redesign society by means of political power. Oliver Cromwell is the most remarkable example in the history of the English-speaking peoples. In spite of the fact that political authorities were very favorably disposed towards the church, if not actually under its control, these attempts were on the whole failures. The Christian leader who actually succeeded in influencing social, political, and economic developments most strikingly was, by contrast, a man who did not reach out for political influence and power, but devoted himself to the tasks of evangelism and church discipline: John Wesley, the founder of Methodism (1703-1791). The religious rebirth which he brought to England is widely credited with having saved that country a bloody revolution such as took place in France.

Today, however, the church nowhere has the ready access to political power once enjoyed by certain popes, nor does it have at its disposal devout, highly-committed political leaders like Cromwell. Its position in society today does not even give it as much leverage for reform as it enjoyed in the days of John Wesley. What then does it hope to accomplish by turning its remaining strength and energies into the field of social and economic development and revolution, where so many much more powerful actors are already present?

The answer is twofold. On the one hand, a measure of *self-deception* is involved. It is hard to imagine that church leaders can really believe that they influence the course of history with their social and economic announcements and appeals. In isolated cases, such as the passage of the Civil Rights Act of 1965, ecclesiastical propaganda and pressure has played an important role, but that was an exception, and already the Civil Rights movement has become the Black Power movement and has wrenched itself out of the hands of all of its ecclesiastical guides—except for those few who would rather betray their principles than lose the illusion of power. To an embarrassingly great extent, religious "leadership" in social action consists in jumping on a bandwagon that is already well under way, and attempting to attract general attention. Nevertheless, religious leaders do seem to be able to deceive themselves and to imagine that they are directing events and making history, when in fact they are only trailing along behind. It is necessary to postulate a certain amount of genuine deception on their part to explain the naïve enthusiasm with which they put their programs forward.

The second part of the answer is the same as that given for the progressive abandonment of objective truth and of basic doctrine: it is a withdrawal from responsibility. The historic Christian faith places a tremendous responsibility on individual Christians *for other individuals*. In a non-Christian or even anti-Christian society this personal responsibility is almost too much to bear. It is easy, in fact psychologically it is almost necessary, to take refuge in structures which divert and distribute individual responsibility to God for one's neighbor.

If Christianity is true, then those who adhere to it have an awful responsibility. To them is committed the task of spreading the News without which it is impossible for man to have eternal life. In evangelically-inclined Protestant circles one is frequently reminded of the Great Commission given by Christ to his disciples before his ascension: "Go therefore and make disciples of all nations . . ." (Matthew 28:19). It is often received as a kind of challenge to meritorious extra duty. Its negative implication is overlooked: If *you* do not do it, it will not be done. The New Testament offers little if any hope of salvation for those who do not know Christ, regardless of whether they wilfully reject him or never hear of him. These conditions are hard ones, and many theologians have proposed various ways in which those who do not know of Christ could still share in the meritorious effects of his work, as "anonymous Christians." The idea that every one will somehow receive a chance is an appealing one, and it takes some of the burden off of the church, but it is not very well founded in the teaching of Christ himself, nor in the rest of the New Testament. It may take the psychological pressure off indolent or timid Christians, who refuse to be witnesses for Christ, but it cannot give any really solid basis for optimism about the fate of those who do not know him.[8]

During the age when the West (which at that time thought of itself as the World) was Christian, at least in name, the responsibility to evangelize did not weigh so heavily on the church as a whole, nor on individual Christians. Everyone in a "Christian" nation may be presumed to have heard the Gospel, or at least to have had the chance. Whether this presumption is true or not is a different matter. Even in the best of "Christian" nations a considerable number of people fail to attend church, or fail to listen if they do attend. There was no more guarantee in the "Age of Faith" than there is today that the church would present them with the message of Christ in a clear and understandable form. But even allowing for the great discrepancy between the theory of a Christian nation, and what the Christianity of that nation looks like in practice, the presumption is not absurd.

Two things have happened in the modern world to shatter this easy complacency and to face the individual Christian and the church once again with the responsibility for evangelism, for proclaiming the Gospel, and leading men and women to Christ. The first is that the West has had to realize that it is not the world. During the nineteenth century, and to a diminished degree up to World War II, Western civilization tended to think of itself as *civilization,* and of all other cultures as more or less developed forms of benighted barbarism, waiting only for the light from the West. The United Nations, as they were organized immediately after World War II, represented the old concept: the World, for practical purposes, included the victorious Europeans and American countries, with a disdained and dormant China added. In the years since 1945, the West has become a minority. In the present United Nations, the United States still pays the bills, but neither the United States nor the West as a whole calls the tune. The "Christian" West has had to recognize that the non-Christianity of the East, the paganism of parts of Africa, and the anti-Christianity of the Communist world are not just transition phases, which will quickly pass away as they get to know us better. We again have to face the Great Commission.

The second shattering thing which has happened to the "Christian" West is *secularism.* The believing Christians are a minority in every country of the once-Christian West. In a few places there is still an aura of Christianity, so that it is not absolutely necessary to face the church's minority status. Nevertheless, it is becoming increasingly harder for Christians everywhere to escape the awareness that the church is a minority, and that convinced believers within the nominal church are a smaller minority still. It is becoming increasingly evident that the responsibility to bear witness to Christ no longer begins on the other side of the Pacific Ocean, as we once comfortably assumed, but on the other side of the street, or even on the other side of the breakfast table.

If Christ has no witnesses other than his Christian disciples here on earth, and if people who fail to accept him have no real grounds for any hope of eternal life, and if finally not only the greater part of the world, but the greater part of the nation and a large part of the nominal church do not in fact accept him, then the conclusion is dreadful, and inescapable. Christians must admit that a large proportion of the people of the world, of their fellow-countrymen, of their fellow church members, and even of the members of their family and of their friends, may very well be lost eternally.

This is not an easy conclusion to face. It can easily drive a person into a despairing depression, or unbelief, or both. To understand and live with the full implications of Christian teaching on the subject demands wisdom and courage. It is hard to face the fact that Christ "came to His own, and those who were His own did not receive Him" (John 1:11). It is hard to have to tie it in with St. Paul's admonition, "We are ambassadors for Christ, as though God were entreating through us" (II Corinthians 5:20). Under such circumstances, it is only natural that much of the church is turning its gaze away from spiritual responsibility to the unconverted, which is so hard to fulfil, to social responsibility.[9]

Responsibility for the individual is too difficult for the churches. It is even too difficult in the area of benevolent care for physical needs, for what used to come under Christian charity has been turned over to the agencies of public welfare. It seems to be impossible for the modern church to bear the burden of being responsible for the fate of individual men's perishable bodies: it must abandon that concern to the State. How then can we expect the church to bear the responsibility for their souls?[10]

A final, and significant, symptom of the church's flight from responsibility for persons to responsibility (or pretended responsibility) for the structures of society lies in the changing direction of ecclesiastical pressures for legislation. The church was certainly involved in society earlier in the century: the ill-fated experiment with Prohibition is a prime example of church-sponsored legislation. In their support of Prohibition, the participating American denominations were engaging in social action just as much as are their descendants who today support civil rights, poverty legislation, and so on, but there was a significant difference. Prohibition was an attempt to reform *individuals* through legislation. It was intended to have a direct, moral benefit on the lives of individuals directly affected. The new movements frankly aim at *society* first, and only secondarily at the individuals within it.

It is not merely a question of tactics; it is more fundamental than that. "God loved the world," Christ tells us in John 3:16, and "the world" is a collective expression, which includes all of society and a lot more besides. This text is, for obvious reasons, a favorite of the social actionists within the church.[11] But Christ continues with a singular: the love of God has the effect that "whosoever believes" (Gk. *ho pisteúon*, the believing one), in the singular, may be saved and have everlasting life. The love of God is for the *world*, but in the New Testament it appeals to *individuals*, challenges *individuals*, and works through *individuals*. Can the church turn from witness to individuals to attempts to reshape society through the state without turning from being a servant of God to trying to play God?

3. *The Direction of Social Action*

One of the most puzzling developments of the mid-twentieth century is the growing Communist-Christian rapprochement. Throughout the whole nineteenth century and much of the twentieth, all branches of the Christian church were determined in their opposition to Marxism, an opposition which became even stronger after the Communist Revolution in Russia. The churches were regarded as bastions of social conservatism. "Theology supports the throne," they used to say in the Kaiser's Germany. The picture was not uniform, the most important exception being England, where the Labour Party still bears significant traces of the role which Non-Conformist piety played in its founding. Elsewhere the clergy, sharing the frustrations, fears, and anxieties of the rest of the population, could on occasion greet revolutions with enthusiasm, as in France in 1789 and in Germany in 1933. Nevertheless the church on the whole played a conservative role, and formed a hard wall of resistance to Communism. In Roman Catholicism this attitude was maintained by Pope Pius XII; his successor John XXIII relaxed it, and the present Pope seems to be displaying an inclination to reverse it.

It has often been charged that the church, particularly Protestant denominations in America, has been subverted by Communist agents. The truth of these charges has been extensively discussed and disputed. They are not our concern here, for if true, they mean that the church is being perverted through a skilful and planned infiltration. What is more significant for our inquiry is the question of whether the church is being *converted* from within, without the use of conspiratorial methods by outside powers.

It does not surprise us that a bishop of the Russian Orthodox Church in the Soviet Union never publicly criticizes the policies of his own atheistic, anti-Christian government, but instead praises them as often as he can. A man who has achieved a high office in a church in a Communist-dominated land is certainly there on government sufferance, if not by government connivance. What does surprise is that such men have been accepted, more or less at face value, by the presumably free and rational members of the World Council of Churches. It is not surprising that delegates from Communist nations often represent their governments' official viewpoint at World Council sessions. It is more surprising that others, presumably free delegates, take similar stands and support similar views.

To some extent this can be explained and made understandable. For decades major elements in the church did rigidly oppose all social change, and defend entrenched privilege; they were indeed reactionary and opposed to all attempts at social progress. Sometimes this was from a genuinely religious dread of violent change, sometimes because important elements in the church were too closely involved with the established powers. A certain reaction to this is inevitable and desirable. The present situation goes far beyond anything that can be interpreted as a healthy—or even slightly excessive—reaction to the errors of the past. The Geneva Conference on Church and Society, together with Pope Paul's *Populorum Progressio,* shows that important, if not to say dominant, elements in the church have picked "rapid social change," i.e. revolution, as the wave of the future, and are trying to ride it.

From the point of view of what the church should be, if it is to be faithful to its heritage and to the tasks which Christ gave it, this is an unworthy policy, in at least two ways. First, it is both deceptive and deceived: deceptive, because the church's spokesmen are evidently trying to give an impression of leading and directing events which they are in fact merely following, and deceived, because by the late 1960's both the Communist economic system and the myth of the natural goodness of the emerging nations are thoroughly discredited. Second, by it the church admits that it has nothing better to offer the world than what the world can devise for and recommend to itself. With that admission, it negates its own reason for existence. That seems to be its deliberate choice.

Within Roman Catholicism, which has only recently begun to loosen up and lose some of its traditional rigidity, it is not yet absolutely clear what is happening (although many qualified Roman Catholic observers are already filled with the gravest apprehensions). Within Protestantism, it is abundantly clear that the major institutions have chosen to continue to live, as institutions, in harmony with the changing world as best they can—even though it means surrendering what was their unique privilege and their reason for existence: possession and proclamation of the saving truth of God. They have made and are making this choice rather than accepting its alternative, which might be to suffer persecution, even death, as an institution, rather than surrender their faith. This alternative sometimes results in what is called martyrdom, and it sounds deadly. Ultimately it is far healthier for the individual Christian and for the church than compromise. Of course, for many Protestant denominations and institutions, the choice was made long ago. The acceptance of theological liberalism, of rationalism as opposed to revelation, of the mass of human presumption which likes to call itself "modern theology," began long ago, and makes the present obvious defections virtually inevitable. It is only because the intellectual apostasy, which began well over a hundred years ago, was not widely recognized by Christian people in general, that they are so shocked by the moral apostasy and political prostitution which they see today.

"Politics," says a U.S. Presbyterian leader, "is the vehicle through which the will of God is done in the world today." The deposed dictator of Ghana proclaims, "Seek ye first the political kingdom." At the Geneva Conference on Church and Society, a Nigerian lawyer proclaims, "For us, the central question is political power in the world."[12] Are these compatible with the statement of Jesus Christ, "My kingdom is not of this world"?

4. Evaluation and Prospects

As believing Christians, we must and do admit that the church has responsibilities in and to society. Although it may be the calling of some individuals, the Gospel does not require a monastic-quietistic isolation from society, rather the contrary. We recognize that there is such a thing as an *unholy* other-worldliness. Concern with the great question of personal salvation can lead and has led to selfish preoccupation with one's own spiritual condition, and to neglect of one's needy and suffering neighbors. The church, particularly at certain times and in certain places, has been reactionary. Christians, their denominations and institutions, and the church as a whole will have much to answer for in this respect when they stand before the judgment-seat of Christ. All this we must confess; we must not merely concede it, we must proclaim it.

But as people committed to the truth, we must also say some other things, not with boasting, but for the sake of the record. Christianity tolerated slavery for hundreds of years, after a Christian emperor had come to power. But it was Christians who began the abolition of slavery and put an end to the slave trade. The beginnings of hospitals, orphanages, and countless other works of human compassion go back, in large measure, to Christian impulses. The missionaries to Africa and Asia went with the colonizers—but for all of that, they took schools, and medicine, and a new concept of human dignity, along with the news of the Son of God who was not ashamed to call men his brethren. We do not like the idea of a puritanical, moralistic,

Christianity-dominated society, perhaps, but we like even less what is replacing it. There is much for Christians to be ashamed of in their conduct, for they are obliged to judge themselves by the standards of Christ. There is not so much with which the non-Christian world has the right to charge them. For the sake of the truth, we must make these reservations, not in the effort to make excuses for Christian failures, but merely to have the facts on the table. In the eyes of the Judge who counts, the record of Christians through the centuries leaves much too much to be desired. That we must confess.

When all this has been said and admitted, we must judge that *the present course of representative Christian leaders, as indicated by publications of the World Council and an encyclical of the present Pope, constitutes a reversal of the priorities of Jesus Christ.* It is a prostitution of the church's mission to preach the Gospel to the whole creation. It is a denial of the basic truths of revelation. It is a betrayal of the One who became a Son of Man that we might become sons of God.

This is not to say that the representatives of the World Council of Churches, not to mention the Pope himself, have in their own minds followed these developments through to their logical conclusions. It is, however, to say that these conclusions will follow, and that we should recognize them, and repudiate the course which leads to them, before they have become inevitable. The branches of Christendom which have been preoccupied with evangelical orthodoxy, with the purity of the faith, with personal salvation, have many sins on their consciences, and have much for which to atone, but the "new direction," is betrayal of our basic commitment and apostasy from fundamentals of the faith. The task of the Christian is to seek first the kingdom of God and his righteousness. That task was assigned by Christ, and no one, be he sociologist, politician, theologian, or church head, can change it.

What prospect does the social substitution have of accomplishing its goals? Will the World Council be able to direct world revolution? Will the Pope become the architect of world economic development? We need not answer these questions. For those who are yet sane, who still have some idea of what is possible in the real world, the answer is clear. The revolution may tolerate the church—for a time. It may even appreciate its support—for a time. But at the end the

Christian church will discover that Marxist revolution has its own goals, one of which is the suppression of religion. It cannot be bribed by a little support from the church. Does the organization church realize this? It does not appear to do so. Perhaps it can still learn, before its chances for learning—and life—are gone.

Notes

[1]*Charity*, the English word derived from the Latin *caritas*, deserves to be rehabilitated. Some needy persons feel that their self-respect compels them to announce, "We don't want charity," and social reformers are fond of telling us that we must make it clear that public aid is a right, and is definitely not *charity*. To this we must say: It may be so, but it is too bad, for charity properly understood is the highest of the virtues (I Corinthians 13:13). *Caritas*, and its Greek counterpart *agápē* are used for the self-giving love of God, and for the kind of human love which resembles it, as opposed to Latin *amor*, Greek *éros*, the passionate love which is so often in reality self-seeking. If he understands what it means, the man who says, "I don't want any charity," is saying a dreadful thing.

[2]Quoted in *Christianity Today*, Vol. XXI, No. 18 (June 9, 1967), p. 923.

[3]*Institutes*, Book IV, Ch. xx, §§ 3-7. Calvin believed that a combination of aristocracy and democracy was the best form of human government, IV:xx:8, but admitted that all forms of government could have divine sanction, and claimed that each form could easily be corrupted: "The fall from kingdom to tyranny is easy; but it is not much more difficult to fall from the rule of the best men to the faction of a few; yet it is easiest of all to fall from popular rule to sedition." Library of Christian Classics edition, Vol. II, p. 1493.

[4]Quoted from the Authorized ("King James") Version of 1611. Modern-language citations are from the New American Standard, Revised Standard, or Berkeley editions, used by kind permission of the respective copyright-holders. To identify the version from which each citation is quoted would be relatively pointless.

[5]Even in this ecumenical era, Presbyterianism remains a highly fragmented thing: its two principal divisions in the United States are the *United Presbyterian Church in the United States of America*, to which Brown and Blake belong, and the more conservative, Southern-based *Presbyterian Church in the United States*.

[6]The *Official Report: World Conference on Church and Society* is available from the World Council of Churches, 475 Riverside Drive, Room 439, New

York, N.Y. 10027, for $1.50 per copy. A highly favorable report was written by John C. Bennett, president of Union Theological Seminary, New York, a participant at the conference, in *Christian Century*, Vol. LXXXIV, No. 5 (February 1, 1967), pp. 137-138. A severe criticism of the conference's pretensions to omniscience, of its demands for dictatorially-imposed social changes, and its approval of violent revolution, was made by Alice Widener in *Christianity Today*, Vol. XI, No. 10 (Feb. 17, 1967), pp. 499-505, and contested by Eugene L. Smith, executive secretary of the WCC in the United States, in the same magazine, Vol. XI, No. 17 (May 26, 1967), pp. 853-855, with a rebuttal by Editor Carl F. H. Henry, pp. 855-856.

[7]Paolo VI, "Populorum Progressio. Lettera enciclica sulla promozione dello sviluppo dei popoli. 26 marzo 1967." *Documenti e Testi*, 1 (Milan: ACLI, 1967), § 87, pp. 35-36. Emphasis mine.

[8]The discussion about the possibility of eternal salvation for those who do not personally believe in Christ, or for those outside the church, to use another term, has a long and agitated history. It should be clear that the New Testament does not categorically deny the possibility. On the other hand, it says very little to support it. It lays great emphasis on the church's obligation to fulfil the Great Commission, and offers no comforting assurance that those whom the church fails will be rescued in some other way.

[9]This combination of great responsibility with great incapacity and lack of success is a tremendous burden for many a devout Christian. The fact is that it is our responsibility to be witnesses, but not to *make converts*. For that the Holy Spirit alone is competent. Anglican scholar James I. Packer treats the problem very thoroughly in his short book, *Evangelism and the Sovereignty of God* (Chicago: Inter-Varsity, 1961).

[10]This is not the place to become involved in the question as to whether it is proper to distinguish so sharply between body and soul. Admittedly, the New Testament views man not as a soul temporarily imprisoned in a body (although sometimes the church has given that erroneous impression), but as a unity of soul and body. The word "soul" used here simply indicates the part of man which is capable of entering into a responsible, personal relationship with God.

[11]Its abuse has been bitingly analyzed by Jacques Maritain in *Le Paysan de la Garonne* (Paris: Desclée de Brouwer, 1966), pp. 50-62.

[12]Cited by Prof. Mario Miegge, "La conferenza di Ginevra 'Chiesa e Societa,' " *Protestantesimo*, Vol. XXI, Nr. 4 (1966), p. 229. This same African told me privately that he puts personal faith first; the published reports, then, give only one side of his interest.

CHAPTER 5

· A CHRISTIAN NATION? ·

Blessed is the nation whose God is the Lord.

PSALM 33:12

Is the United States a Christian nation? This question is often asked today. It can be asked for many reasons. There are those for whom it is obvious that the United States *is* a Christian nation, and who want it to live up to what they think that ought to mean. It is also asked—and answered negatively—by many sincere Christians who want to shock people into giving up their merely cultural, habitual Christian coloration and into coming to grips with the real nature of Christian faith. It is asked by members of religious minorities, who have felt discrimination and disregard for their own sensitivities in the automatic way many American institutions take a kind of generalized Protestantism for granted. It is asked by the advocates of a new moral anarchy, for whom Christianity (like civilization) spells restraint, but who do not want to tackle both religion and patriotism at once, and so try to disentangle them a bit and get at them one at a time.

No one is really happy with the idea. There are plenty of Americans who still fall into the first category. They are convinced that this nation was founded by God's help, that it still exists "under God," and that it will continue to prosper only as long as it recognizes God and shows him reverence. These people, who would answer the question in the affirmative, are not very happy with the *kind* of Christianity Christian America puts into effect. Our national drives have been satirically portrayed as greed and sex, and that caricature comes terrifyingly close to the truth. The cultural Renaissance into which America has surged after World War II has rapidly turned into a pornographic and nihilistic swamp that would have made a decadent Roman satirist blush. To say that honesty, either verbal or financial, is a characteristic of our public administration, either at the national or at lower levels, would be naïve, to say the least. And as to foreign policy, surely no Christian would want to concede that our preferred melange of self-interest, opportunism, ruthlessness, and humanistic idealism is based on the teachings of Christ. Our domestic policies are usually based on the broadest kind of appeal to self-interest.

The United States may have a great deal of Christianity deep down. There is evidence of this. There is much to indicate that something basic in America is still healthy, both in a spiritual and in a moral sense. But wherever it is and whatever it is doing, it is not setting the tone. It is not giving the direction to mid-twentieth-century America. And it is not immune to disease. There is plenty of reason to think that America has a large reservoir of Christian faith, of sound morality, and of idealism. But there is also a great deal of reason to fear that this reservoir is in danger of being polluted.

If we can say that America is, for the moment, a Christian nation, this is not a thing in which we can take comfort. Alexander VI, the infamous Borgia pope, may have been a Christian in some formal sense, but he was certainly no credit to Christianity. The Roman Catholic Church of his day also produced a Savonarola—but Alexander was pope, and Savonarola was burned at the stake. Even those of us who want to claim that America is a Christian nation must admit with tears that we are approaching a situation in which we will burn our Savonarolas and crown our Alexander Borgias.

Then there are Christians—the second category—for whom America is still too much a "Christian" or "Christianized" nation. If the Christian faith is in fact a personal matter, depending on individual commitment and discipleship, then living in a nominally Christian culture may be a tremendous handicap. The typical American child grows up with the impression that a Christian is what one is if one's parents do not happen to be Jews, or the much rarer Moslems, Buddhists, etc. That kind of Christianity certainly will not stand the tests of either time or eternity. From this point of view, it would be better to shuck off all pretense that the United States is a Christian nation. We should call it "a pagan nation, inhabited by a minority of committed Christians." This is a realistic attitude, and it has the advantage that it makes people face the problem. It makes them realize that living in a Christian civilization is no free ticket into the City of God. Yet few Christians can adopt this kind of grim realism without a real sense of sorrow. To condemn the nation, in effect, in order that at least some may be saved from the general wreckage, is no easy choice. Even a great evangelist like Billy Graham, whose calling is to summon men from complacent self-satisfaction to make an honest decision before God, cannot face the choice; at his crusades the old and ambiguous image of a Christian America is constantly reëvoked.

What about religious minorities which resent the fading image of a Christian or even a Protestant America? On the one side, they have a certain amount of history in their favor. The United States was not, in fact, founded as a Christian nation. A certain religious orientation was more or less taken for granted by the Founding Fathers, it is true. It would not have occurred to them to contest the existence of God or the necessity of dependence on him. It was not their purpose to form a secular, anti-Christian state. Still, they had no intention of establishing any particular form of Christianity. Many of them were merely vaguely Deistic in their convictions. The "Christian America" for which they laid the foundation resulted from their tolerance, but not from their deliberate design. On the other side stands the fact—which ought to be obvious, but apparently is not—that a religion must have *some* character if it is to exist at all. If the social and educational life of a community is not to be purely and aggressively secular, it has to take on some distinct tones, which will naturally be those of the majority, or of the most influential and vocal minority. The attempts on the part of certain religiously-inclined minority groups, among them many Jews, to forbid public expressions of Christianity, is short-sighted to say the least. Intolerance for the majority's religious expressions also undermines the majority's moral convictions, and to encourage this is a short-sighted policy for any minority.

The United States is certainly not free of prejudice and intolerance. There is much of which we have reason to be ashamed. On the other hand, the religious—and irreligious—freedom of the United

States is unparalleled. The Protestant churches of the United States send far more than their proportionate share of Protestant missionaries abroad. The financial contributions of the Roman Catholics of America are a principal bulwark of the Roman church around the world. When the nation of Israel found itself confronted with a unitedly hostile Arab world in 1967, it was America's Jewish community which immediately provided a stream of cash and volunteers. The most diverse religious communities flourish in America. Naturally not all of them enjoy the same kind of semi-official status of a kind that Protestantism does. But they must enjoy something much more important in order to be able to flourish as they do.

From the point of view of history, the members of minority religious traditions who object to all references to America as a Christian nation are right. From the practical point of view, their objection may seem a needless kind of pedantry. Christian America is not free of intolerance, but it offers a far different kind of hospitality to all religions from that offered in secular Russia—or secular Nazi Germany.

Finally, we should consider the position of those anarchists who attack the tradition of a Christian America in an effort to overthrow all the traditional restraints implied by Christian moral values. From one point of view the evangelical Christian could easily say, "Let them have their way." The moral standards of the Christian faith are meaningful, in the last analysis, only to Christians. Of course the practical ethic of the Golden Rule has a certain utility for any society, but the ethics of the Sermon on the Mount make sense only in the light of a Last Judgment. The Christian has no real leverage by which to demand or expect Christian moral standards from those who do not believe the premises of Christianity. From this perspective, Christian ethics are only for Christians. Nevertheless, this is not the whole story. If the Christian were allowed to be concerned only for the eternal salvation of his fellowmen, then he could legitimately ignore the temporal life of those who reject the Gospel. However, this is precisely what the advocates of the "social Gospel"[1] accuse the orthodox of doing: preaching salvation and neglecting the ordinary physical needs of those about them.

A basic conviction of the Christian is that physical needs cannot be distinguished from moral and spiritual ones. In a seminal work, Abraham Kuyper, one of the outstanding Calvinist thinkers of the last hundred years and at one time prime minister of Holland, stated the fundamental immorality of merely giving welfare aid without adding a moral dimension to it. Of course it is necessary to prevent physical starvation: that is our duty before God. But merely to feed men's bodies without feeding their spirits is, in the last analysis and in its results, a disastrous undertaking. Kuyper's short book, *Christianity and the Class Struggle*,[2] is seventy years old, but is even more pertinent now than when it was written.

If moral and spiritual needs cannot be isolated from purely physical ones—and this is a basic conviction of biblical religion, one that is expressed by Jesus himself—then the Christian cannot legitimately ignore the morals of his community and confine himself to those of his limited Christian fellowship. Therefore the Christian must deny the oft-repeated charges of the immoralists, who seek to throw off the repressive restraints, as they call them, of "Puritanism." (The historical phenomenon of Puritanism had much that was unattractive, but in modern parlance, any moral standards which do not bend flexibly under the slightest pressure are known as Puritanism.) People living in a society which has been formed by Christian ethics, even of a watered-down sort, often express resentment at the restraints which that society imposes on their unbridled self-indulgence. In fact, however, if they found themselves living without restraint in a society without the Christian ethic, they would soon discover that they had lost far more than they gained.

One significant problem confronts both the immoralists and the minority religious traditions in their differently motivated attempt to break up the still more-or-less Christian orientation of American society. An individual may forsake a certain ethical or religious system in order to embrace another, equally complete or even more complete. This we call conversion. But a society cannot be converted so easily. It is much easier to destroy an existing set of values than it is to build a new one. For example, the humanists who so strongly object to the heritage of Christian values in America claim to have a better set of values with which to replace it. (In the case of some ostensibly humanist anti-Christians, such as Mrs. Madalyn Murray O'Hair of public school prayer fame, one may question whether the better set of values actually exists.) Nevertheless, it will be much easier to destroy the values we still have than to replace them with anything new.

If American and European society is to have any generally accepted value-system, it must be something akin to that of Christianity, because that is the only one that is sufficiently well-known, sufficiently pervasive, and sufficiently well-founded to command much respect. It may be possible for enthusiasts of other systems to discredit Christianity and to reduce or virtually to eliminate its influence on American society, but it will not be possible for them to provide an effective substitute short of a new system artificially imposed by force. This is what happened in Nazi Germany, and it is what happens in Communist countries—but no one can say that that takes place by reasoned discourse, by persuasion, or as a result of a growing popular conviction. In fact, a more or less orthodox Christian system can theoretically afford to be more tolerant than can many others—precisely because it lays such stress on *individual* conversion and *voluntary* commitment. In practice, the most Christian societies, for all their moralizing and their puritanical attitudes, have often permitted their citizens greater freedom of behavior than non-Christian ones.

The rather evident need for some system of values to order men's relationships with one another means that if it does not come from within—and Christianity is the only real candidate to do this on a large scale in the "Christian" West—it will be imposed from the outside. In a 1964 debate at Harvard University on the subject of Billy Graham's evangelism, Professor James Luther Adams, a noted authority in the field of Christian ethics, reproached the evangelist for dealing only with individuals, and for making no attempt to change the conditions of society by influencing legislation. Dr. Harold Ockenga of Boston countered Professor Adams with the question, "How far would you go in coercing moral behavior by law? As far as the Socialists? or as the Communists?" Unfortunately the question was received both by Professor Adams and by much of the audience as an unworthy attempt to discredit him by suggesting that his goals were similar to those of Socialism or even of Communism. But the question, apart from its unhappy innuendo, was fair enough.

The new immoralists like to present the case as though it were a choice between the arbitrary restraints of traditional Christianity and responsible human self-determination. The argument often seems to be, "Christian restraint is unworthy. Promising rewards and threatening punishment is a disgraceful way to influence behavior. Remove

the restraints, allow people to exercise their freedom, and their conduct will be more responsible, more charitable, more moral." Unfortunately it does not work that way. The real choice is between the
responsible freedom of Christianity (or, in this realm, of some simi-
larly inner-directed ethical system) and between unbridled license,
moral chaos. The condition of unbridled license is unstable, and is
terminated by the order of tyranny—either imposed from within, by
those who can no longer stand the chaos, and who have become willing to accept tyranny rather than continue longer in it, or from outside, by those who find a disordered and unprincipled society an easy
prey for aggression. The real choice then, is between personal responsibility and tyranny. There is a certain inconsistency in the fact
that a defender of freedom like Professor Adams will support the
enforcement of morality by church-supported legislation. He does so
to counteract what he considers the lack of social responsibility and
the preoccupation with personal salvation of Billy Graham's approach, but to rely on government-regulated morality rather than
on personal religious conviction is to invite a tyranny far more repressive than anything the Puritans ever imagined. There is a strange
kind of blindness here. We find other writers, nominally Christian,
who object violently to the slightest control on even the most pornographic literature to be printed in America, but who write tolerantly
or even approvingly of the Marxist puritanism that they find in the
Soviet Union.[3] Perhaps this inconsistency is not as great as it seems:
perhaps it is another example of the rejection of personal, interior
moral responsibility before God, which cries out for the imposition
of some kind of restraint from outside.

A rather distressing aspect of the attack on traditional values, one
that is all too seldom recognized, lies in the fact that many people
are not at all ashamed to attack the whole fabric of Christian values
merely in order to insure their own license to do as they please. This
is admirably illustrated by the late Aldous Huxley:

> I had motives for not wanting the world to have a meaning;
> consequently assumed that it had none, and was able without
> any difficulty to find satisfying reasons for this assumption. . . .
> The philosopher who finds no meaning in the world is not con-
> cerned exclusively with a problem in pure metaphysics; he is

also concerned to prove there is no valid reason why he personally should not do as he wants to do, or why his friends should
not seize political power and govern in the way that they find
most advantageous to themselves. . . ."[4]

Motivation similar to Huxley's, but usually less frankly expressed,
can be recognized in many of those who feel that they have a mission
to liberate America from those residual restraints imposed by being a
"Christian nation."

An examination of the reasons why people think that America is
or is not, or wish that it were or were not a Christian nation, is illu-
minating, but does not answer the question. Whatever the reasons
behind the question, it remains a valid and a difficult one.

In one very important sense, the United States is not and has never
been a Christian nation. Perhaps over half of the American people
are affiliated, in one way or another, with a Christian church: this
does not make the nation Christian. Although church attendance is
better among Roman Catholics in most of the United States than it
generally is among Protestants, and better among Protestants in some
regions than in others, it is doubtful whether more than a substantial
minority of Americans give even one hour a week to God in Christian
worship. Under such circumstances we can hardly speak of being
a Christian nation. Even among those who are officially church members, and who attend churches with some regularity, it is probable
that only a minority really know what the Christian faith is all about,
or make a serious effort to live according to the teachings of Christ.
It is clear that Christian morality does not influence our government
policy, which we have previously characterized as a strange and unstable melange of ruthless pragmatism, unprincipled self-interest, and
optimistic, humanistic idealism. We stamp IN GOD WE TRUST
on our coins, and now we also print it on the dollar bill as well; but
in practice we rely on our armaments and alliances. When it comes
to a crisis, we really trust neither. A great many suggestions have been
put forward about what really motivates America, from "the arrogance of power" through avarice for material wealth and an obsession
with pleasure to a love of peace and freedom, but no one would seriously say that it is motivated by a concern to love and obey God.

All these objections are valid. On the other hand, there is a sense

—despite Christian hypocrisy and all the valuable contributions of non-Christians to America—in which we can call the United States a Christian nation. It is, for better or for worse, the most Christian among the world's major nations. Other countries may in fact have an established Christian church, but it is no secret that the United States has the highest church participation, the greatest number of foreign missionaries per capita, and the largest contributions to Christian churches, *by far,* of any of the major Western nations. The civilization which we have in the United States is a product of Western Christianity. It may be a degenerate product, or it may be, as others would see it, just on the verge of breaking the shackles which Western Christianity has fastened on it, but it is at the present time indisputably a product of the Christian church. It does not take a majority to give a society its character. A convinced minority is quite sufficient. The number of convinced Christian believers in the United States is small, but it is doubtless considerably larger than the number of those *committed* to any alternate system of values. The proportion of committed Christians in the whole American population is without a doubt larger than that of committed Communists in the Soviet Union. If Christianity—Christian theology, Christian morality, Christian ideals—does not give American society a distinct character, then it will not have a character at all, for there is nothing else that is in a position to do so. There are opposing candidates, all the way from idealistic evolutionary humanism through the "Playboy philosophy" to what must be described as a virtual cult of evil, but none of them is in a position to impress a real character on our country—at least not yet. If Christianity is not in a position to teach the country any virtues, it is too bad: it will still be blamed—and responsible—for America's faults. In this rather vague sense, then, it can be said that the United States is Christian.

This conclusion is unfortunately too vague and too poorly defined to be of much value. The advocates of a non-Christian America will not be pleased at being told that we *are* a Christian nation, and will remain so for some generations, because of our heredity, about which we can do nothing. Those to whom the expression "a Christian America" is a mark of honor and something devoutly to be sought after will hardly be satisfied with the kind of Christian-ness which we have admitted in the preceding paragraph, which is—like the religion of so many nominal Christians—a habit without conviction, and perhaps not even a particularly well-loved or comfortable habit at that. It is necessary to be more precise in our terminology, and to ask ourselves exactly what the whole concept implies.

1. *The Idea of a Christian Nation*

The idea of a Christian nation goes back, in principle, to ancient Israel. Each of the peoples of the ancient world had its own god or gods, but with the Hebrew people the situation was different. Their God was indeed their *own* God, but he was also the *only* God. It was important for Israel to choose the path of service and fidelity to him, but it was much more important that he had chosen Israel. It was not that they were sufficiently wise or sensitive to have sought out the only true God among the maze of the idols of the ancient Near East, but that God—for reasons known only to himself—chose them from among all the other peoples of the earth.

This is an important distinction. In biblical terms, a people cannot become God's people by deciding to serve him: it becomes his people because he calls it forth. God called Israel out of Egypt (Hosea 11:1). Israel had a considerable degree of racial and social homogeneity, but the experience of being chosen by God has left an indelible mark on them, one which far surpasses their common racial and cultural heritage in its ability to shape their destiny. Even if, as most Christians believe, the spiritual Israel has replaced the Jewish nation in God's plan, physical Israel still enjoys a most remarkable place among the nations, as the events of June, 1967, so clearly showed. The church, by contrast, had no ethnic or cultural continuity prior to being called out by God. As St. Peter writes, addressing the "aliens," i.e. the Christians, scattered throughout Asia Minor, "You once were not a people, but now you are the people of God" (I Peter 1:1, 2:10).

In their origins, then, Israel and the church are similar, in that both began with their calling forth by God. There is a difference, inasmuch as Israel was a people before it was chosen (or at least before it was called out of Egypt, when the call of God became unmistakable in its clarity), whereas the church became a people in the act of being chosen. The difference before their callings becomes negligible in the light of the momentous reality of what it means to be *elected* and called by God.

Unfortunately the very reality and virtual tangibility of this divine calling has had the same adverse effect on both Israel and the Christian church: they have come to take it for granted, to treat it as a matter of course, of something which is theirs by right, even by habitual usage, with many privileges and no obligations. In the early days of the church, most Jews were Jews by the accident of birth. Converts to Judaism did exist, but were comparatively few in number, and the Jews made no active attempt to win them. Judaism, with its exclusive monotheism and its complete rejection of the Roman imperial cult on which the Empire set such store, could have appeared as a potential threat to the Roman authorities if it had had a strongly proselytizing tendency. It did not, and hence it was tolerated as a *religio licita* (lawful religion), even though the Jews resolutely refused to participate in the official worship of the Empire.

At the very beginning, Christianity was regarded by the Romans as a variety of Judaism, and for a time it too enjoyed Judaism's protected status. When the Jews of Corinth brought St. Paul before the Roman proconsul Gallio and charged him with disrupting their religion, Gallio replied, "If it were a matter of wrong or of vicious crime, O Jews, it would be reasonable for me to put up with you; but if there are questions about words and names and your own Law, look after it yourselves; I am unwilling to be a judge of these matters" (Acts 18:14-15). Soon, however, the Romans came to distinguish between Christians and Jews. The Christians attracted their attention not least because of their zeal for making converts, and eventually serious persecution began.

Even before Christianity secured official toleration in 313, the church had begun to acquire a share of merely nominal members—children of believers who became church members merely because their parents expected it of them. Nevertheless, the ever-present threat of persecution discouraged even believers' children from making a purely formal commitment without any conviction behind it. The Emperor Diocletian, who ruled from 284 to 305, reorganized the administrative structure of the Roman Empire and made a great effort to arrest its decline. For example, he introduced a rigid scheme of price controls to bring an end to the increasing inflation and progressive debasement of Roman money. The death penalty was decreed for those who violated it. This Draconian measure did not succeed in ending the inflation, but it virtually strangled trade and commerce. In the ideological realm, Diocletian sought to reëstablish the spiritual unity of the Empire by striking at the church, its largest and most dangerous body with a distinct ethos of its own.

Diocletian's persecution was not only more brutal than that of his predecessors. It was also much more systematic, better planned, and it lasted longer. The number of martyrs was great, but so was that of the "lapsi" (those who gave up the faith rather than face persecution) and even of the "traditores" (those who turned over the Holy Scriptures to the persecutors on their demand). Despite its severity and its duration, the persecution could not crush the church. It was continued into the reign of the Emperor Galerian in the East, but his death in 311 and the military successes of Constantine in 312 eventually brought respite. The Edict of Milan, dated in 313, gave legal toleration to Christianity.

It was not long before the Christian inclinations of the new Emperor became known. This resulted in a flock of conversions to the church favored by the absolute lord of the whole Empire (Constantine became sole ruler in 324). It is very hard to be sure whether Constantine's conversion was genuine, or rather whether it was genuinely to Christianity. He certainly was converted to something. Despite the scepticism of modern writers like Gore Vidal, it seems likely that it was genuine, but it certainly produced a rash of nominal imitations.[5] Under the Emperor Theodosius I, Christianity became the state religion of the Roman Empire in 380. Thus it was the Roman Empire, in its late and decadent phase, which created "Christian Europe." The Empire was Christian in a way in which the United States has never been—formally and officially.

Following Constantine, the various European peoples were "converted" to Christianity, in a long process which finally concluded when the ruler of the Lithuanians, the last pagan people of Europe, married the Queen of Poland in 1386. But whether it was Chlodwig and his Franks (about 500), Vladimir and his Russians (987), or Jogaila (Polish *Jagiello*) and his Lithuanians, there is something very suspicious about the claim that a whole people has been converted— in other words, perhaps the problem is that Europe became Christian but most of the Europeans did not.

The concept of a Christian nation in the biblical sense, by analogy with Israel, would be that of a nation which had chosen, as a nation, "to serve the Lord" by following his call. But no such nation exists. Perhaps the Puritans and Pilgrims were on the way to establishing one, but their vision was soon diluted by immigrants who did not share it, and their own fervor rapidly cooled. In the biblical sense, the Christian nation is not a nation at all, but the church—that is the community which corresponds today to ancient Israel. The New Israel is spiritual.

2. A Nation Under God?

The concept of "a Christian America" is in the first place not biblical, in the second place hardly likely to be attained, and in the third place, if it were attained, it would probably go a good deal farther than most of its sentimental advocates wish. Intrinsically, it is impossible to legislate Christian conduct. The reason is simple. Unless the conduct results from the willing obedience of the human heart, it is not Christian. Where public law commands conduct in conformity with Christian principles, and where lack of conformity is punished by law, the Christian will of course obey the law at the same time that he conforms to his Christian principles. But mere obedience to the law will prove nothing about a man's inner convictions, since it is effectively secured by the threat of legal sanctions. By enforcing a certain conformity to the laws of God through the medium of enforced government regulation, a "Christian state" would probably produce resentment and rebellion in the hearts of its citizens, and thus drive them farther from Christian obedience rather than bring them closer to it. This experiment has been tried from time to time, and these results have usually been obtained. Two examples from American experience illustrate this.

In the United States, Prohibition was a religiously motivated attempt to enforce a kind of moral improvement on the general population without convincing them of its necessity or desirability. Because Prohibition was such a dismal failure, attempts are made by the current generation of "liberal" Christians, who have no objection to the use of alcohol, to blame it on the fundamentalists. Actually it was an example of Protestant cooperation more or less across the board, and the Protestant liberals of that generation were as deeply involved in it as any fundamentalists, while some of the most conservative Protestants, especially among the Lutherans, opposed it. Instead of reducing the demand for and the use of beverage alcohol, Prohibition increased it. It converted thousands upon thousands of wine- and beer-drinkers to hard liquor, and gave a tremendous impetus to organized crime and to government corruption. It certainly reduced the general moral level of the country. Of course, we cannot blame Prohibition alone for this. The hostile popular reaction to Prohibition resulted from already-present factors which would have had an effect even if Prohibition had never been enacted.

This is not the place to consider whether those evangelical Christians who supported the Prohibition Amendment had sound theological reasons for doing so.[6] The problem which concerns us is not whether the Christian has a right to drink alcohol (concerning which the Bible seems plain enough), but whether the church ought to encourage society to legislate compulsory abstinence for all its members, Christians, Jews, Moslems, atheists, and all the rest. Today "liberal" Protestants recoil in horror at the memory of Prohibition, which they look upon as an intolerable attempt to interfere with human freedom. But in reality the current fervor of many liberal Protestants for civil rights legislation has much in common with the old zeal for Prohibition. Quite apart from whether civil rights legislation is a desirable or necessary thing for society and whether it is dictated by Christian principles,[7] there is the fact that, like Prohibition, it is an attempt to enforce moral behavior before and without providing any foundation in moral conviction. It is argued that by requiring the mixing of the races in schools and in housing patterns, prejudice can be dissipated. This works, to some extent—just as Prohibition, thoroughly enforced, reduces alcoholism—but the results are only superficial. There is in fact a growing amount of evidence that one effect of the civil rights struggle and of the legislation it has produced has been to *increase* racial prejudice and hostility.

We must recognize and admit that much of the opposition to the civil rights movement has been based on prejudice and selfishness. (No doubt much of the opposition to Prohibition was also based on self-interest.) We do not wish to deny that the civil rights movement has a better moral case to support it than Prohibition did. The point is that in both cases the results seem to be the opposite of what was desired.

Why has this happened? Why has the attempt to legislate racial equality and harmony been followed by a terrible deterioration in interracial relations, just as Prohibition was followed by an increase in the abuse of alcohol? The answer is clear. Kuyper was quite right when he stated that welfare benefits, without a moral foundation, may ultimately harm rather than help those who receive them. The converse is also true. Prohibiting immoral actions (drunkenness, racial intolerance) without establishing an adequate, understood, and accepted moral foundation for the prohibition will ultimately harm rather than help the cause for which it is done.

If Christianity *cannot* be legislated, what becomes of the concept of a nation under God? Must we abandon it entirely? Must we produce a completely *lay state,* in which the laws enacted by man do not correspond at all to the laws of God? No, it is impossible for any state to be completely indifferent to all the laws of God, for many of them are written upon the human heart and simply cannot be disregarded if society is to exist at all (Romans 2:14-15). A most instructive example is furnished by the fact that the Soviet Union, which promoted free love, easy divorce, and general sexual looseness immediately after the Revolution, soon reverted *for practical reasons* to a much more puritanical morality than we have in the West.

This much, then, a state, any state, *must* do. This much it will do, with or without encouragement from the Christians. But, if it wishes to call itself a nation *under* God (*before* God would be a better expression, signifying *responsibility* rather than mere *subjection*), it can do more. The government can show by its public statements that it recognizes that it is not itself absolute. An attitude of reverence and gratitude towards God can be cultivated. This, according to St. Paul, is a minimum which he requires of all men, and without which he will consign them to folly and madness (Romans 1:18-32). The right of churches and religious associations to exist and to function freely can be recognized. It is certainly legitimate to encourage worship by making the legal day of rest coincide with the majority's day of worship. In an age when taxation takes progressively higher percentages of each individual's income, it is proper for church contributions to be tax-free and tax-deductible. The attitude of the state towards the church can be one of respectful and benevolent non-interference. All this is right, even necessary, if the state wishes to exist *before* God and not *against* God.

Although this is a difficult distinction to make, it may even be necessary for the state to draw the line about what it is willing to recognize as a religion. In fact, with the proliferation of cults in the United States, it is evident that not everything which wishes to call itself a religion can be granted government toleration and encouragement. It is surely to be hoped that the U. S. Supreme Court will not dignify Dr. Timothy Leary's L.S.D. cult by acknowledging it to be a religion and according it the protection of the First Amendment against the narcotics control agencies. Naturally the power of the state to discriminate in religion can be abused, as it can in every other realm of life. There seems to be no way to avoid it, if society is to preserve its sanity.[8]

The state then may and should provide a climate in which the church is free to evangelize, to build up its congregations, to instruct them, to practice charity, and otherwise to fulfil its proper mission. It can take care not to expand its own activities, particularly in the area of social welfare legislation, in such a way that it completely supersedes the church. It can attempt to avoid placing Christians before difficult conflicts of conscience. It can afford a certain protection to religion from abuse and insult by anti-religious propaganda (although here we begin to tread on thin ice); finally, it can afford a somewhat more extensive recognition to the historic Christian faith than it need show to every transitory phenomenon which calls itself a religion.

If it has done all these things, the state will have done well. It will have avoided the condemnation which comes from rebellion against God and insult offered to him. At the same time it will not have made the cardinal error of trying to take upon itself a task which properly belongs to the Holy Spirit: that of identifying the true doctrine of Christ to the seeker and of bringing him to the point of accepting it. It will not pretend to an absolute separation of the religious and political spheres, for it will recognize that man is a unity, and that the spiritual cannot be neatly severed from the physical—except by death. It will not strive for an absolute consistency and impartiality in dealing with all religions, for while such a thing may be possible in theory, it is never so in practice. It will try to be considerate of both the majority and the minorities, and neither to insult nor to use compulsion with either.

The United States, during its less than two centuries of existence, has done an exemplary job in most of these respects. There is at one and the same time greater fervor of belief and greater freedom for all varieties of unbelief in the United States than in any other major nation. This does not make it the Kingdom of God on earth. Those who make this identification are misguided and ultimately dangerous to both the nation and the church. But it is a place where the Christian has considerable liberty to hear and obey the voice of his King. For this, he is to be grateful. For this, he owes his country a great debt of thanks. He will pay this debt with love, but he will never forget that neither the United States, nor any other nation of this earth, is the blessed "nation, whose God is the Lord."

Notes

[1]The term "social Gospel" was coined by Walter Rauschenbusch (1861-1918), and combined a reduced concern for salvation with a kind of optimistic faith in social and economic progress. Rauschenbusch's spiritual heirs proceeded to go beyond his *combination,* and to *substitute* social progress for conversion.

[2]Kuyper's book first appeared in 1895 and has been frequently reprinted, most recently by Hein (Grand Rapids: 1950).

[3]For example, *Christian Century* editor-at-large J. Claude Evans certainly would not write about censorship in the United States, if it existed, with the same tolerance, if not actual approval, which he shows for it in the Soviet Union. "A Paradigm for Russia," *Christian Century,* Vol. LXXXIV, No. 21 (May 24, 1967), pp. 679-680.

[4]Cited in Arnold Lunn and Garth Lean, *The New Morality* (London: Blandford, 1964), pp. 12-13, and used by permission.

[5]See A. H. M. Jones, *Constantine and the Conversion of Europe* (London: Hodder and Stoughton, 1948), for a good account. Vidal's scepticism is expressed in his fictionalized autobiography of the last pagan Emperor, *Julian* (New York: New American Library, 1964).

[6]It is of course impossible to base an absolute prohibition of the use of alco-

holic beverages on the Bible; Jesus drank wine, as did his earliest disciples, and even Calvin received part of his salary in wine. It is conceivable, however, that the abuse of alcohol is or could become so severe a social problem that Christian love would require its entire prohibition. Some of those religious leaders who supported the Volstead Act did so for this reason, but many others, misguidedly I believe, interpreted the New Testament in such a way as to require total abstinence.

[7]The author is convinced that civil rights legislation was and is necessary to terminate segregation in the United States, although perhaps not the sort that has been enacted into law. While racial segregation is not explicitly forbidden in the Bible (neither is slavery), pride and contempt for others are forbidden. A legal policy of segregation expresses and perpetuates such attitudes, and is therefore to be condemned and fought. It is not inconceivable that under certain conditions the Christian can or should tolerate segregation, but he must always recognize that in principle it is incompatible with the Christian view of man and of his duty to his fellows.

[8]The Christian recognizes the right of the state, in principle, to suppress a religion which it considers a threat to the public peace. To the extent that this right is exercised against the Christian religion, as is being done at present in the Soviet Union, the Christian can only bear witness to his faith and trust to God to vindicate him and his testimony.

CHAPTER 6

· WHAT IS LEFT OF CHRISTIANITY? ·

I know your deeds and your toil and perseverance, and that you cannot endure evil men, and you put to the test those who call themselves apostles, and they are not, and you found them to be false; and you have perseverance and have endured for My name's sake, and have not grown weary. But I have this against you, that you have left your first love.

REVELATION 2:2-4

What is left, then, of "Christianity"? Is there any structure that we can still clearly recognize as Christian? Is there any teaching that is still accepted as essential? Is there any morality which we can unreservedly call Christian?

Only a few years ago the expressions "Christian" and "Christianity" caused no confusion when they were used. They may have evoked a sympathetic or a hostile response; they may have aroused loyalty or resentment, but no one was in doubt as to what they meant. It was taken for granted that not only the learned theologians and the great saints knew, but that the ordinary man in the street, whether a church-goer or not, also knew or could quickly find out if he decided that he wanted to know.

Today the word "Christian" is mysterious. No one knows what it really means. "Christian theology" is a free-floating kind of thing, which seems to include everything, including what used to be called blasphemy. "Christian morality," on which both "orthodox" and "liberal" Christians, both Protestants and Catholics, used to be in more or less general agreement, is completely adrift. Things which used to be considered virtues (such as sexual continence, love of country) are presented as either indifferent or wrong. Things which used to be considered evils (such as insurrection, blasphemy, pornography) are presented as inoffensive or even good. Church organization is in disorder, with people of the most diverse beliefs sharing in each other's communion services, teaching at each other's seminaries, participating in each other's important decisions. The situation in Christian doctrine, morality, and church organization is aptly described by Heraclitus's words of two and a half millenia ago: "Everything flows and nothing abides; everything gives way and nothing stays fixed."

This state of affairs is becoming increasingly evident to the ordinary church-goer. He does not have to attend a far-out seminary or to read one of the avant-garde religious journals like *Renewal*. The ordinary denominational monthlies, to which his church urges him to subscribe, are usually proof enough. The most distinguished general Protestant publication in America, *The Christian Century*, presents some of the wilder if not the wildest examples of modern religious radicalism alongside of articles which represent healthy Protestant thinking in line with the historic Protestant confessions of faith. By the very variety of its contents, the *Century* exemplifies the diversity, if not to say the utter confusion and chaos, of Protestant thought today.

The contact which a typical church-goer has with formal theology may be limited. He may do no more than attend church on Sunday, and may never participate in a church discussion group or see a religious paper. Even so, he can hardly avoid sensing the restless flux of current Christian thought and life, because in all probability it will be brought right into the worship services he attends. Whether the church is turned over to a protest group to stage a quasi-religious "happening" or whether electric guitars and bongo drums are brought in for a "folk mass," he will have plenty of evidence that "everything flows and nothing abides."

We must be careful not to misunderstand. The same words can be used to support traditionalism or radicalism. The late Pope John XXIII said, "The substance of the ancient doctrine, contained in the 'deposit of faith' is one thing; its formulation is quite another." This statement has been used by Catholic conservatives to emphasize the need for preserving the substance of the ancient doctrine, and by radicals to justify their most extreme "reformulations." The important thing is not whether the phraseology is new or old, but whether it corresponds to and correctly translates the priceless heritage of God's revelation of himself.

Christian faith, however orthodox and biblically sound it may be, will have no meaning whatsoever if it is not communicated to twentieth-century men and women in such a way that they actually understand it. Catholics of the Middle Ages and later could take refuge in the concept of "implicit faith" (belief in whatever the church teaches, even if one does not know what it is), but that is clearly impossible today. No Protestant church (with the exception of a few tightly-disciplined groups) has a sufficiently clear grasp of its own faith for any Protestant to be willing to trust himself to it implicitly, and a similar situation is developing with great rapidity in the Roman Catholic Church. In such circumstances no one can depend on "what the church believes." He has to be sure that his faith is personal. (Note that to have a *personal* faith does not mean that one has a faith which is different from everyone else's; it means that one's faith is personal because one personally knows it, chooses it, and holds to it.)

If we are unwilling to seek and to accept new ways of *expressing* the Christian faith, there is a great danger that we shall end by merely repeating formulas which are not even understandable, much less meaningful, to anyone who is not completely steeped in our own esoteric tradition. In the current theological and intellectual situation, however, there is a much greater danger that if we allow the expression of the faith to become fluid, we shall in fact lose its substance. There is a sense in which it is possible and legitimate to seek other ways to formulate the meaning of the Incarnation of Christ than that chosen by the Council of Chalcedon in 451.[1] The problem is that our theologians, in their attempts to produce a "meaningful restatement," are actually producing something that can in no sense be reconciled with the original creed. John XXIII intended to safeguard both the historic faith and the freedom of modern man to express it in contemporary and relevant language, but modern theologians are clearly abusing this freedom. Many of their interpretations or restatements are mutually irreconcilable with one another and have very little resemblance to the faith of Christians through the ages. If there is rank confusion among both the Christian laity and the non-

Christian public about what the word Christian actually means, professional theologians must bear a considerable share of the blame.

Where did the trouble begin? How did the nature of Christianity come to be something mysterious and unknown? Paradoxical as it may seem, much of the confusion results directly from the attempts of theologians to make the Christian faith understandable and palatable. It is a commonplace that Christianity has never been "easy to swallow." The preaching of Jesus to his fellow-Jews was not an unmitigated success, nor was the missionary activity of early Christians in the Roman Empire. Historians estimate that when Constantine the Great saw the vision in the sky in 312, perhaps ten per cent of the population were Christians. That was after two hundred and seventy years of missionary preaching by enthusiastic and dedicated men ready to die for their faith. Today the situation is not so different. The reason why Christian preaching is not accepted is not wholly or even principally because it is not understood. It is also because it is not liked. In most cases it is not that Christianity has been tried and found wanting. It has been found difficult and not tried.

Many theological attempts to make Christianity understandable have a genuinely *missionary* motive. Theologians, concerned that people are not accepting the message of Christ, try to express it in language which is easier to understand and to accept. Unfortunately there is an easy transition from this legitimate and necessary task to an attempt to make Christ's message more acceptable by leaving parts of it out or by changing them drastically. Many theologians make it without even being aware of what they are doing, especially if they are not firmly committed to a definite creedal position. Sometimes they feel that if they can only get people to "join the church," get them involved in some activity, it is all right to make the message as inoffensive as necessary. Afer the new members have signed up, they can be presented with the full message.

Quite apart from the fact that this underhanded approach is incompatible with the Christian's responsibility to the God of truth, it also does not work. Usually the amplification of the message never comes. The evangelist, pastor, or theologian who tries to get people safely "hooked" before giving them the full treatment often discovers that by the time they are hooked he has forgotten what he wanted to say.

1. The "Essence" of Christianity?

One of the outstanding and most appealing of attempts to make Christianity more easily acceptable was Adolf Harnack's *The Essence of Christianity*,[2] perhaps *the* classic work of liberal Protestantism. Harnack, one of the most brilliant theologians of the late nineteenth and early twentieth centuries, earned his fame by decades of thorough scholarly research. He had no need to write a theological thriller in order to make a name for himself. Unlike many other theological innovators, Harnack was a man of reverence for God as well as of zeal for theological change. As a result, we can more easily believe in his sincerity than in that of those modern theologians who gain their fame solely by their radical repudiation of some essential doctrine.

Harnack believed that the essence of Christianity lies in the teaching of Jesus rather than in his person. Jesus, according to the great German liberal, taught about the fatherhood of God and the brotherhood of man. Our task is to worship God as Jesus did. This kind of a restatement of Christianity requires one to overlook or ignore the extent to which Jesus' *teaching* centered on himself as the only means of access to God the Father (e.g. John 14:6, "I am the way, and the truth, and the life"). Only a few years after Harnack wrote, Albert Schweitzer clearly demonstrated that Jesus presented himself as the Messiah and as the coming Judge of all the world, and that there is no legitimate way to separate his teaching about the Father and his moral counsels from his teaching about himself.[3] Schweitzer was unwilling to accept Jesus' messianic claims as true, and rather than face the implications of his unwillingness by repudiating Christianity, or by continuing to teach theology while rejecting Christ's teachings about himself, Schweitzer resolved to live a life of practical imitation of Christ, in whose theological teachings he did not believe.

Since Schweitzer, theologians have admitted that they cannot claim that Christ taught only the fatherhood of God and the brotherhood of man. Clearly he would never have been crucified if that had been his whole message. Nevertheless the appeal of a simplified kind of Christianity like Harnack's is so great (at least to theologians) that it constantly reappears. Sometimes new theological arguments are brought forward to support it, but more often than not it is merely presented to the church and the world in the confidence that so few people know the contents of the Bible that such a distortion is not likely to be challenged. Therefore Harnack's liberal "classic" is still relevant, because it represents a kind of faith that is often popularly mistaken for historic Christianity.

Harnack remains but one representative, and the most distinguished and irreproachable one, of a host of theological writers who have contributed to making the concept of Christianity all but unintelligible. In Harnack's case, we must admit that he *intended* to clarify the situation. Unfortunately, his "liberal" reduction of Christianity to what he called its essence was not a simplification but a substitution. Liberal Protestantism is not Christianity at all, but a new religion. This was clearly demonstrated by a great American conservative Protestant scholar of the inter-war period, J. Gresham Machen. His short book, *Christianity and Liberalism*[4] remains very useful, because Harnack-style liberalism is not yet dead, even though, theologically speaking, there is no justification for it. "The evil that men do lives after them"; this is true of theologians as well as of Roman dictators.

Liberal Protestantism is truly a child of nineteenth-century optimism of faith in progress and in moral as well as biological evolution. Man was held to be good and to be getting better. Nothing so radical as redemption was necessary: a certain amount of indulgence on the part of a grandfatherly kind of God and proper education would be quite sufficient to save man from the consequences of his "mistakes"—sin was no longer seen as a problem to human perfection. Thus liberal Protestantism felt that men and women can and should worship God as Jesus did, and that no special sacrifice on Jesus' part was necessary to reconcile them to God.

On the European Continent, World War I dealt liberal Protestantism a blow from which it never recovered. A world which could destroy the flower of its young manhood in four years of senseless carnage simply could not be thought of as a world of constant evolutionary progress. The liberal Protestants' intuition was better than their logic. On the vast scale required by the principle of evolutionary progress, the death of so many million soldiers does not necessarily mean anything. There was no compelling logical reason to abandon faith in progress, but fortunately it was largely abandoned—the evidence was psychologically, if not logically, convincing. The world and the human race can and do go backward as well as forward.

In the United States, which did not pay so high a price in blood and suffering in World War I and which reaped tremendous profits in business, industry, and finance, this liberal illusion hung on longer. The Depression and World War II destroyed it as a theological position. Under the withering criticism of "neo-orthodoxy," especially of Reinhold and Richard Niebuhr, the naive theology which identified national progress and expansion with God's providential plan in history has shriveled and disappeared. But this optimistic faith in human goodness among theologians returns to plague us in the naive confidence which assumes that with time all political enemies must become kindly friends. The belief that the Soviet Union has been mellowing in its attitude towards the United States is supported less by evidence than by the optimistic conviction that, being human, the Soviet leaders too must inevitably improve with time. This faith has occasionally been shaken by Soviet actions in Czechoslovakia and the Middle East, but it seems to recover as time passes.

In another way, the old liberal Protestant progress-philosophy is reappearing, coming in as it were by the back door of the Christian Communist dialogues. Although the Communists have given themselves and the world plenty of examples of man's capacity for evil, they still assume the fundamental goodness of man. Some avant-garde Christian theologians (such as America's Harvey Cox) who would reject this faith as applied to the American "Establishment" accept it for the Soviet one. It would be unthinkable for them to say that the United States government is working to bring about the kingdom of God—but they seem to be able to say it for the Soviet Union.

This strange defect of vision must not be interpreted as a symptom of pro-Communism. It is rather the result of the correction of the old progress-philosophy by *limited* and *selected* experience. The selfishness and arrogance which can be found in American society are harder for them to overlook, because they are closer at hand. They persistently overlook the fact that Communist society may be—and is—consistently far crueler and more dishonest, because it operates without the partial correctives of American democracy and of our remainder of Christian mentality. This fact should not cause us to mistake the loyalty of such theologians. Often enough they are so much more critical of free America than of Communist Russia precisely because they feel that America ought to be so much better. That is, they are comparing America as it exists in the mid-twentieth century to the messianic dream of the Pilgrims or at least of the Social Gospel. About Russia they cherish no such illusions—therefore they can praise the Soviet Union's dubious accomplishments while denigrating our own because they fall short of the messianic vision. Thus via the "dialogue" with the Marxists, liberal theology is falling back into its old and beloved error: belief in the fundamental goodness and inevitable perfectability of man.

2. Save the Church!

The efforts of modern theologians are both more radical and less rational than Harnack's. Harnack, we have seen, at least *intended* to clarify Christianity for the non-Christian. With modern writers like Bishop Robinson, the same purpose can be discerned, but in addition there is a strong desire to change the church. In *Honest to God* the "missionary" intent may still predominate, but in *The New Reformation?* the revolutionary purpose is clear.[5] If the nineteenth century was the great century of Protestant missions, the twentieth century is the century of curialism and church politics, not only in Roman Catholicism, where they have a long tradition, but also in Protestantism. The goal is to save the church, as an institution, whatever it costs.

The doctrine, preaching, and teaching of a classical liberal like Harnack reveal a commitment to the cause of the *truth* (as he erroneously saw it), even if it must be at great cost to the church. For this reason Harnack was vehemently opposed by many officials in the Lutheran church in Germany: they were not so opposed to his beliefs as such, but sensed that they represented a danger to the church as an institution. The modern radicals, by contrast, are in fact committed to the *church* but not to truth. In their desire to reform doctrine and practice they make hardly any pretense to be trying to bring them into conformity with truth as such, but rather with what twentieth-century man will buy.

In other words, in the "new theology" of Protestantism (of which we shall let Bishop Robinson serve as an example) the desire is to insure the survival and influence of the church. Perhaps the "new theologians" genuinely hope that if only the institutional church can somehow survive the present crisis, it will later be able to devote itself in peace and quiet to the recovery of the essential doctrinal commitments it jettisoned in the effort to survive. Their principal concern, however, is simply to save the church.

Church officials, from the lowest administrative levels to the highest, have never been noted, as a class, for their theological clarity and brilliance. Neither World Council of Churches Secretary Blake nor Pope Paul VI is likely to be remembered as a theologian. On the other hand, church officials usually have a sharp sensitivity for the practical interests of their institutions. In the case of the "new theologians" many officials must sense that their goal is somehow to pull the church through her present crisis. Therefore they tolerate or even encourage their radicalism.

Somewhat the same thing is happening in Roman Catholic circles since the Second Vatican Council and *aggiornamento*. Much of the updating of Roman Catholicism also stems from the unconscious or calculating desire to enable the church to triumph over the challenges of the modern world, at *whatever the cost in truth*. Protestants must realize that while certain reforms within Roman Catholicism are intrinsically appealing to Protestants, the calculating motive behind them may make them unhealthy both for Roman Catholicism and for Protestantism. To "save the church" at the cost of commitment to the historic faith is no salvation at all, for a church which has been "saved" by this method is no longer the church of Christ.

Harnack's liberalism threatened the church as an institution because of his commitment to truth. The prevailing mentality of his age, with the apparently irresistible triumph of science and apparently unbroken progress still to come, made him misunderstand what really is true, but his zeal for truth was genuine. In the case of liberalism, the danger to the church and to Christian faith results from the superficiality and inaccuracy of the truth as liberal theology sees it. With the radical "new theology," the danger is precisely that truth itself is given up for the sake of institutional continuity.

When a great man of the liberal generation, Albert Schweitzer, faced what he felt were insuperable doctrinal difficulties in the church of his day, he withdrew from his posts in the church and in theology and went into the jungle as a missionary doctor. He was unable to resolve the question of the truth of Christianity satisfactorily, but it did not occur to him to go on within the organized theological establishment without an answer to it. Twentieth-century theologians talk a great deal about honesty (e.g. *Honest to God!*); they like to play with the thought of giving up their bishoprics, their pastorates, their academic chairs and titles, and becoming an impoverished and scattered band of radical Christians. But it is no accident that they do not do it. Bishop Robinson suggests it in *The New Reformation?* but so far no radical theologian of note has done anything as practical as what Schweitzer did.

The motives behind the radical theological attack on historic Christian doctrines are presented as (1) a concern for the truth in the light of modern science and biblical scholarship; (2) a concern for modern man, whom the traditional church is not helping; (3) a desire to practice the New Testament principle of love for one's fellow-men. In reality *none* of these is the real motive. The shallowness of their alleged concern for truth can be demonstrated by the cavalier way in which "new theologians" deliberately misrepresent historic doctrines. The concern to help "modern man" find his way into the church is denied outright by Paul van Buren, while others, from Bishop Robinson to T. J. J. Altizer, in fact direct what they have to say not to the world outside the church but to the church. Finally, the desire to put the principle of love into practice cannot be very strong if in fact its preachers confine themselves chiefly to doctrinal agitation and to ecclesiastical manipulations, neither of which do much toward its fulfillment. The professors remain firmly seated on their chairs, the pastors continue in their pulpits, the bishops keep their robes. Even the former Episcopal bishop of California, James Pike, did not resign from the duties of his office to engage in practical labors of love, but to enjoy the untrammeled freedom of the Center for the Study of Democratic Institutions to continue his doctrinal, dogmatic, intellectual agitation. It is quite consistent that Pike has tried to retain the status of a bishop (although some Episcopal leaders hold that he has forfeited it), precisely because his struggle is *for* the institutional *church* and *against* the content and the truth of the historic Christian *faith.*

For this reason a man like Pike is never subjected to the same kind of widespread official church disapproval that Billy Graham constantly meets. Pike threatens Christian truth, but he is devoted to pulling the church through its protracted crisis—somehow, anyhow —even if it costs it every major doctrine. Graham is committed to the Christian message, but to the structure of the church, he is largely indifferent; he would probably be willing to see every *visible* church collapse if the *invisible* church, the invisible community of those who believe the historic faith, could continue to grow. Graham deals with individuals, despite his technique of mass evangelism, and he is respected by individual Christians; Pike deals with structures and is respected by the hierarchy.[6]

The desire on the part of church functionaries and theological professors to *save the church*, whatever the cost in truth, is neither creditable nor promising. It would be wrong to suggest, as Peter Watkins does in *Privilege*, that there is a calculated attempt on the part of cynical clergymen to preserve their positions of power and prestige. In most cases it is much more likely that they genuinely feel that the church has great social value and ought to be preserved. The difficulty is that ultimately the worth of the church depends on the truth of its teaching—unless we are willing to accept it merely as a kind of opium for the people, which is useful because it keeps people happy or in line, regardless of the truth of the claims by which it does it. The conscious or unconscious dishonesty involved in attempting to keep the church alive and effective although one does not accept its claims makes it an unworthy undertaking. It is also fundamentally unpromising because in the long run the church's effectiveness depends on its credibility. One of the most obvious factors in contemporary Protestant theology is the *credibility gap*. If Christians and non-Christians alike reach the point where they no longer trust theologians to deal with them on the basis of truth, but fear that they are being manipulated by them, then there will be no chance of the church preserving itself, no matter how frantic its attempts at *aggiornamento*.

The efforts of an Anglican bishop like Robinson, an Episcopalian like James Pike, a Baptist like Harvey Cox, or a Roman Catholic like Leslie Dewart are not to be compared with those of Peter Watkin's mythical, neo-fascist clergy in *Privilege*, at least not as far as their integrity is concerned. Each of the above-named theologians is acting out of the conviction that the traditional doctrine is far less important than the "life of the church." In *Privilege,* reactionary clergymen cynically make use of a confused "pop" singer to start a half-revivalistic, half-fascist national awakening. Perhaps the movie's weakest feature lies in its assumption that modern clergymen could be so efficiently calculating. Unless we are willing to concede to them a kind of cynical benevolence like that of Dostoyevsky's Grand Inquisitor, its clergy are fundamentally selfish schemers. Modern theological radicals are by no means selfish plotters. The tragedy lies in the fact that the ultimate result of their good intentions is not so different from that of the evil scheming of Watkin's clerical conspirators.

The "save the church" policy which sacrifices doctrine and a concern for truth automatically promotes the increase of hierarchical and administrative power. The anti-dogmatic Bishop Pike of California is a vehement critic of Roman Catholicism as well as of the teachings of his own church. It might therefore seem a blow to his work that his successor as bishop of California, C. Kilmer Myers, has openly come out in favor of recognizing the Pope as "the chief pastor of men." Actually it is a logical consequence of Pike's efforts. Pike and others like him strike at the foundations of personal faith by attempting to discredit the historic doctrines of Christianity. His successor is then in a position to plead for the great power-structure of the papacy, which is less concerned with winning individuals' *trust* than their *obedience*. It is no accident that this is taking place during the reign of the politically astute and theologically superficial Paul VI, rather than under his predecessors John XXIII or Pius XII. The Roman church is having its own problems about doctrinal integrity and theological credibility. Whether it can digest the kind of Protestants who would accept the pope for reasons of expediency rather than truth is certainly open to question. It seems more likely that the support of such Protestants can only further confuse the situation within Roman Catholic theology and doctrine.

3. *"Christian" Doctrine?*

The result of this conceptual confusion, caused in large measure by theologians themselves, has been a general retreat from doctrine.

A simple dictionary gives "Christian doctrine" as the first definition of Christianity, but this is a definition which does not enlighten us, for today we must ask, "What is left of Christian doctrine?" Is Christian doctrine still Christian? The question seems to imply a tautology. How can something be Christian unless it is Christian? Although false teachings and teachers abound throughout Christendom, the real problem is not so much the presence and presentation of false, i.e. non-Christian, doctrines within the churches, as that real Christian doctrine is nowhere to be found.

A characteristic of the church in our day—of the whole church and of each individual church—is the *avoidance of doctrine*. In churches and in church-related schools (both Sunday schools and the regular schools and colleges maintained by the churches), there is a growing reluctance to teach anything specific and definite about the Christian faith. This reluctance is not shared by the so-called "cults."[7] Groups like the Mormons and the Jehovah's Witnesses do not appeal because their teachings are simple, easy to accept, and in line with the modern mentality. None of these things is true. Much of their effectiveness in making proselytes comes from the fact that they have a distinct doctrine of which they are not ashamed. In general they do not try to veil the points at which their doctrine clashes with modern assumptions, but rather adopt the attitude: "That's what our teaching is. If you feel that you can't accept it, then don't. But the responsibility for the consequences is yours."

Protestant churches, on the other hand, tend to apologize for their doctrines, to push them into the background. How often a preacher or teacher is heard to say: "That is what the church has taught, but of course we do not expect you to accept it if you find it difficult." There is some justification for such diffidence when the doctrine in question is an uncertain or a non-essential one. (An example might be the question about whether the Christian is obliged to give a tithe of his income to God, as is prescribed in the Old Testament. This is a case where the New Testament principles binding on Christians are not absolutely clear. However, even in this case, the important point is not whether the tithe is difficult for a modern man to accept, but whether God requires it.) Today we find this hesitancy not only on disciplinary questions and on peripheral doctrinal issues, but on important doctrines like that of the Virgin Birth of Christ and on absolutely essential ones such as the Resurrection. By suggesting to his listeners that he will condition his preaching on their response of hostility or acceptance, a preacher inevitably gives them the idea that right and wrong is determined by their response. Faith becomes a "personal matter" in the wrong way: each individual's opinion becomes the standard for the content of faith. Faith becomes no more than what the late Paul Tillich meant, namely, that which one takes seriously and without reservation. Even Tillich would not have accepted the idea that what one man takes seriously is automatically as good as the next man's—but this impression is frequently given from the pulpit, and is viewed as intelligent and tolerant broad-mindedness. This is the most destructive nonsense imaginable. Christian faith must be personal in the sense that each person individually understands the historic faith and personally commits himself to it, but not in the sense that he decides what it should be.

Nowhere is this foolishness more obvious than in the informal religious discussion, now often conducted on an ecumenical basis. The legitimate and in fact necessary discussion about how individuals can come to grips with the God who reveals himself in Scripture becomes a silly swapping of ideas on "what I think God is like." On the one hand, every individual's conception of God, of, if you prefer, that which he takes most deeply and seriously, has a certain validity and is not to be ridiculed or dismissed lightly. Every human attempt to attach meaning to life, whether it be the vast, idealistic philosophical edifice of a Hegel or the blatant egocentricity of a D. H. Lawrence, deserves our respect to the extent that it represents a man's honest effort to find a light in the darkness of human ignorance. Of course there are attempts which are so frivolous or dishonest or both that they deserve no respect. It is more important to realize that there can be a vast difference between an *honest attempt* to give meaning to human life and the true meaning itself. Honest inquiry is never a substitute for knowing the truth. Christians of many centuries and denominations have frequently adopted an arrogant, insensitive attitude towards those whose views differed from theirs. In times past it seems to have been all too easy for Christians to accuse everyone who disagreed with them of intellectual dishonesty and of a lack of moral integrity. Today the mistake is more likely to lie in the other extreme: we accept as honest, sincere, and even "courageous" religious formulations and restatements which are nothing but the product of a fertile and frivolous imagination.

Acceptance of the criterion of "sincerity" in a theological discussion is dangerous, just as it would be in scientific research. Of course, if someone who is contributing to the discussion is evidently frivolous or insincere, his contributions ought to be dismissed. But if his sincerity cannot be impugned, his views are not necessarily valid for that reason. Sincerity is a relatively worthless standard here, because it is something which is almost impossible to judge, and because it can be quite independent of the facts. Fundamentally, any meaningful discussion of Christianity must be based on the historic faith and its standards, i.e. on the Bible itself and on the great doctrinal formulations of Christian history, as well as on the disciplined experience of the church and individuals today.

The different, half-ashamed attitude adopted by many churchmen towards all doctrine results in an emphasis which can be summed up in the slogan, "Christianity is a way of life." To the extent that it is directed at those for whom Christianity is nothing but an intellectual game with no practical consequences, the slogan has merit. To teach by word alone without examples is useless and ineffective: actions do speak louder than words. On the other hand, many actions require words and concepts, not only to explain their meaning, but even to give them a meaning. The execution of a convicted murderer after a trial in which he has had ample opportunity to defend himself is quite a different matter from the vengeful lynching of a suspect by an enraged mob. The actions are similar, and the result is identical, the death of a man, but the *words* of the prosecution, the *words* of the defense, and the *judgment* of the court create a vast difference between them.

A Christian who is not living his religion is either a bad Christian or a false one, it is true. But we may say with equal vigor that one who does not communicate (witness to) and teach his religion is either a disobedient Christian or a sham one (see Acts 1:8, and the "Great Commission" of Jesus to his disciples, Matthew 28:20). Part of the Christian's inheritance is his right to know what he believes and why he believes it. Jesus himself told his disciples, "No longer do I call you slaves; for the slave does not know what his master is doing; but I have called you friends, for all things that I have heard from My Father I have made known to you" (John 16:15). The major problem with doctrine in Christian churches today is that it is virtually non-existent. This represents a fundamental and ultimately fatal apostasy. The Christian and the church are morally bound to have a clear idea of the Christian faith and to proclaim it clearly to the world. The present confused babble of the theologians is not only irresponsible: it is a betrayal of this obligation.

The "Great Commission," in which Jesus commanded his followers to teach and make disciples of all nations, makes it clear that the present deemphasizing of doctrine is not due to any lack of a clear commandment from God. It is likewise not the result of a lack of doctrine to be taught. Despite all the variations of Christian doctrine through the centuries and in various confessions and denominations, there is a very substantial body of teaching on which there is fundamental unity. The fact that men as different in temperament, education, and cultural background as Augustine and Luther should have so much in common is remarkable. Many similar parallels could be drawn, bearing witness to the fact that there is a reality behind their beliefs, a reality which moulds the faith of such different individuals to itself and gives it a relatively harmonious form. There was never a time in the history of the church without fanatics, fantasies, and heretics, but there still remains a common current of conviction which runs through the centuries and bridges the great denominations.

Doctrinal Differences

It would be both dishonest and useless to pretend that there are no real and significant differences which divide the major confessions and denominations. It has sometimes happened that the church has split over trivial matters or even mutual misunderstandings, and that the breach has continued long after the real reason for it has been forgotten. In general, however, the major divisions within Christendom are not over trivialities, but over serious matters. Before turning our attention to the vital beliefs which orthodox Christians of the major historic confessions have in common, we shall do well to look at a few of the issues which divide them. In so doing, we should bear in mind that the theological distinctions are not always actually the cause of a division or of its continuation. (For example, the Christological controversies of the fifth century, which plunged the Eastern Roman Empire into civil disorder and contributed greatly to the loss of Egypt and Syria to the Arabs, derived in large measure from a revival of nationalistic feeling in those countries.)

Eastern Orthodoxy and Protestantism reject the accepted Roman Catholic doctrine of the primacy and infallibility of the pope. Although both of the great non-Roman Catholic branches of Christendom might have been willing to accord some kind of a primacy of honor to the Roman bishop, they could not and cannot do it as long as he claims an authority which seems to them to infringe on God's. Many of the major doctrinal differences between Eastern Orthodoxy and Protestantism on the one hand and Roman Catholicism on the other result directly from papal claims and definitions. For example, the doctrines concerning purgatory and indulgences, which both the Eastern churches and the Protestants reject, have been so firmly fixed upon the Roman church by papal pronouncements that it is difficult for Rome to deëmphasize or withdraw them, despite considerable dissatisfaction with them within her own ranks. In many issues, Eastern Orthodoxy agrees with Rome in practice but denies it the right to make authoritative, binding decisions. Thus the Eastern churches observed the *feast* of the Assumption of Mary long before the Latin church of the West, but they repudiate the *dogma* of the Assumption promulgated in 1950 by Pope Pius XII. Eastern Orthodoxy accepts and encourages the veneration of the "saints,"[8] especially of Mary, a thing which Protestants uniformly reject, but the Orthodox and Protestants are again closer together in their advocacy of the principle of justification by faith and their criticism of the Catholic doctrine of grace and of individual merit.

There are also matters on which Protestants agree with Roman Catholics and disagree with Eastern Orthodoxy. Chief among them is the doctrine of the double procession of the Holy Spirit: the Nicene Creed, in the version used by both Catholics and Protestants, says of the Holy Spirit that he "proceeds from the Father and the Son." The phrase "and the Son" was not in the original creed, but was introduced in Spain in 589, in France in 767, and in Rome in 1014;[9] the Greeks reject it, and made of it a major bone of contention in the great East-West schism which began in 1054. Roman Catholicism and the chief Protestant confessions officially agree in teaching the doctrine of election or predestination, for which the Eastern Church has had little use—although particularly on this point there is great inconsistency among both Catholics and Protestants. Despite their official endorsement of the Augustinian position on predestination, shared also by Thomas Aquinas, Roman Catholics incline in practice to an endorsement of the freedom of the human will. On the Protestant side, the rejection of predestination by the Catholic humanist Erasmus was echoed two centuries later by John Wesley, founder of Methodism, who called it an "awful doctrine," and modern evangelists like Billy Graham share the Erasmian-Wesleyan perspective.

These doctrinal differences are not small things. To some extent they can be explained away, and to some extent the conflicts and crises result more from an unhealthy overemphasis of one position or the other than from an absolutely irreconcilable conflict. Nevertheless, basic conflicts remain. The teachings of Scripture cannot be both sufficient and insufficient for salvation; justification cannot be both by faith alone and by faith together with works; the pope cannot both have the right to define dogmas as necessary for salvation and also be an imposter with no authority. Christians cannot forget or ignore these differences, nor is it honest to establish some kind of an institutional unity which pretends that they do not exist. What is possible—if the great branches of Christianity have enough in common—is to live by what unites us and agree to live with what divides us. What we have in common is really very great.

Doctrinal Similarities

The differences between the various Christian denominations and confessions are only suggested in the preceding section, not exhausted. Because what unites us is more important than what divides us, it is important to recognize that a few paragraphs hardly suffice even to enumerate the great common convictions which unite all Christians properly so called. Those which follow are not the only convictions which Christians share, nor are they even necessarily the most important ones. Unfortunately (such is the virulence of theological controversy and strife) even a compressed list such as this will not meet with complete approval by all those who consider themselves orthodox, biblical Christians, and many will no doubt look in vain for a particular doctrine which they consider more important than some of those given. Nevertheless, in order not to be guilty of never passing beyond the vague generalization, it is necessary to be specific.

In the preceding pages an allusion was made to the common faith shared by Augustine and Luther. Those readers who know something of the history of Protestant-Catholic polemics will immediately suspect a Protestant attempt to repudiate all that happened in the Dark and Middle ages as sub-evangelical and degenerate. According to this view, medieval Catholicism really was unfaithful to the great tradition of the Fathers of the Church, and it was Luther and the Reformation which reestablished the contact. This highly simplified picture is not absolutely without a basis in fact, for medieval religion was quite a different thing from the Christianity of the early church, and Luther did rediscover something that was lacking. Few sixteenth-century Roman Catholic scholars could have competed with John Calvin in knowledge or appreciation of the Church Fathers. Nevertheless, we must also admit that not only Thomas Aquinas but many later and lesser medieval Catholics also inherited and developed something from Augustine and the early church, and that there were tremendous differences between the evangelical church under Luther and Calvin and the early church under John Chrysostom and Augustine. If we attempt to list a number of great figures of church history who shared a common faith, and produce names like Basil of Caesarea, Ambrose, Augustine, Chrysostom, Bernard of Clairvaux, Francis of Assisi, Luther, Calvin, Zinzendorf, Wesley, many legitimate objections can be made. There were vast differences between these men; there are others who might equally legitimately belong to the list, such as Thomas Aquinas, Ignatius Loyola, and Francis de Sales, whom the Protestant finds hard to list but whom he cannot entirely omit with a clear conscience.[10] We must not oversimplify and create an artificial and forced consensus between great Christians of the past and present. Yet if one thing stands out when one studies the writings and lives of such men, it is that they knew and served the same Lord, and that they shared one faith and one hope. From the faith and hope which they and the whole historical community of Christian believers have shared, the following doctrinal points are selected as examples:

(1) The reality, personal nature, and power of God. In a day when slogans such as "the death of God," "the God beyond God," "the depth of being," and more like them are bandied about, it is necessary to be reminded of what the Epistle to the Hebrews says, first, "he who comes to God must believe that He is," by which God's reality is affirmed, and second, "and that He is a rewarder of those who seek Him," which clearly points to his personal nature and his power (Hebrews 11:6). Vague generalizations about God as "Someone in the Great Somewhere" are entirely worthless, in fact, harmful. It is necessary to recognize that he is personal, that he has a distinct character, that he can be known and in fact must be known by us if we are to fulfil our true destiny. The necessity to know God and the possibility of knowing him depend on (2).

(2) The existence, authority, and understandibility of a true revelation of God in the Bible. It is absolutely crucial that we recognize God as the One who acts in history, in real space and time, and who reveals himself in authoritative language which we can understand. In one of the rather few mystical experiences described in the Bible, St. Paul says that when he met Christ on the Damascus road, Christ spoke to him "in the Hebrew dialect" (Acts 26:14). It was not just a piece of descriptive embellishment for Paul to mention the fact that Christ spoke Hebrew (actually, the Aramaic of first-century Palestine). It means that even in this tremendous encounter between the Risen Son of God and the man who was to be his foremost evangelist and theologian, an encounter to which Paul owed his own salvation and to which we owe a good part of the New Testament, something was said which could be repeated and which can be understood. It was not an ineffable experience which cannot be described: there must have been much about it which could not be and has not been conveyed in human words, but Paul did not dwell on that aspect of it. He told his noble audience, Festus, Agrippa, and Bernice, what he had heard in Hebrew, and they understood. They did not understand fully and deeply enough to accept it, as far as we know, but the basic content was understandable.[11]

(3) The estrangement of man from God caused by a real fall in space and time. The doctrine of the fall of man is one that most readily lends itself to a mythical interpretation as an interpretative description of the human condition; this might be acceptable if the

account in Genesis 3 were all that we have, but St. Paul, in Romans 5:12-21, makes it clear that his understanding of redemption depends on a real, unique fall into sin. The doctrine of the fall is extremely important, because it enables the Christian to rebel against the present human condition, against the evil, injustice, and suffering in the world, without rebelling against God. The situation which Camus describes in *The Plague,* in which God permits suffering and death, does not please God any more than it pleases man. God permits it because he allows man to act significantly, and allows the consequences of the fall to take place. If the Genesis account of the fall is merely symbolic or mythical, then (a) Paul is wrong in attributing man's bondage to death to Adam's sin, and also wrong in attributing man's new life to Christ, and (b) God created man fallen, which says something very bad about God and something fundamentally hopeless about man. The present state of development of evolutionary thought makes this doctrine a difficult one to understand and to reconcile with scientific theories or the origin of human life. Nevertheless, it is so integral to biblical theology that it cannot simply be dropped if it seems to be objectionable in the light of certain developments in modern thought and science. Furthermore, aside from a real fall in real history there is no way to escape the conclusion that God is pitiless and that man is damned by nature.

(4) The incarnation of the Son of God by the power of the Holy Spirit on the Virgin Mary, so that he was perfect man and perfect God. Speculation about whether or why God *had* to become incarnate in order to redeem man may be left to others: the point is that he *did* do so. This divine entry into human history is irreversible, and it gives man a glorious heritage. The type of supposedly Christian theology which seeks to "understand" Jesus Christ by divesting him of his divinity is but another stage in man's age-long rebellion against God and rejection of his grace. The unity of the historic church on this vital doctrine is monolithic.

(5) The sacrificial and substitutionary death of Christ; his resurrection, ascension, and his ultimate return to judge the world. At different times and in different confessions there have been tendencies to center theology and piety on either the Incarnation or the Atonement, but neither does justice to the Christ-event if taken alone. The great events of Passion Week would take on quite a different

scale if the Man who went through them were not also the Son of God. On the other hand, being the Son of God is not an empty, static dignity. In the Atonement, God in Christ revealed what he is like: the Incarnation took place in order to make the Atonement possible, and cannot be separated from it.

(6) The significance of human moral and spiritual choices. Hell has been called "the greatest monument to human freedom." The teaching of Christ and the faith of the Christian church have always emphasized the eternal significance of choices made here and now. Christ came to bring the promise and the possibility of forgiveness to a world of men who were dead in trespasses and sins, but it is there only for those who will accept it. One of the most pernicious theories to beset Christianity is that of universalism, which holds that all men will ultimately be saved. Although some biblical and philosophical arguments can be brought forward to support this position, surely the whole tenor of Christ's teaching is against it. In a strange way, hell is necessary for human significance. If no man, no matter what he did, could finally rebel against God, but all men were ultimately to be brought back into harmony with God through a kind of irresistible grace, then all the moral and spiritual struggles of men would have no more meaning, in the last analysis, than the wrigglings of hamsters in a laboratory cage. Likewise, heaven does not exist simply as a reward or a bribe, but it is the inevitable expression of the love of God. It certainly is possible for Christians to be excessively other-worldly, but the kind of pseudo-piety which claims that eternal life is not important is simply out of touch with God's gracious purpose for man.

Many other doctrines could be listed, dealing with the nature of the church, prayer, the sacraments, the ministry, Christian conduct, social responsibility, and so on. Even though Christian groups are divided on these issues, there is still more agreement than one might expect. But these can be left aside for the moment, for what is important to us is simply to note that there is a considerable and important body of doctrine about which the whole church has always been in substantial agreement. The flight from doctrine is not due to any lack of doctrines to be taught: it is an anticipatory stage of a real rejection of basic principles of the Christian faith.

4. The Churches

The tragedy of the Christian churches today is that they can continue to exist as *institutions* when the spiritual life has gone out of them. The institutional life of a church does not appear to depend on its spiritual vitality. Over the centuries, all the major churches have developed a number of secondary functions and resources which enable them to continue to exist, and in some cases to appear to prosper, without in the least fulfilling the task that Christ assigned to them.

From the biblical point of view this surprising fact is not so surprising. In the New Testament the church appears as a kind of beachhead established by Christ in enemy territory, for the world, in a real sense, in under the control of sin and the devil. The church is not the company of those men who have resolved to distinguish themselves from the majority of mankind by being especially good, by taking special care to discharge their responsibilities to God. It is rather the group of revolutionaries who have flocked to Christ's banner in revolt against the age-long rule of sin and of the fear of death (Hebrews 2:14-15). The Christian knows that his cause will eventually be victorious, for it is God who controls the ultimate destiny of the world, not Satan. But this ultimate victory is not yet evident. Before it is consummated, there is still to be much suffering and struggle. The church can come to terms of peace with the world in which it lives only by being untrue to its calling, which is to witness to the lordship of Christ in a world which is under the tyranny of the power of darkness.

Unfortunately the church consists of ordinary people, who do not like to be unpopular. Therefore there will always be a strong temptation for the church to accommodate itself to the world, to reduce the "unnecessary" friction, and finally to abandon its calling and duty in the world. There is no need for the Christian to seek to be unpopular, nor is it right to attribute any hostility which he may encounter to persecution. Plenty of us behave in ways which would earn us hostility whether we were Moslems, Buddhists, or humanists.

The Christian has an obligation to remove all sources of unnecessary hostility, so that the Gospel of Christ will get a hearing instead of being rejected unheard. However, beyond a certain point hostility cannot be eliminated, because fundamentally the Gospel crosses up the world and shocks man. The Christian's task is to do his best to make sure that when non-Christians are shocked, it is by the message of the Gospel and not by the behavior of Christians.

If the churches of today make one consistent impression on the world around them, it is not that they are a committed fellowship dedicated to the transformation of the world. It is rather that they represent a kind of pressure and interest group, determined to preserve itself and its privileges and prerogatives at all costs. The radically secularizing theologians, such as Harvey Cox, are quite right in their attempt to get the churches out of their self-serving rut of perpetuating themselves and back to the task of serving the world into which God sent them. While the evangelical Christian must condemn the secularizers for depriving the church of the one real possibility it has of serving the world, that is, for changing the Gospel to the point where it no longer can bring salvation, he must accept with sorrow the accuracy of their diagnosis. If the orthodox Christian resists secularization simply by defending the church or Christianity, he will be doing much the same thing as many radical theologians. To save the church by preserving its historic faith is much better than to attempt to save it by abandoning the faith, but it is not enough to meet the challenges of today.

Both Roman Catholicism and liberal Protestantism cut a dismal figure when faced by the depraved, anti-Christian challenge of Nazism, and they have not done so much better vis-à-vis Communism. Evangelical Protestantism, on the other hand, has failed miserably to contribute to social justice and improve racial relationships in those racially troubled areas where it has traditionally enjoyed a powerful position, such as the American South and the Republic of South Africa. The general conduct of the churches is not one to inspire the ordinary observer with the impression that they can show him the life which Christ came into the world to bring.

Fortunately, while God works with institutions and nations, he begins with individuals. Often in the history of Israel it seemed that the whole nation had become faithless, yet through a faithful remnant, God was able to restore the whole nation to health and continue to use it in his plan for the redemption of mankind. As we look at the church as a whole, and at individual confessions and denominations, we must say that the doctrinal and institutional structures are riddled with decay. We must say at least this much, if we are unwilling to say that the official structures are *causing* the trouble. This is a black picture, yet as we look more closely, at particular individuals, at particular congregations, we can see that even today there are faithful remnants.

What remains of Christianity is not easy to find in its theologies, in its academic controversies, or in its institutional structures. Yet something does remain, and in God's providence it will be enough to preserve the church, so that "the gates of hell shall not prevail against it."

Notes

[1]The Creed of the Council of Chalcedon, held in 451, gave the fullest and clearest definition of the two natures of Jesus Christ, whom it defined as fully God and fully man.

[2]Adolf Harnack (von Harnack after his knighting by Kaiser Wilhelm II in 1914) lived from 1851 to 1930 and was the outstanding German theological scholar of his generation. The German original, *Das Wesen des Christentums,* was published in 1900. The English translation is titled, *What Is Christianity?*

[3]Albert Schweitzer's book, *The Quest of the Historical Jesus,* first appeared in German in 1906 under the title *Von Reimarus zu Wrede.*

[4]First published in New York in 1923 by Macmillan and reprinted by Eerdmans, Grand Rapids, in a paperback edition in 1960.

[5]We must use the word "missionary" with reservations. Bishop Robinson's desire to win people to the Gospel may be sincere enough, but his Gospel is no longer genuine, and thus his "mission" is mission only in terms of its *function,* but not of its *content.* In this sense we can also speak of the Communists as showing "missionary" zeal. For a critique of Robinson's position, see O. Fielding Clark, *For Christ's Sake* (Wallington: Religious Education Press, 1963); Leon Morris, *Religionless Christianity* (London and Chicago: InterVarsity, 1964); the most thorough treatment is in Eric L. Mascall, *The Secularisation of Christianity* (London: Darton, Longman and Todd, 1965, and New York: Holt, 1966), Chapter 3, "Emotion Recollected in Tranquility."

[6]Dr. Graham, because of his individualistic emphasis, may reasonably be criticized as having an inadequate theory of the church, but at least he begins at the right place, i.e. with the individual Christian. Some theologians spend a great deal of time speculating about the true nature and proper role of the church without having themselves come to terms with what it means for an individual to be a Christian.

[7]The expressions "sect" and "cult" are often bandied about as terms of abuse. As used here they are intended to be purely descriptive. The great sociologist of religion Ernst Troeltsch reserved the term "sect" for groups which are functionally and socially (rather than doctrinally) exclusivist and voluntarist. Thus the Mennonites, whose doctrines are not so different from those of the major Protestant churches, are often called a "sect." American Protestants who are exasperated when Catholics ask them, "To what sect do you belong?" have the right to point out in reply that in the United States the Roman Catholic Church, being exclusivist and voluntarist, is also a sect, while many Protestant groups, in which membership is habitual and involuntary, better fit Troeltsch's definition of a church. The term "cult" is used to refer to a group with basic theological divergences from historic Christianity. Thus the Mormons, who teach that man is made in the physical image of God, are a cult, and so are the Jehovah's Witnesses. The term is reserved for groups which have something in common with historic Christianity. Islam is a religion, not a cult; within an Islamic frame of reference, one can speak of Moslem sects and cults.

[8]Protestantism follows St. Paul's practice of calling all Christian believers saints, and does not reserve the term for those who have been canonized by popular consent or by official church action. Cf. Romans 1:7, I Corinthians 1:2, II Corinthians 1:1, Ephesians 1:1, Philippians 1:1 and Colossians 1:2 for examples of Paul's terminology.

[9]Karl Heussi, *Kompendium der Kirchengeschichte,* 12th ed. (Tübingen: Mohr, 1960), pp. 186-187.

[10]Thomas Aquinas (1225-1274), the greatest theologian of the medieval church, built much of the foundation for the tremendous edifice of Roman Catholic theology, which has proved so difficult for the Reformers and their successors to dismantle. Ignatius Loyola (1491-1556), founder of the Jesuits, and Francis de Sales (1567-1622), both of them outstanding men, were effective opponents of the evangelical cause.

[11]For an insight into the importance of the phrase, "in the Hebrew tongue," as well as of the vast significance of a unique, historic fall for the meaningfulness of man and the mercy of God, I am indebted to theologian and pastor Dr. Francis A. Schaeffer.

CHAPTER 7

· CAVEAT EMPTOR ·

Beloved, do not believe every spirit, but test the spirits to see whether they are from God; because many false prophets have gone out into the world.

I JOHN 4:1

"The trouble with this country," a self-appointed "bishop" and radio preacher once said, "is that there are too many false prophets." He continued, "They ought to pass a law and make them put signs on their churches, 'Devil's Church. This Way to Hell.'" In the present situation, it would indeed be a great help if churches were so identified. Christ asked his auditors in the Sermon on the Mount, "What man is there among you, when his son shall ask him for a loaf, will give him a stone?" (Matthew 7:9). What Jesus did not expect his listeners, drawn from the curious and generally unconverted Jewish general public, to do, his self-styled twentieth-century disciples constantly do. Men and women come to the churches seeking understanding, meaning, knowledge, love, God. What they will receive is anybody's guess.

A few years ago a brilliant young German attorney spent a weekend in the home of an American minister working in Switzerland. The attorney, like approximately half of West Germany's adults, was a baptized, confirmed Lutheran; like the vast majority of those baptized, confirmed Lutherans, he had not been inside a church in years. The American minister, by his theology, could be called a fundamentalist; in his approach, not only to theology but also to individuals, he shows a greater awareness of what the twentieth century is and means than any eager radical or secular theologian. He understood where the young attorney was: his examinations just completed, he stood on the threshold of an active, successful, and fundamentally meaningless career. There was no fixed reference point in his life, whereby to evaluate the successes of the past or the exertions of the future. After a few hours, the attorney suspected, for the first time in many years, that God might really be there. He was not merely interested: he was shaken.

Friday and Saturday were spent at the minister's home; Sunday he went back to Zurich, and there, for the first time in many years, expressed a desire to go to church. The church was one-quarter filled, chiefly with elderly women. The congregation straggled through some ancient hymns. The learned preacher, graduated from Zurich's well-known theological faculty, preached a twenty-minute sermon as complicated as it was trivial. The attorney's believing friend, who had only reluctantly accepted the proposal to go to church, could almost read his thoughts on his face: "I haven't been wrong. This *is* what the church is really like. That other one, up in the mountains, is some kind of a freak or a fanatic."

How many times a week do similar things take place in churches around the world? How many people come, of a Sunday morning, hoping to receive bread, and receive a stone? They happen all too often. A perpetual problem for the Inter-Varsity Christian Fellowship and for similar small groups of convinced, dedicated, "ordinary" Christians is to find churches to which they can send new Christians with a clear conscience, or to which graduates can go on leaving the university. Members of I.V.C.F. groups are "ordinary" Christians in the sense that they have no distinctive or peculiar doctrines. Their faith is the faith of the historic creeds and the great Reformation confessions, taken seriously. And that is the difficulty—because the organized churches, in large measure, do not take it seriously.

As a result, some of the most sensitive, most deeply committed, most *orthodox* Christians attend no church. These are not people of the type who say, "I can worship God just as well on the golf links as in some stuffy church." They are people who realize that according to God's commandments, they should be worshipping him with a congregation and who are deeply pained by their inability to find a serious, consistent, and living congregation. They know that their failure to find the "right" congregation does not excuse them from their responsibility, but they recognize somehow that to attend the churches which are available might sap their faith rather than strengthen it.

This is a terrible thing for the churches. It means that the very people who are most deeply committed to the calling of being disciples of Christ exclude themselves—or are excluded—from the congregations which need them most. It is all very well to be religious, but one must not be fanatical. If there is any place where *enthusiasm* is less welcome than on the theological faculty, it is in church. We are all familiar with the problems caused by an excess of enthusiasm: they are often described to us by a society and an educational system devoted to an optimistic, humanistic, evolutionary atheism. They can be real: much evil has been done and is still being done under the cover of religious enthusiasm. The Arabs deluded themselves into still another ill-fated holy war against Israel; Protestant clergy can still be set upon by Catholic mobs in some Latin American countries; Northern Ireland is developing its indigenous brand of fanatical Catholic-baiting. But we must be realistic: is an excess of enthusiasm, an excess of moral seriousness, an excess of piety, the threat to the churches in the final third of the twentieth century?

It would be good if we could say that the church is but a shadow of its former self. That suggestion is appealing, but an examination of church history forbids it. The "former self" never existed: that is to say, the church has never been free of the most serious, and at times the most sordid, problems. They existed in the New Testament. St. Paul's first Corinthian letter is a dreadful catalogue of theological and moral disorder which no modern suburban church could match. On the one hand, this is frightening. It means that there is no "pure church" to which we can return by historical investigation. The Reformers, particularly John Calvin, thought that they were restoring a corrupted church to its early purity. What they accomplished, in the eyes of many of us, was a good thing and a necessary thing. Evangelical Christians cannot succumb to the romantic dream of a Christian Europe, united under a single pope, but without the Gospel, without the Bible for the people, without all those evangelical imperatives which the Reformation rediscovered. On the other hand, it is clear that whatever Calvin and Luther accomplished, it was not a return to primitive Christianity. Perhaps they captured the essential spirit of the early church in an adequate way, or even the best way, for sixteenth-century Europe, but they certainly did not restore the church of the early centuries. If they had, it would not have been an unqualified success.

The church has never been an unqualified success. That may offer us some comfort as we wrestle with the complex of problems which seem so much beyond us. Somehow, out of this puzzled, perplexed, and indolent mass we call the church, God is going to produce a triumph. Through it, he is going to bring his purposes to light, "in order that the manifold wisdom of God might now be made known through the church to the rulers and the authorities in the heavenly places" (Ephesians 3:10). We ought to recognize this; in fact, we virtually must recognize it, if we are not to lose heart entirely.

But we cannot let the matter rest there. "For they are not all Israel who are descended from Israel," writes St. Paul (Romans 9:6), and not everything is church which goes by the name church. Individuals are recognizing this. When a serious Christian moves from one community to another, he may make no effort to stay within the same denomination, but he will seek a new congregation which is faithful to the same Lord. In the Roman Catholic Church and in the more ritualistic, more tightly organized of the Protestant churches, such church-hopping is frowned upon or condemned outright. Yet even when a really awakened Roman Catholic remains firmly within the boundary lines of his own fold, he may be found straying via radio, television, or the printed word to find the preachers and teachers who most clearly speak to him of Christ, regardless of label. Unfortunately many people who were once awake to the meaning of the Christian faith, who were once committed, simply give up. They abstain from public worship, and take no part in official Christianity. Thus the official church is left too often to the lukewarm—to those too lethargic to be grieved by its faults and too bland to throw it over. There is no conceivable way of obtaining statistics, but it is not inconceivable that more believing Christians are absent from the main-line churches of a Sunday morning than are present.

The secular theologians have recognized the problem, and they, in their own way, are trying to save the church, trying to make it relevant to man in the twentieth century. Sadly (or happily, if one considers their theology), attempts to make the church relevant by making it relevant do not work. The organized churches are turning to ever more drastic expedients. Not all of them are as weird and potentially blasphemous as that in which a Harvard theology professor joined the prophet of L.S.D. to stage a Pentecost happening— even the tolerant *Christian Century*[1] took offense at that. But these radical measures hardly produce more than a flicker of renewed interest, which quickly fades. As a matter of fact, it is the orthodox, even the *extreme* (or should we say *consistent?*) groups which can still stir the imagination and fire the blood of twentieth-century people. Among the standard kinds of churches, it is the orthodox, the evangelistic, even the "fundamentalist" groups which advance—not excluding the enthusiastic, pentecostal fellowships on the evangelical side, nor the stern, militant *Opus Dei* movement among the Catholics. Alongside of them the fervent sects and established cults continue to move ahead. All these, at one side of the field, outrace the lethargic machinery of the official, established churches, despite all its efforts to convince itself that it is playing an ever greater role in the shaping of the world. From the other side, the machinery of the church is being overwhelmed by the fantastic pseudo-religions spawned by drugs and unreason, all of which appear more attractive than mediocre ecclesiastical bureaucracy. The orthodox believers, shaved off from the major bodies by an intolerant liberalism, go their lonely but self-confident way. Church machinery is mobilized to condemn them, but no voices are raised against the non-religious or pseudo-religious radicals.

In this situation, individuals are not buying the products their churches offer. Radical theology is intended to appeal to the laity, and indeed, it sells books, and occasionally fills lecture halls. It can fill up the "Letters" column of *Time Magazine*. But it does not fill the churches. Yet theological production is in high gear. State universities are adding departments of religion, if not of theology. Theological tracts become best-sellers; bad bishops become popularly-acclaimed pundits. Where does the consumption come from? Who is creating the demand?

At the risk of oversimplification of a complex issue, two suggestions will be made: first, a significant portion of the radical theological literature published is sold not to people who want to find their way into the church, but who are trying to talk themselves out of it.

Again, there is no way to obtain statistics, yet it is quite probable that a relevant book like *Honest to God*, despite its supposedly evangelistic intent, has eased many more people out of the churches than it has brought into them. Second—and this is more important for us here—a vast amount of theological production is for internal, or rather ecumenical consumption. In an earlier century, Protestants and Catholics, Lutherans and Reformed, Calvinists and Mennonites all worked overtime in preaching, publishing, and disputing, in an effort to convince their opponents, or at least to *convict* them of error. Today, those same groups (with the exception of the Mennonites) are still writing and talking, but they are not disputing. In large measure, they are no longer trying to convert or convince (perhaps too few of the writers are themselves converted and convinced), but simply to "see what people are thinking," to stimulate, to entertain.

Sometimes people read a religious book in the hope of finding something that is worth believing. In Protestant-Catholic polemics, the divines read each other's books in order to refute them. The attitudes are different, but they have this in common: they are both attentive, and they both take what is read seriously. For one type of reader, it offers a precious hope, for the other, a dangerous menace, but it is certainly not *merely* stimulating. Never, since the days of the most vehement Reformation controversies, have Catholic and Protestant theologians read each other's works with greater voracity, or with fewer apparent consequences. In a sense this is too bad; in another sense, perhaps it is just as well, for much of what is being produced, if understood, accepted, and digested, can do little good but much harm. All of the ecclesiastical establishments are in this business, but one market stands out: the theological production of the Roman Catholic Church, considering its great size, is not spectacular, but today, in our tolerant, ecumenical age, its theological appetite is insatiable. Roman Catholicism is ravenously consuming Protestant theology. It is in effect similar to what would happen if the Soviet Union suddenly removed all import restrictions and gave its citizens gold rubles with which to buy Western products. The rush would be unimaginable. And something like that is the attitude which Roman Catholics seem to be taking towards Protestant theology.

Unfortunately, when an "underdeveloped" area is exposed to the products of a more highly developed one, it does not necessarily make wise investments. (Do not take the metaphor too literally; Roman Catholic theology is not to be considered "underdeveloped." In the light of much modern theological "development," it would be better to remain underdeveloped.) Transistor radios are sold in underdeveloped countries, and Western music is played on them—but it is the music of the Beatles and their successors, not of Bach, Beethoven, and Brahms. If a later generation has enough interest to try to evaluate what happened in Christianity in the second half of the twentieth century, it may find the vast Roman Catholic market, suddenly opened to Protestant theology, to have been flooded with the theological equivalent of transistor radios playing the Rolling Stones.

1. The Situation of the Buyer: Roman Catholicism

When Martin Luther and his co-laborers burst onto the theological scene in 1517, the Roman Catholic hierarchy was not buying. Luther and his followers were condemned and excommunicated, and if the pope had had his way, worse things would have happened to them. Now, after almost four and a half centuries of bitter mutual antagonism, the church of Rome is showing an unprecedented openness towards Protestants. This is a remarkable development, and most of us greet it with enthusiasm. But we must look beyond the atmosphere of good feeling which it has produced to ask ourselves what is causing it, what it means, and where it is taking the church.

Is Roman Catholicism "on the move" because it has finally caught some of the insights of the Reformers? Or is it in retreat and seeking allies wherever it can find them, even among its former enemies? Does it feel that Protestantism no longer threatens it and that it can afford to be magnanimous? Or is it giving up its rivalry with Protestantism because that rivalry taxes its dwindling strength? Is it turning a friendly ear to the other side because it recognizes Christian truth in Protestantism, or because it is no longer very concerned for truth at all? In other words, is it a sign of health or sickness that Catholicism is willing to listen to Protestants?

The question is an important one. An action which appears to be praiseworthy in itself (openness towards Protestantism) may, in the last analysis, be harmful if it is undertaken for the wrong motives. Protestants can hardly be pleased at being accepted by the Roman Catholic Church if the reason is that that church is now willing to accept anything from Orthodox Judaism to L.S.D.

For centuries, Roman Catholicism has claimed to be the only authorized and effective guardian of Christian truth. According to its own tradition, one church was founded by Christ and endowed with the gifts of the Holy Spirit, and that is the church which we know today as the Roman Catholic. The tremendous changes which have taken place from the days of the early church to the present are seen as God-willed and God-guided developments, which expand the Roman church's possession of divine truth rather than endanger it. Although there are some problems with this tradition, especially in view of the slow development of the power of the papacy and of the long centuries when major church figures seem not to have suspected the extent of its importance, Catholic apologists have been able to make a fairly reasonable defense of it. One wonders how they will succeed in integrating present-day reversals of traditional doctrine into the picture of harmonious growth, but that is another question.

The skill with which advocates of papal authority and Roman Catholic tradition have pleaded for an organic, God-directed development has failed to convince everyone. In every age there have been those who considered the claims of a single bishop to supreme authority to be a sure indication of the corruption of the church, and perhaps even the work of the Antichrist. Pope Gregory I (590-604) indignantly reproached Patriarch John the Faster of Constantinople for calling himself the universal bishop; Gregory did so to defend the rights of all the bishops, himself included, and not because he wanted the title for himself. For this reason he enjoys considerable respect among Protestants, who look on the "development" of the early church into the Roman papacy as a degeneration which well-nigh destroyed it. In contrast to the Catholics who see an unbroken tradition of harmonious development, classical Protestantism distinguishes three ages of the church: (1) the Formation of the Church, from its founding by Christ through the age of Pope Gregory I; (2) the Deformation of the Church, the Dark Ages and Middle Ages, from Gregory to Luther; and (3) the Reformation of the Church, from Luther onwards.

Although Roman Catholics would not like to think of the Middle Ages as the time of deformation, it is clear that the Reformation which Luther sparked beginning in 1517 was not confined to Protestantism. Roman Catholicism also changed, in part in reaction, in part as a continuation of developments which were already under way before Luther arose. However long the Reformation of the church, as viewed by Protestant tradition, may have lasted, it seems clearly to be over now. For Protestantism, at least, this present age is clearly an age of deformation, and for Roman Catholicism perhaps not less so.

Within the Roman Catholic Church, the anti-Reformation Council of Trent (1545-1563, with long recesses) brought about significant changes—or, if you prefer, developments. Trent went so far in rejecting everything that Luther taught that it impoverished Catholicism, and made it unnecessarily rigid, even from the point of view of its own tradition. Valuable elements of the common Christian heritage were eliminated for no better reason than because Luther praised them. What resulted was no longer "catholic" in distinction to the narrowness and Germanness of Luther: it was Roman Catholic in a way that it had not been before. Luther did not merely lead the Protestants away from traditional Catholic Christianity; he also drove the Roman Catholics off in the opposite direction. So significant were the changes which Trent introduced in its effort not to change, and so reactionary and conservative were the Protestants in their efforts to reattain the original purity of the early church, that Professor Heiko Oberman of Tübingen likes to speak of the Catholic Reformation and the Protestant Counter-Reformation.

Protestants have been forced to admit that Luther, Calvin, and the other Reformers did not simply recover the primitive purity of the church, as they sought to do. Protestantism was quite a different thing from early Christianity. One can argue that substantially it is the same, but it is evident that Protestantism, just like pre- and post-Tridentine Catholicism, bears the marks of its passage through time. In the last three decades, Protestants have become more and more conscious of the importance of tradition for them and their churches —so much so that we now have the anomalous situation in which Protestants appeal to "holy tradition" while Catholics cry, "Back to the Bible!" Protestants are being forced to face the fact that it is impossible for a church to live by the Bible alone: every church, by the very fact that it exists, develops a tradition and at least to some extent lives by the tradition it develops.

Roman Catholics, at the same time, are becoming more and more sensitive to the dangers and possibilities of self-contradiction inherent in their development hypothesis. They found ways to argue against the contention of Protestant (and some Catholic) historians that the papacy had gone against orthodox doctrine and thus disproved papal infallibility when their opponents spoke of the "Causa Honorii" or the "apostasy" of John XXII.[2] But it is harder to argue against the changes wrought by Vatican II and *aggiornamento*. Perhaps a skillful canon lawyer can argue that this too is just part of the harmonious, forward development, but the general public cannot be convinced that it is not a change of direction and a repudiation of tradition. To the extent that it shakes Protestant controversialists in their anti-Catholic stereotypes and has forced them to stop saying, "Rome can never change," this development is good. But change for the sake of change is not necessarily a positive thing: Protestants and Catholics alike must ask themselves whether these changes represent growth or decay.

Reform-minded Roman Catholic historians like Hubert Jedin and Josef Lortz[3] have drawn the attention of theologians to the way in which the Counter-Reformation narrowed and restricted Catholicism. It is easy to understand why the sixteenth-century Catholic church felt it necessary to do this: it was either form a strong front against the Reformation, or surrender to it. As a result, those Christian truths which were emphasized by the Reformers (justification by faith, the authority of the Bible, the sovereignty of God) were neglected and even denigrated by the Roman counter-Reformers. In consequence, the Roman church got itself deeply mired in legalistic and authoritarian thinking—so much so that some historians say that the conquest of the church by the Roman Empire, which began under the Emperor Constantine, was finished at Trent.

Under the circumstances, it is easy to understand why many Roman Catholics appreciate the new open-mindedness of their church, which permits them to acknowledge and appreciate some vital aspects of the Christian heritage which had previously been rejected simply because they were praised by the Protestants. It is significant that Roman Catholic scholars in two fields, biblical studies and church history, have been at the forefront of this development. Roman Catholics, turning more readily to the Bible itself instead of to their traditional commentaries, have discovered it to be the legitimate source of some "Protestant" ideas. Church historians, trying to understand why the Reformers acted as they did, have been forced to recognize that their reasons were far better than the embattled popes and cardinals of that age could admit. Unfortunately, precisely because such scholars have stimulated a new openness, Roman Catholicism may be dangerously naive vis-à-vis Protestantism today. The Protestantism of Robinson is not that of Luther, nor is Pike's anti-Catholicism anything like that of Calvin.

Scholars in the Roman Catholic Church have been dealing with individual problems in their relationship with the Bible and with Protestantism; they have been dealing largely with the message of the New Testament itself and with the Protestantism of 1545. Today, however, neither the Roman Catholic hierarchy nor the laity are faced with Protestantism as Luther or Calvin envisaged it. If hierarchy and laity are encouraged by the good things their scholars tell them about Luther and Calvin to lend a favorable ear to their modern Protestant successors, they are in for trouble. Modern Protestantism has no right to trade on the goodwill some Catholic scholars are discovering for the Reformers of the sixteenth century. If Luther and Calvin were right in their major emphasis, then modern liberal and radical Protestantism is dead wrong.

It is good that Roman Catholicism is willing to modify its attitude of traditional hostility towards Protestantism, but caution is in order. The cleavage between the Gospel as preached by Luther and systematized by Calvin on the one hand and the atheistic "gospel" of an Altizer or the secularized Gospel of a van Buren[4] on the other is far greater than that between Luther and his Catholic opponent Eck or between John Calvin and Ignatius Loyola.[5] Roman Catholics who are willing to be open-minded towards Protestantism must be careful of what they recognize as Protestant.

Twentieth-century Roman Catholics must be cautious about Protestantism, at least about liberal or radical Protestantism because it could be deadly medicine for them. There are indications that the noxious influences within modern Protestantism are spending themselves, and that within Protestantism a healthy reaction is setting in, one which will preserve at least a part of the Protestant church. But these same influences can still wreak great havoc within Catholicism, where no defenses against them are in existence. In fact, since Roman Catholics are not used to having to discriminate between orthodoxy and nonsense in the teachings of their own priests, the Protestant seeds of decay could cause even more damage among Catholics than they have caused in Protestantism. (This is not to say that the teachings of Roman Catholic priests have in fact always been orthodox in the past, but merely to point out that the laity are not used to suspecting them of heresy as a matter of course.)

From a very early date in the history of Protestantism, individual Protestants have had to learn to make their own judgments on orthodoxy and heresy, on sin and morality. Luther himself, and Calvin, and a few others of stern mettle such as John Knox, spoke with considerable self-confidence and authority, but even they never claimed to be *the* authority—even if they sometimes acted like it. The great Protestant leaders frequently contradicted each other, and their opinions were challenged by their subordinates—frequently on minor matters, and occasionally on major ones. There was no legally established authority on which the ordinary Protestant could rely, nor could he go very far in the direction of implicit faith. Thus, for a Protestant, the erosion of formal standards of orthodoxy (such as that which was formalized in 1967 in the United Presbyterian Church in the U.S.A., with the downgrading of the Westminster Confession) is not so crucial, for there never has been a really authoritative Protestant structure on which he was accustomed to rely. Protestantism has had extremist theologians for centuries, and the average Christian has had to learn how to recognize them and avoid them. When churches and congregations have failed to do this, there have been major disruptions—the "Unitarian departure" in New England is a case in point: all or virtually all of the Congregational congregations in the vicinity of Boston were swept away by what was then modern thought, and became Unitarian. Despite such individual examples, Protestants and Protestant congregations have shown an ability to preserve a certain stability in the face of theological foolishness among some of their teachers and leaders.

Within Roman Catholicism, the situation has always been different. Those who were heretics—at least by the standards of the Roman church—were eliminated, often by means which will not be discussed here. Protestantism has not been completely free from inquisitorial tendencies, but with some exceptions Protestant zeal for doctrinal purity has not generally resulted in such drastic measures as the stake, the scaffold, or imprisonment. Recent Protestant heresy trials, when successful, have done nothing more drastic than deprive the suspected heretic of his position and his revenues, and usually they provide him with enough free publicity to more than compensate him for their loss. An awareness of this situation is surely one reason why the Episcopal Church failed to take any action against Bishop Pike for his own repudiations of the Christian faith. This failure, which has parallels in most other Protestant denominations, may well be the most practical course for a church to take—but it exposes it to reproach for duplicity and indifference to truth.

It is repugnant to every concept of human liberty and dignity to say that a man should be punished or persecuted for his ideas and opinions—but it is also repugnant to reason to say that a church cannot dismiss a teacher who is undermining its own intellectual foundations. It has no right to persecute him, but it certainly has no obligation to furnish him with a salary and a pulpit. This seems obvious, yet such is the temper of our times that it is difficult for a church to act in accordance with such a logical principle. Roman Catholics have kept their heads on this particular issue longer than Protestants. A more or less effective system to safeguard the purity of doctrine has existed within Catholicism for centuries. (Probably it is breaking down today, but that is a different question.) With all its advantages for the perpetuation of the Catholic church and faith as that church understands it, this very effectiveness has its detrimental side. First, many radically-inclined teachers have dissimulated and failed to show their true colors, in order not to lose their appointments. Thus Roman Catholic theology could be hollowed out from the inside, without its being apparent. Only this can explain the rapid collapse of Catholic theology in several important areas. The ranks of apparent orthodoxy have long contained a repressed fifth column, which is now beginning to emerge. Second, the ordinary church member has not cultivated the ability to discriminate between the various theological views proposed to him by ordained, officially approved theologians. To confront the typical Roman Catholic with what his own theologians are saying today is bad enough: to confront him with the bewildering maze of modern Protestant theology is to invite madness.

In short, Roman Catholicism must beware of too free a contact with Protestantism because it is not in a position to survive it. If Catholicism were immune to the spiritual and moral problems of the mid-twentieth-century world, the dialogue might not be so dangerous. But Catholics have not built up the same immunities as Protestants. Suddenly to expose them to all the Protestant viruses may produce a theological epidemic of unparalleled dimensions.

2. *The Product Offered: Present-Day Protestantism*

One major difficulty faces the Catholic who wishes to engage in ecumenical dialogue. That is: how to define Protestantism. To come to terms with one branch of it may not mean much in terms of a reunification of the church. The situation has never been freer as far as the possibilities of dialogue are concerned, but the positions of the dialogue partners are so unclear and so poorly defined that what begins as a dialogue may quickly become a confused babble.

Orthodox Roman Catholicism has a great deal in common with *orthodox* or *evangelical* Protestantism. (The terms *orthodox* and *evangelical,* applied to Protestantism, mean substantially the same thing: *orthodox* draws attention to conformity with the ecumenical creeds, while *evangelical* stresses the primary importance and seriousness attached to the Gospel.) "Liberal" Protestantism, by contrast, and even more so, modern existentialist Protestantism of the Bultmann and post-Bultmann schools, is in deadly opposition to all orthodox Christianity, whether Protestant or Roman Catholic. On theological grounds, we would expect the most fruitful dialogue to take place between open-minded, orthodox believers on both sides of the Protestant-Catholic line. Instead, the Catholics find themselves in dialogue with Protestant liberals if not extremists. The evangelical Protestant, looking at the company the Catholics are now keeping, can only ask, "Don't they know what they're doing, or have they quit believing what they still profess?"

The answer seems to include a bit of both alternatives. In the spring of 1963, an unprecedented ecumenical assembly was held at the Harvard Divinity School in Cambridge, Massachusetts. Roman Catholic scholars and officials, led by Cardinals Bea and Cushing, conferred with Protestant scholars and educators in an atmosphere of mutual respect and appreciation. Unfortunately it was an unbalanced dialogue. No representatives of the conservative, evangelical wing of Protestantism were invited, and when representative evangelical theologians asked to be allowed to attend, they were refused. The official reason given was that it was to be a meeting of scholars, and supposedly there are no real scholars among the evangelicals. This is a strange attitude to adopt, particularly at Harvard Divinity School, which for decades was known as *genuinely* liberal, i.e. willing to accept anyone who was academically competent, regardless of his doctrinal convictions. As a result of liberalism of this kind, which is unfortunately all too rare, a very significant proportion of evangelical Protestant theologians have earned doctorates at Harvard.

Even if the implication that evangelicals have no scholars were true, it would hardly have been justification for excluding them from the colloquy. Roman Catholic Cardinal Richard Cushing, like the late Harvard Divinity School Dean Samuel Miller, an authority on practical theology, is better known as an administrator than as a scholar, and they were moving powers in it. The real reason seems to have been given by Professor G. E. Wright in a conversation with one of the evangelicals who was denied admission. Wright is himself rather a conservative as far as theology is concerned, but like many conservatives who have won respect in the liberal academic establishment, he is very chary of fellowship with those who are to his right —not merely the so-called fundamentalists, but also the more moderate evangelicals. He remarked that the conference could not afford to bog itself down with questions such as whether Adam had a navel.

The humorous gibe about Adam's navel is used against evangelicals in the same way that the angels-dancing-on-a-pin disputation is presented as typical of Roman Catholic scholasticism. Both gibes have a certain justification. Evangelicals certainly have tended to involve themselves in endless arguments on subjects about which there can be no real knowledge. On the other hand, neither liberals nor extreme radicals are free from this fault either. Furthermore, the question of Adam's navel—or at least the question about organic evolution and Creation which lies behind it—is definitely *not* irrelevant. In fact, for contemporary theology it may well be *the* crucial question. Twentieth-century theology is making a great effort to be man-centered, and to derive its doctrine of God from the way he interacts with man, rather than to have some kind of theoretical theology independent of man. Therefore today the question of the evolutionary or non-evolutionary origin of man is extremely relevant: is he a creature, i.e. the work of a Creator's hand, or a statistical accident?

As a result of the exclusion of the conservative Protestants, the Roman Catholics found themselves dealing with a spectrum of Protestantism which was significantly shifted to the left. It is a strange thing that in ecumenical encounters men who believe all the great ecumenical creeds and in addition hold to the verbal inspiration of Scripture should be systematically excluded, while those who reject not only the authority of the Bible but also the literal meaning of the creeds, should be included. The Harvard discussion included nominal Protestants whose theology is hardly different from a kind of religiously-colored humanism. Professor Georges Florovsky, Russian Orthodox, expressed doubts that European Roman Catholics like Cardinal Bea really knew the religious convictions, or lack thereof, of some of their Protestant dialogue partners. This was probably true in some cases, but if it is the only explanation of why Roman Catholics are in dialogue with liberal and relativist Protestants and not with orthodox and conservative ones, then Roman Catholic theological awareness leaves a very great deal to be desired. The fact that no real clash occurred between the presumably orthodox Catholics and the liberal and even humanist Protestants must indicate that something is wrong on the Catholic side as well.

A single ecumenical event is not a reliable guide to the way the whole dialogue is going, of course, but it is not unfair to cite this example, for it is rather typical. One reason why Catholics are less often involved in dialogue with Protestants who share the same fundamental theological convictions than with liberals is the fact that the evangelicals themselves are often reluctant to engage in mere discussion. One of the chief ground-rules of contemporary dialogue is "no proselytizing." One may discuss all one likes, but one must be careful not to try to convince one's discussion partner. At an ecumenical discussion center for clergy outside Boston, one Protestant minister was told that he was not a suitable candidate for ecumenical discussions because he was a convert from Roman Catholicism. (The place is Protestant-run.) In other words, one may talk, but one is not allowed to become convinced and to change one's mind.

The Protestantism which is for sale to Catholics on the ecumenical market, then, is a one-sided kind of Protestantism from the leftward end of the theological spectrum. For this reason alone, Catholics who are interested in a real dialogue which might contribute something to them might do well to try to talk to precisely those Protestants who do not want to talk to them, or who, if they do, want to convince and convert them.

Aside from the fact that in the dialogue as it now exists Roman Catholics are exposed to the unhealthiest and least biblical side of Protestantism, there is also the very important—and perplexing— matter of the divisions within Protestantism. A particularly common gambit in the old days, when Roman Catholics were actually trying to convert Protestants, was to point to the hundreds of different Protestant denominations which exist in the United States. To judge by the figures given in various official counts is somewhat mislead- ing, for although there are over two hundred different Protestant denominations in the United States, the vast majority of Protestants fall into a relatively few classifications: Lutherans, Reformed, Episco- palian, Baptist, Methodist, and Pentecostal are terms which cover most of them. Even when this work of classification has been per- formed, however, several different divisions remain. Naturally the Catholic, used to thinking in organizational and structural terms, looks at these divisions. As a result he often overlooks the fact that within contemporary Protestantism *denominational divisions are rela- tively meaningless.*

Protestantism is sorely divided, it is true, but the gaping wound in its body is not one of denominational division. *The great division is between those who believe the Bible and those who do not.* (Note well that the expression is "believe the Bible," not "believe *in* the Bible." The Bible is not an object of faith, but it bears witness to what must be believed. In the same way, the Greek and Latin ver- sions of the early creed confess, "I believe *in* God, in Jesus Christ, in the Holy Spirit," but continue, "I believe the holy, catholic church." This small but important distinction is not evident in the common English version of the Apostles' Creed.) Almost every Protestant denomination has "liberal" and "evangelical" members and churches; there are few denominations which are wholly one or the other. The *authority and trustworthiness of the Bible* is the crucial issue in Protestantism today, beside which all others are of lesser importance.[6]

Many people would prefer to see the crucial question placed elsewhere, for example in the area of Christology, i.e. our understanding of Jesus Christ. There is some merit in this suggestion, because a Christian believes *in* Christ in a way in which he does not believe *in* the Bible. It is true that Christ is the center of our faith, but it is also true that we have no sure means of access to him other than through God's Word, i.e. through the Bible. When Billy Graham was invited to speak at Harvard in 1964, a local minister who was very much opposed to him was asked to introduce him. On the night of his lecture, the minister appeared in a black suit and clerical collar, a thing not customary in his denomination and most untypical for an evangelistic meeting in the United States, apparently to make it clear that he looked upon himself as speaking for his church. After bestowing some not very convincing words of praise on Dr. Graham, he went on to chide him "for talking so much about the Bible, when I would prefer to hear more about Christ." The audience, which was certainly not particularly pro-Graham, was a bit taken aback by this introduction, but not the evangelist himself. He went to the podium, opened his large Bible, and said, in effect, "After what you have heard, I must apologize to you for reading from the Bible, but I know no other book that speaks to me so well of Christ . . ." At the burst of applause and laughter from the audience, the minister turned bright red: his luminous face, above his round, white collar and black clerical suit, made him look like an upside-down German Imperial flag. In the last analysis, the doctrine of Christ is more crucial than the doctrine of Scripture, but basically the two are not separable.

Others would like to see the crucial dividing line placed in the area of the doctrine of God. Two theologians already cited, the late Tübingen professor Karl Heim and the American pastor and lecturer Francis Schaeffer, both insist on the fundamental importance of one's concept, or better, knowledge, of God. For Karl Heim, the whole of mankind is divided into those who know that the personal God of the Bible is real, and those who are unaware of this fact, or resist it. Schaeffer believes that much of the most sophisticated theology, but also of the simplest and most straightforward "evangelical" kind, is carried on without answering the question of the reality of God. As a result, people can go forward at evangelistic rallies to "make a personal decision for Christ" without being in the least convinced that God is real. This distinction is obviously more basic than the doctrine of Scripture, more basic even than Christology, but it is a distinction on a different level. The question of the reality of a personal God, or of Christology, divides believers from unbelievers, Christians from non-Christians. The question of the authority of Scripture divides sound teaching and good theology from false teaching and bad theology.

There is a difference in seriousness here. There are Christians who believe in the personal God of the Bible and who accept Christ as God and Saviour while holding, at the same time, a very low view of the authority and reliability of the Bible itself. Such a thing is possible, even common. There will undoubtedly be a great number of bad theologians who manage to find their way to heaven. But the fact that it happens is a dreadful thing, because bad theology takes its toll. A happy inconsistency may prevent it from destroying the one who devises it and teaches it, but through him it can have a most pernicious effect on others. Normally, of course, a low view of the authority of Scripture also affects the one who holds it, and leads to a low view of Christ, but the inconsistency of the human intellect is such that this logical connection is not always there.

It is necessary to say that the liberal-evangelical chasm is absolute *in the realm of theology*. There are many theological "liberals" who are really true Christians, because Christianity in the individual depends on the attitude of the heart towards Jesus Christ, and this is not always consistent with one's theology or one's morals. There are Christians who offer bad examples of theology, just as there are Christians who offer bad examples of morality. God will deal with both classes, but he will deal with them as a father with his children. Liberal *theology*, by contrast, is not a defective kind of theology, in the same way that a "liberal" Protestant or a "liberal" Catholic may be a defective but nevertheless genuine Christian. *It is another religion*. The so-called "new morality" of Bishop Robinson and Joseph

Fletcher is not a defective variety of Christian morality, but a masked rebellion against God. The Christian who wishes to preserve both his sanity and his charity in dealing with theological liberals and radicals must keep both facts in mind: first, a Christian may have a low (liberal) theology and/or a low (permissive, hedonistic, relativistic) morality, and still remain a Christian; second, no low theology is Christian theology, and no low morality is Christian morality. A believing Christian with either a low theology or a low morality is in for trouble in his own life, and will cause trouble in the lives of others. (Of course, we are speaking of the extreme case: a Christian with low morality or theology is an extreme example of the situation of the average or good Christian, for no believer has a flawless theology or morality. It is better to be an inconsistent Christian than no Christian at all. In the wide spectrum of human types, we can also encounter people with impeccable theological positions and with high moral standards who in the last analysis are not Christians, because they have no personal faith in the One whom they correctly profess.)

The liberal-evangelical chasm is the greatest reality in Protestant theology today. It places all theological dialogue under a dark shadow, particularly dialogue with Roman Catholics, who are more used to judging a man by the standards of his church than by what he himself in fact represents. Since some Presbyterians are biblical Christians, while others are relativists and even anti-Christians, one must seriously ask oneself just what it means to have a dialogue with Presbyterians. The same chasm exists in Roman Catholicism, of course; it is only now coming into clear evidence, but it has apparently existed for some time. Within Roman Catholicism the shibboleths which are used to try to distinguish the true Christians from the merely nominal adherents and actual pagans are different, but the cleavage is there too. The public pronouncements (not to mention the private lives, which were worse in an earlier age) of some of the highest Roman Catholic dignitaries bear evidence that all that is Catholic is not necessarily Christian. Under such circumstances, the real area for dialogue is within the denominations, not between them. To approach it differently, constructive dialogue should take place between the genuinely believing elements in the different denominations, and not between the officialdom of each denomina-

tion. Of course it is much easier to arrange a dialogue between officials than to arrange a Christian-pagan dialogue within a single
church, especially if, as sometimes happens, the pagan is a bishop
and the Christian a layman. Protestantism is so deeply divided on
this very basic issue that it is meaningless to try to have an official
dialogue with a Protestant church. The only thing that this can
accomplish is to bring Protestantism's schizophrenia into Roman
Catholicism as well.

3. The Radical Pig in the Protestant Poke

The fact that the Catholic-Protestant dialogue usually involves, on
the Protestant side, more career ecclesiastics and church politicians
than committed Christians (the two are not mutually exclusive, but
they are by no means synonymous) casts suspicion on the discretion
and discernment if not the orthodoxy of the Roman Catholic dialogue partners. Because of its own centralized structure, the Roman
Catholic Church naturally tends to think of dialogue in church
terms. But if Protestantism is to be taken seriously—and that is what
a dialogue ought to mean—then the Protestant conception of the
church must be taken seriously: the church is the *invisible* fellowship of all true believers. This *invisible* fellowship is precisely what
is *not* represented in most ecumenical discussions. Protestants as a
whole are growing more and more estranged from both their church
bureaucrats and their theologians. Indifferent and nominal Protestants are growing estranged from them because they represent the
church, in which they basically are not interested, and committed,
concerned Protestants are turning away from them because they do
not represent the church. That is to say, in the eyes of committed,
evangelical Protestants, many bureaucrats and most well-known theologians may represent an institution, but not the church of Christ.

Is there anyone who does represent the true church in the eyes of
evangelical Protestants, or who could represent Protestantism in ecumenical dialogue? The answer is difficult, because people who could
typify committed, grass-roots Protestantism are examples, not representatives with official powers. The name which most readily comes
to mind is that of evangelist Billy Graham. Dr. Graham has no eccle-

siastical authority, and in a sense he represents no one but himself: he has had no greater official powers conferred upon him than have been conferred upon any other minister, and less than any Methodist or Episcopal bishop. But can we name one, or even a group, of Methodist or Episcopal bishops who are known and respected by as many Methodists and Episcopalians as Billy Graham is? To be a bit fanciful, let us imagine two booths set up at a state fair to offer spiritual guidance and counsel. If Graham were put in one, can we imagine any Protestant theologian or church executive who could even begin to compete with him in the other booth? Of course, if we put Bishop Robinson in the other booth, he would soon gather a crowd of interested conversationalists. But can we imagine a man concerned about eternal life, seriously troubled with a problem of guilt, or wondering whether God is real, turning into Robinson's booth rather than Graham's?

The illustration is not as frivolous as it may seem. People like Billy Graham and Norman Vincent Peale, to name another, have very different approaches, but both are committed to the historic, evangelical Protestant faith. People who are interested in religion listen to Robinson; people who are desperate about life, about themselves, listen to forthright and clear believers like Graham and Peale. If we were to attempt to turn either of these two ministers, one Baptist, one Reformed, into an authorized spokesman for Protestantism, we would be making a serious mistake. (Each of them has occasionally been consulted as a spokesman, and the results were sometimes embarrassing.) The point is simply that a man who attempts to speak the truth about Christ, about heaven and hell, sin and forgiveness, love and duty, as the Bible teaches it, represents something quite different from those who feel themselves competent to remake the church and society in their own image, and to initiate a self-conscious new reformation.

It would be quite wrong to try to make the position and approach of either Dr. Graham or Dr. Peale the basis of a new Protestant consensus. From the point of view of an evangelical theologian, each of them may be criticized for a tendency to put everything in the service of his own chief concern—in one case evangelism, in the other, combining mental with spiritual well-being.[7] Both of them have at times taken strong stands in opposition to Roman Catholicism; neither of them is loath to see a Roman Catholic converted to evangelical Protestantism. Protestant church leaders and well-known theologians, on the other hand, are quite reluctant to do anything which might endanger their amiable and interesting dialogue.

If Roman Catholicism is to avoid poisoning itself on the new ecumenical diet, it must be very careful not to ingest the radical theologies which are destroying Protestant church life and doctrine. If they recognize that the believing, spiritual Protestants (if we may use this expression) are turning their backs on their ecclesiastical and theological leadership, just as spiritual Catholics turned their backs on certain aspects of the Roman hierarchy in the Middle Ages, they will quickly recognize the futility of a serious dialogue with those who no longer represent a living church. In the Protestant view, the church only exists where there is a real, personal faith in the risen Christ. By such a standard, many Protestant ecumenists cannot be said to represent the church. It is not our place to pass judgment on the faith of individual Protestant theologians, yet it is only honest to say that in the statements of many Protestant leaders there is nothing which bears witness to Christ or glorifies him, and there is much that witnesses to a thousand other things.

By listening to the ecclesiastically and academically authorized spokesmen of the Protestant church establishment, Roman Catholicism not only exposes itself to virulent doctrinal errors against which believing Protestants are trying to quarantine themselves. It is dealing with people who would really represent Protestantism only if the Roman Catholic view of the church as an organized, visible unity were true. But Protestants who have a logical right to speak only on the grounds that that for which they stand is assumed to be false cannot be profitable discussion partners. To confine the discussion to official Protestantism isolates Roman Catholicism from the real spirit of biblical, evangelical Christianity, which has some very important things to say to it. A Protestant who believes so strongly in the Gospel of Christ as he understands it that he will try to convert the Roman Catholic away from the rather different view of the Roman church is an unpleasant dialogue partner, but a Protestant who does not believe it enough to make such an attempt is a worthless one.

Much of the Protestant church establishment now wants to work with Roman Catholicism. It even seems to set great store on the approval and honors which the Roman Catholic Church can confer. Evangelical Protestants, on the other hand, level severe criticism at Catholicism and charge that it still needs drastic reformation from top to bottom. When an evangelical Protestant talks to Roman Catholics, he always has the hope that their church can be re-formed according to the Word of God. Roman Catholics can never be out of harmony with this hope, although they will not usually concede that Protestants can tell them how to do it. To turn away from the evangelicals because the evangelicals continue to criticize them is to deprive themselves of a kind of friction which could be quite beneficial.

"Liberal" and radical Protestants, on the other hand, do not want to reform Roman Catholicism according to the Word of God, but to conform it to the world of man. This is a course to which no Roman Catholic can agree, unless he wants to give up all claim to being a Christian. Evangelical Protestants have always charged Roman Catholicism with being too humanistic, with putting human wisdom and human standards in place of God's. Naturally Roman Catholics resent such charges, but they have an obligation to take them seriously. The evangelical or orthodox Protestant approach to what Roman Catholicism is doing today must be to say, "It is moving, indeed, but is it moving in the right direction?" The other class of Protestants, the ones who love the dialogue and who never say anything rude, are gleefully crying, "Yes, yes! More, more, and faster, faster!" Roman Catholics ought to be aware that if they take Protestantism en masse, they will be buying some kind of a radical pig in a voluminous poke. Protestantism has a lot to offer Catholicism; some of it can be bitter medicine, but healthy. But it is not offered by the Protestant establishment, because that is only a second-rate copy of the Roman Catholic one, with practically all of its model's faults and few of its virtues. The biblical and evangelical spirit of Protestantism can still be found, but it is necessary to look hard. The market-place of religious dialogue has not benefitted much from the vaunted Protestant business ethic: it is still like an Oriental bazaar. In it, there is much to be found that is of great value, but the old motto holds: CAVEAT EMPTOR—Let the buyer beware!

Notes

[1]*The Christian Century,* Vol. LXXXIV, No. 21, May 24, 1967, pp. 703.

[2]In 638 Pope Honorius I and Patriarch Sergius of Constantinople cooperated with the Eastern Roman Emperor Heraclius in publishing the *Ekthesis,* a document intended to reconcile the Monophysite Christians with the orthodox church. In 681, the Sixth Ecumenical Council condemned Pope Honorius as a heretic. For three centuries afterwards each new pope anathematized Honorius on taking office, until the case was eventually forgotten. It was raised again in 1870 when the decree on papal infallibility was being discussed. Pope John XXII (1316-1334) propounded the view that after death the soul sleeps until the day of the Last Judgment. He was condemned by the faculty of the University of Paris and forced to recant under pressure from the King of France. In both these cases, defenders of papal infallibility deny that the pope was speaking *ex cathedra.*

[3]These two German church historians have been in the forefront of the re-evaluation of the Reformation and Counter-Reformation. See Lortz, *Die Reformation in Deutschland* (Freiburg: Herder, 1949, 3rd ed.), and Jedin, *Geschichte des Konzils von Trient* (Freiburg: Herder 1951, 1957). Their careful, sensitive evaluation of the spiritual and ethical values actually at stake in the Reformation and Counter-Reformation has been swamped from both sides—by uncritical Catholics buying everything that is Protestant simply because it is different, and by half-hearted Protestants seeking to gain from Roman traditionalism and authority what they themselves lack in personal conviction.

[4]Thomas J. J. Altizer, *The Gospel of Christian Atheism* (Philadelphia: Westminster, 1966); Paul van Buren, *The Secular Meaning of the Gospel* (New York: Macmillan, 1963). These two men are on the extreme, radical fringe of Protestant theology, it is true. Therefore it is all the more significant that the general Protestant church press is so much more generous to them than it is to a conservative Protestant like Billy Graham.

[5]The founder of the Jesuit order and the great French Reformer were contemporaries and fellow-students in Paris.

[6]The doctrine of verbal inspiration holds that the direction of the Holy Spirit in the writing of the Scripture extends to the words and not merely to the ideas. It does not hold that the words themselves were dictated; they were chosen by the human writers, but the Holy Spirit guided their choice to preserve them from error.

[7]The present writer differs from Dr. Graham in some important respects, particularly with regard to the presuppositions implied in his "invitation sys-

tem." The invitation system as practiced by Dr. Graham and some other evangelists minimizes the importance of grace in personal conversion and over-emphasizes the role of the human will. It sometimes produces "decisions for Christ" on the part of people who are not sure that there is a God. Despite this reservation, which is shared by many Reformed theologians, he would wish to make plain his great respect and affection for Dr. Graham, who is proclaiming the Gospel as no one else in this generation.

Chapter 8

· UNANSWERED LETTERS
TO ROME ·

But the Spirit explicitly says that in later times some will fall away from
the faith, paying attention to deceitful spirits and doctrines of demons . . .

St. Paul to St. Timothy, I Timothy 4:1

Few questions perplex the conservative Protestant today more than
this: what must I think about Roman Catholicism? Before World
War II it was easier. In Protestant eyes Rome did not seem to have
changed for the better at any time in her long history. Having made
a wrong turn sometime back in the Dark Ages, she had rejected and
spurned those who tried to set her right and in some cases had persecuted and killed them. In 1870 the first Vatican Council had passed
its decree on papal infallibility. This was a blow to all those who
hoped for some kind of a reconciliation between the church of Rome
and the Protestants. Catholicism seemed to remain inflexible. As late
as 1950 Roman Catholicism was increasing rather than reducing its
conflict with Protestants in another area, that of the veneration of the
Virgin Mary. In the bull *Munificentissimus Deus* Pope Pius XII
declared her bodily assumption into heaven to be an article of faith,
necessary to be believed for salvation.

Up through 1950, then, Rome seemed to be intent on pursuing
her own course, and increasing her claims to unique authority, dis-
dainful of all her rivals. Protestants therefore looked on her with
suspicion, hostility, and apprehension. In some these feelings were
based on ignorance of Catholic teachings and on lack of personal fa-
miliarity with individual Catholic leaders; in others they were based

on actual knowledge or experience of some of the less attractive features of Roman Catholicism. Then suddenly, almost overnight, all this changed. On the one hand, the situation of all the churches was becoming so precarious that inter-church conflict began to seem an insupportable luxury; on the other, the Roman church itself began going through such a series of sweeping changes, some of them virtually revolutionary, that Protestants could no longer say, "Rome can never change." Even some of the most hidebound and categorical anti-Romanists on the Protestant side have been forced to reevaluate Rome and their own attitude towards her.

The applause with which many non-Roman Catholics greet changes, even radical ones, within the Roman Catholic Church must seem to mock those Catholics who loved their church as it used to be, and as they had been led to expect that it would always remain. The situation of converts to Catholicism, who thought that they would find in it stability and authority lacking in Protestant denominations, has become almost ironic. But for all Catholics who love their church, it must be a bitter thing to have to accept compliments on having "finally caught up" from those whom one had always thought to be deficient in Christian knowledge, faith, and piety.

Nevertheless, Protestants are at least fellow-Christians. If they greet the changes within his church with approval, a Catholic may think that their approval is motivated by Christian considerations. But when the non-Christian, secular world also begins to praise Rome for its "progress," the loyal Catholic will find it perplexing if not actually alarming. Since the non-Christian world must, by its very nature, be hostile to the church, what are we to think when the world begins to applaud the church for its "progress"? Naturally we do not want to fall into the error of those who never feel like true Christians unless they succeed in making themselves thoroughly disliked by everyone around them. But the problem is real. Jesus warned his disciples that the world would hate them (John 15:18). When the world stops booing the church and begins to applaud it, its enthusiasm ought to arouse the Christian's suspicion. When even committed Marxists join the ostensibly "neutral" secular press in their praise of the course the Roman church is taking, all those who are concerned about her fate and destiny, Catholics and Protestants alike, had better take notice.

For the conservative Protestant the situation is perplexing. There was a time when Protestants rejoiced at any difficulties which befell Catholicism, on the principle that Catholicism's loss was Protestantism's gain. Naturally they would not have rejoiced at the news that a Catholic mission had been burned in Africa, but in "Christian" Europe, they felt, anything that hurt Rome benefitted them. If this evaluation ever was true, it is true no longer. The situation of all the churches in the world now resembles that of the mission station in Africa. There are no longer any Christian societies, if ever such things really existed. Of course, the situation of an established church, such as the Church of England, the Church of Sweden, or the Roman Catholic Church in Spain, is different from that of a merely tolerated church in a Communist state, but the peace and freedom which the churches enjoy in Western democracies, and the government support which in some cases is theirs, are deceptive. Even in Western countries many of the most influential circles, controlling education and the communications media, are thoroughly alienated from Christianity and are determined to eradicate it. Their methods are less repressive than those in the "people's democracies," but the ultimate goal is the same.

Under such circumstances we are beginning to see that, as Professor Hermann Sasse writes, "In spite of all divisions and separations, the Christians and the churches of whatever denomination are bound together by the strange solidarity of a common history. They experience the same joys and disappointments, successes and failures. *Great spiritual movements, healthy or unhealthy, spread through the whole of Christendom irrespective of denominational borders.* It is by no means so as it was believed forty years ago that the fall of one church means the rise of another. They are all confronted with the same enemies, the same emergencies. Together they rise, together they fall."[1]

Of course, recognition of this solidarity does not end inter-confessional controversy. It does not end the attempts of members of one church to persuade members of another to change sides. It does not even end the attempts by various church bodies to use the leverage of government support to favor their own goals at the expense of other Christian bodies. But it does mean that even the most convinced, fire-breathing evangelical Protestant and the most dedicatedly ultra-montane Catholic must recognize that something is at stake for each of them in the fate of the other's church, even though on the level of *Christian* controversy they criticize or even condemn it.

Thus the Protestant who looks at the changing Catholic Church has a divided mind. Of course, if he is a "liberal" Protestant, of the sort to whom theological truth is an unimportant if not a meaningless concept, then he can look with glee on the ease and thoroughness with which many Catholics are abandoning the traditional dogmas and traditional moral teachings of their church. But if he is an evangelical Protestant, concerned for the historic Christian faith, his response is more problematic.

On the one hand, he can be glad that the Roman church is beginning to yield on some of the principles and practices against which the Reformers protested: the reading of the Bible is encouraged, services are being conducted in the language of the people, preaching and congregational singing are encouraged, even clerical marriage seems a real possibility. On the other hand, for all his hostility to Roman authoritarianism and to the kind of Catholic tradition which seemed to make a mockery of the simplicity of the Gospel, he always recognized that traditional Roman Catholicism, like classical Protestantism, was committed in principle to the sovereignty of the Triune God, to the divinity of Jesus Christ, to his miraculous works, his saving death, and his real resurrection, to his second coming, and to the authority of the Bible as the Word of God. Now, as the conservative Protestant rejoices that Roman Catholicism seems to be abandoning some of the accretions which only a few years ago were being fervently defended as priceless parts of the "Catholic heritage," he also is beginning to notice that along with the unnecessary, undesirable, and even wrong elements, the Catholic church is in danger of abandoning not only those things which made it distinctively Roman Catholic, but also those things which are simply Christian.

In a traditionalistic institution, change is a hard thing to control. At the beginning of the Reformation, both Luther and Calvin found that some of their more enthusiastic followers wanted to run wild. As early as 1522, less than five full years after the posting of the Ninety-Five Theses, Luther had to deal with "fanatics" and "heavenly prophets" and with his own colleague Carlstadt, who threatened to disrupt his work of reformation right in his own town of Wittenberg. John Calvin and the Swiss Protestants felt it necessary not merely to suppress the Spanish physician Michael Servetus but to execute him when he came to Geneva in 1553 bringing anti-trinitarian and Ana-baptist agitation. Calvin and his colleagues were aware of the dangerous precedent they were setting in executing a man for heresy, an act which has embarrassed their followers to the present day, but they were convinced that Servetus' views, if permitted to spread, would completely overthrow Christianity.

Luther and Calvin, faced with extremists in their own "reforming" camps, were forced to take or at least to permit the same kind of repressive measures which they criticized when the Catholic church employed them against Protestants. They felt that it was absolutely necessary to prevent their Reformation from losing all coherence and becoming chaotic. Although they knew quite clearly what they wanted and were both strong, determined men with almost unlimited influence among their followers, neither Luther nor Calvin could fully master the radical tendencies in their own camps. It is doubtful that any single reform-minded leader within the Roman Catholic Church today is as powerful a personality or has as clear an idea of what he wants as they did. It will not be surprising if the Catholic attempts at reform produce eccentricities as dangerous as the unitarianism of Servetus or the vagaries of the "heavenly prophets."

With this in mind, the evangelical Protestant must be inclined to warn his Catholic partner of the danger of going not merely too far, but completely off the deep end. Protestants have always had to admit that Roman Catholicism has had certain absolutely fundamental principles in common with them throughout all their mutual controversy and animosity. When changes in the Catholic church seem to threaten the loss of fundamental Christian principles, then the evangelical Protestant cannot rejoice, even if the Roman church is less trouble to him because of it.

The paradox is this: Protestants have long objected to the power of traditionalism within Roman Catholicism, applying to Catholic traditionalism the strictures of Jesus in Matthew 16:6ff. Yet precisely this Roman traditionalism preserved evangelical values within the Roman Catholic Church when liberalism was destroying them in Protestant churches. By remaining stationary while Protestantism disintegrated theologically, Catholicism for a time looked as though it could end by being more evangelical than the so-called evangelical churches after their bouts with liberalism. But now traditionalism, so long the object of Protestant scorn, is being abandoned by Catholics, and with it there is great danger that the evangelical doctrine which Roman Catholicism did contain (though embedded in and often obscured by human traditions) will be lost with it.

Nevertheless, having said this, having warned Catholics of the danger that their *aggiornamento* may result in chaos rather than in constructive reform, as has happened all too often to Protestant churches, the Protestant must still, paradoxically, assert that in some areas the reforms are too shallow and too few.

Catholics may well demand of Protestants, "How can you criticize us when your own church is in such disorder?" Our answer can only be that we criticize not on the basis of what our churches are, or what we ourselves are, but on the basis of what the Bible teaches that the Church of Christ should be. No Protestant, in criticizing Roman Catholicism, can legitimately claim that his own denomination is above criticism. Most of us have had even severer things to say about our own Protestant leaders, whose salaries we pay, whose orders to some extent we must follow, and the blame for whose excesses we must bear. But the fact is that for the Protestant who listens to the Bible as to the Word of God, questions arise about Rome which cannot be shouted down by enthusiastic ecumenical cheering. If the standards of the Bible itself cause us to criticize the superficial, politically-motivated ecumenism which characterizes the World Council of Churches, they also force us to try to be honest about the difficulties which we still have, even with the Catholicism of Catholics whose heart seems definitely to be in the right place, i.e. with those who do believe in the transcendent, triune God, in his divine Son, and in his authoritative and reliable self-revelation in the Holy Scriptures.

Enough has been written by Protestants criticizing the church of Rome. Some of it is intended to win over disillusioned Catholics, some to frighten wavering Protestants away from Rome, some to encourage Protestant smugness and self-righteousness. Some of it is even written in an admirable desire to get at the essence of Roman Catholicism and to see what it really is and where it is actually going. Finally, in our ecumenical era, there are Protestants who romanticize the Roman church, putting it in a better light than most of its members would.

The purpose of this chapter is neither to fortify Protestants nor to convert Catholics. Its purpose is to explain as clearly as possible some of the most important reasons why consistent Protestants reject Roman Catholicism and are suspicious of Catholic overtures, despite all the good reasons to form a united front against anti-Christian forces.

In order to do this, it will be necessary to deal with *real* Protestant objections, which cannot always be done gently. They are of two kinds. Firstly, we have definite theological objections to the system of religion which is Catholicism. These might be said to constitute an evangelical criticism of Catholicism. They result from the basic differences between Roman Catholics and evangelical Protestants on the fundamental nature of the Christian faith. To understand the position of each side better does not minimize these differences: it increases them. That is to say, one cannot reconcile the basic "evangelical" views of Martin Luther with the fundamental "Catholic" ones of the Council of Trent by understanding each of them better. A deeper understanding may help one better to appreciate the sincerity and the Christian intention of both parties, but the views themselves cannot be harmonized. Here understanding can bring a measure of sympathy, or perhaps even conversion, but not the reconciliation of opposites.

Secondly, there are practical objections to Roman Catholicism. These are based, broadly speaking, on the experiences Protestants have had with Catholic practice, especially with Catholic power. We can also call these historical objections. Here understanding can help bring about a reconciliation. Often the practice of individual Catholics, of Catholic leaders, and frequently of Catholic power structures has been out of harmony with the teachings of the Roman Catholic Church itself. If a Protestant sees that what he criticizes in "Roman Catholic practice" is in fact also condemned by Roman doctrine, it can help him overcome some of his antagonism and hostility. Nevertheless, the facts of Catholic history are such that more than an explanation and a retroactive criticism is required from the Catholic side before the Protestant can forgive, forget, and perhaps most important, overcome his suspicion of what the Roman church is likely to do in the future. There are some areas where the Catholic church must confess and repent.

At this point it is important to admit that Catholics have reasons to mistrust Protestants. Who has the greater reason for hostility and mistrust is a question which it would take a great deal of work by superhumanly impartial scholars to answer. We do not propose to answer it, and certainly will not deny that Catholics have reason to suspect Protestants, individually or collectively. We merely wish to make it clear that if a Roman Catholic wants to understand *why* neither the jovial and fraternal fellowship of John XXIII nor the suave diplomacy of Paul VI have overcome Protestant suspicions, he must consider the long history of Protestant experiences. As he examines the Protestant charges, he is sure to find many which he feels are wrong or overdrawn. There, patience and honesty may help the Protestant to overcome his suspicions and to retract any distortions and false charges. But an honest examination will reveal to the Catholic major areas of Catholic behavior for which he must feel genuine shame. There he himself must be willing to face the facts and to try to take constructive steps to undo the damage they have caused. If the Catholic can understand that Protestants are not just being surly and spiteful when they reject the Pope's extended hand of fraternity, he will be able to contribute something to making the desired fraternity a real possibility.

1. *Theological Objections to Roman Catholicism*

Although there were many earlier signs of theological and religious unrest, we generally date the beginning of the Protestant Reformation from the day that Luther posted his Ninety-Five Theses on the door of the Schlosskirche in Wittenberg in October, 1517. At first all that he wanted was the correction of certain abuses, particularly the elimination of the hawking of indulgences as it was being practiced by the Dominican monk John Tetzel. Since Luther was an Augustinian friar and since Wittenberg itself had a splendid collection of relics, the church authorities including Pope Leo X at first thought it was only a monks' quarrel.

Initially it might have been possible for Leo X to have forestalled a serious conflict by the introduction of a few timely reforms. But the reaction of the higher clergy and of the Pope to Luther's initial proposals convinced him of the necessity to go further. He discovered more and more faults in Roman Catholicism, some going right to the heart of its system of salvation. Finally he challenged not merely a few corrupt practices but the whole system which permitted and produced them.

In recent years numerous changes have been adopted by the Roman Catholic Church. Many of them correspond rather closely to Luther's initial proposals. Indulgences, which were somewhat reformed in the wake of the Reformation, have more recently been quite severely curtailed. The liturgy has been changed; the Mass is said in the language of the congregation; there are many other examples. These changes have attracted the attention of many Protestants, but they do not in fact touch the heart of the Roman Catholic system, where many of the fundamental problems to which the Reformers objected continue to exist. The impact of nineteenth- and twentieth-century liberalism on the Roman Catholic Church has brought some salutary changes, but all too often it has destroyed things which still continue to appeal to evangelical Protestants without in fact answering their major objections. These objections can be summed up in one phrase, "too much."

The "Too Much" of Roman Catholicism

Viewed superficially, the main difference between Roman Catholicism and traditional Protestantism seems to be that Catholicism has more of everything, from a few more books in the Bible to many more officially canonized saints, from a few more sacraments to many more well-established practices of piety, asceticism and devotion. Most Protestant churches have ministers, some have bishops, but only Rome has the Pope. Protestants have God himself to whom they can pray, and his Son Jesus Christ as their only Mediator; Roman Catholics have not only the Persons of the Godhead, but also Mary, the Mother of the Lord, angels and saints, all of whom are thought able to intercede for them, and thus in some sense to mediate between man and God.* When a man dies, Protestants feel that the time to witness to him and to pray for him is past, and try to comfort his survivors, but Catholics can do more: they continue to pray, to offer Masses, and to gain indulgences for him in the conviction that he can be helped even beyond the grave.

Viewed in this way, what we may call ordinary, everyday Catholicism seems to have everything that everyday Protestantism has, plus some extras. It has the doctrine of the Triune God and of his only-begotten Son, who became man, died for our sins, and rose again; it teaches the forgiveness of sins, the hope of eternal life; it too claims an inspired, authoritative Bible; then in addition, it has much besides.

Protestants should admit that many of the disciplines and practices which Catholicism encourages are good. The half-hearted Protestant is often more easily estranged from his church than the half-hearted Catholic, who is constantly brought back to it by the requirements of Sunday Mass, of confession, and of an obligatory minimum communion attendance. Physical attitudes, such as kneeling, and ascetic practices, such as fasting, will remain useful in the spiritual life of man as long as he continues to be a body as well as a soul. All too often Protestants have cut themselves off from sources of strength because of their dread of appearing to be Catholic.

Nevertheless, to say that Roman Catholicism offers too much, that it is too complicated, too ornate, or too strict, is only the beginning of the evangelical objection to the Catholic system. Behind these many "extras," offerings, which taken individually may not be wrong, the evangelical sees a false perspective: first things are no longer put first, but often are placed so far in the background as to be forgotten and invisible.

The False Perspectives of Roman Catholicism

Why should evangelical Protestants object to an extra bit of zeal, to an imaginative form of devotion, to some practices which may do

---

*Mary's title of *Theotokos,* literally, "the God-bearer," has been rendered into Latin as *Deigenitrix,* and then into modern languages as "Mother of God," an expression which is theologically correct but prone to cause confu-

no evident good but which can seemingly do no harm? The answer
is that by offering this "too much," and by encouraging, or even de-
manding that its adherents make use of it, Roman Catholicism may
deprive them of those things which are really *necessary*. Even if one
accepts the traditional Catholic distinction between the extreme
"veneration" (*hyperdouleia*) offered to Mary and the worship (*lat-
reia*) which is legitimately offered only to God, one fears that such a
distinction becomes quite obscure in practice. In Catholic theory one
calls upon a saint only for intercession and calls upon God for effective help, but the difference at times seems more theoretical than
real. This veneration is not expressly condemned in the Bible, but it
is certainly not condoned. Both the Old and New Testament contain
so many assurances of God's own readiness to hear and respond to
our prayers that the search for saintly intercessors would seem super-
fluous to say the least. And no Catholic can deny the fact than in
practice—aside from the Mass itself—prayer to Mary and the other
saints is often more common than prayer to God himself.

But the charge that it is disproportionate is not the only reason for
a Protestant to challenge the "too much" of Catholicism, of which the
invocation of the saints is a good example. For what may appear to be
merely an "optional extra" not only neglects but imperils an essential
Christian doctrine, that of the *sufficiency* of Christ. When Christ
himself says, "Come to me" (Matthew 11:28), does the Roman
church have the right to add, "and to Mary"? Does it not thereby
challenge the adequacy of coming to Christ? This clearly happened
in one strand of medieval piety, which portrayed Christ as a stern,
severe Judge who could be swayed only by the intercession of his
gentle mother. This picture is not merely an "amplification" of the
New Testament vision of Christ: it is a perversion of it.

Burdens to Christian Belief

For Protestants then, the "too much" of Roman Catholicism may
not merely imperil one's Christian perspectives, but may actually

---

sion and misunderstanding, seeming to give her a place equal to or in a sense
superior to that of her Son, and to lend plausibility to such titles as "Mediatrix
of all grace," and even "Co-Redemptrix."

threaten one's foundation. In one respect this does threaten the essentials by binding the foundation to things which are unnecessary and difficult to believe. If there is any truth at all in the charge of certain avant-garde theologians that fundamental Christian doctrines are rendered inacceptable by being tied to outmoded and unnecessary concepts, how much more are they endangered by being tied to the whole galaxy of beliefs and practices which make up popular Roman Catholicism!* To encumber the Gospel with excess baggage is to make the error of the Pharisees, whom Christ reproached with creating unbearably heavy burdens and loading them on men's shoulders (Matthew 23:4). If the "extras" ever keep someone away from Christ it is a serious matter indeed.

The Danger of a False Trust

More serious even than this charge is the suspicion that the Roman Catholic system promotes a false kind of trust. It is hard to deny that a proliferation of secondary devotions alongside of our basic devotion to Christ can represent a threat to our understanding and appreciation of his unique authority, his love for us, and his power to save those who trust in him. Personal *trust* is implied in the Greek word *pistis,* usually rendered into English as "faith." When the New Testament speaks of faith as leading to salvation, it does not mean *mere* intellectual assent to the truth of Christian teachings, although this is included. It means a personal relationship of confidence in the One about whom Christian doctrine revolves, i.e. in Jesus Christ. Where the system of doctrine is such that it draws our attention elsewhere, whether to other intercessors, to a sacramental system, to an authoritative hierarchy, or to any other substitute object of trust, there is a real danger that the essential element of personal trust in Christ will be downgraded and even destroyed. It is for this reason

---

*To be fair we must admit that sometimes this variety and comprehensiveness is precisely what appeals to many people. Popular Catholicism in a sense offers something for everyone. The conservative Protestant must abandon the modern theologian's utilitarian argument that it will not appeal to people and ask the more basic question of whether it is New Testament Christianity.

that the Apostle Paul inveighs with such vehemence against the Judaizing Christians in his Epistle to the Galatians. They had accepted Christ, but they insisted on continuing to observe certain Jewish practices as *necessary* for the Christian. In their own eyes they were only completing the Gospel, but in Paul's eyes what they did made it into no Gospel at all (Galatians 1:7), and made Christ of no benefit to them (Galatians 5:4).

A basic difference between the psychology of the evangelical Protestant and that of the serious Roman Catholic lies in the area of assurance of salvation. To the Catholic, the Protestant's talk about being "saved" often seems presumptuous, but to most Protestants it is a necessary consequence of the Gospel. It is not based on any human confidence in oneself as worthy of salvation or as immune from falling back into serious sin; on the contrary, it is based on a recognition of the power and the love of the Christ whom he has come to know as his Saviour. The Protestant's confidence that he will not be lost is not confidence in his own virtue, but in Christ's strong, patient, and powerful love. For him the Catholic's lack of assurance does not mean that the Catholic is humbler, but that his theological system has directed his attention away from the Christ it acknowledges to a host of other persons and things, each of which may give some spiritual satisfaction but none of which can give a confident assurance of final salvation. In Protestant eyes, a Gospel without assurance, a Gospel which *requires* works and which leaves even the pious and earnest believer in doubt as to his salvation is no Gospel at all, but in Paul's words, a renewed submission to a yoke of bondage (Galatians 5:1).

The charge that this tendency is inherent in the Roman Catholic doctrinal system is not lightly to be made. It may not come from any sense of Protestant superiority: "We have it, and you don't." It must be put forward with a sense of deep concern and sorrow for a church which has produced so much devotion and self-sacrifice for the sake of Christ but which in so many cases has not enabled its members to see him in such a way that they could be really confident of their eternal destiny. For the Catholic the Protestant sense of assurance may appear to be an enthusiastic or even an arrogant presumption; but for the Protestant its lack must appear to be a lack of saving, confidence-inspiring faith, one which brands the Roman Catholic system, taken to its conclusions, as "another Gospel." It is therefore a charge not lightly to be overlooked.

It is because of this, not because of confession, clerical celibacy, or any other lesser matter, that a serious Protestant cannot respond with unbridled enthusiasm to Catholic appeals to form one Christian fellowship. His heart must respond to the genuine warmth of the Catholic offer of Christian friendship, but he owes it to his Catholic counterpart not to forget the real danger which he sees in the Catholic system. The enormity of this charge, that Catholicism can turn into "another Gospel," is like a leaden cloud on the ecumenical horizon, but it is precisely this which is at the heart of the controversy between believing Protestants and believing Catholics. Therefore we cannot overlook it.

(i) *The theory behind a false trust.* For all evangelical Protestants, the principal reality of Christianity may be summed up in the words of the Old Testament prophet Habakkuk, cited by St. Paul, "The just shall live by faith" (Romans 1:17, Habakkuk 2:4). Orthodox Roman Catholics and orthodox Protestants alike are in full agreement that the necessary and sufficient requirements for our salvation were fulfilled by Jesus Christ. The disagreement comes in the understanding of how this work done by Christ is applied to the individual Christian or is appropriated by him. Protestants, following what they see as the clear teaching of the Bible, hold that Christ's saving work is applied to the individual *only* through faith and *adequately and sufficiently* through faith. In theological terminology, this is called the doctrine of *justification by faith* or *by faith alone*: hence the Reformation watchword, *sola fide*.

The Reformers considered this basic doctrine a recovery of New Testament and early Christian teaching, a contention which is supported today by Catholic scholars such as Hans Küng and Karl Rahner. Over against the Reformers' position, the Counter-Reformation Council of Trent presented a very complicated concept of justification. It taught that justification must be preceded by a *disposition* or *preparation* on man's part to receive God's grace. This involves his acceptance of the truth of the statements and promises of revelation. Faith is thus minimized, tending to be mere intellectual assent. This is insufficient to produce justification, which is accomplished first in baptism, then subsequently in repentance and confession, and which is not once-for-all, but goes on through a man's entire earthly life. In this way, the Council of Trent rejected justification *sola fide*.[2] The complexity of the Tridentine formulation did leave the door open for later Catholic scholars to assert that justification *sola fide* is in fact Catholic teaching, but throughout most of the four centuries since Trent such an interpretation would have seemed fantastic.

Theology makes a distinction between the faith which is believed (*fides quae creditur*) and the faith by which one believes (*fides qua creditur*). Both are necessary: one must have a content to one's faith, certain specific doctrines which are accepted as really true. On the other hand, it is not accepting the content, i.e., the specific doctrines, which constitutes the saving relationship with God. It is rather the personal relationship of trust in Jesus as Lord and Saviour.

After the period when Protestant orthodoxy flourished, Protestantism tended to veer more and more away from the specific doctrines which make up the content of faith, and to be concerned with faith's subjective side: with the emotional experience of trusting, of believing, of being converted, of being "saved." The outstanding German theologian of the Romantic period, Friedrich Schleiermacher (1768-1834), spoke of a sense of absolute dependence as being the most important thing in religion; Paul Tillich (1886-1965), who was indebted to Schleiermacher, talked of "ultimate concern." The important thing about such Protestantism is that the specific content of faith is lost and has been replaced by vague and non-rational feelings.

Within Roman Catholicism, on the other hand, the emphasis has been put on the faith which is believed, i.e. on the objective content. The number of doctrines which the Roman Catholic must believe has been frequently increased. The most recent example, as we have seen, was the 1950 proclamation of the dogma of the bodily assumption of Mary into heaven. If "faith" as elaborated and expanded in this way becomes a list of things to be accepted, it becomes farther and farther removed from the trust sense of *pistis* in the New Testament.* In Protestant eyes, because medieval and later Catholicism

---

*To avoid confusion, let us repeat that trust does not exclude accepting doctrines as true; in fact, trust without doctrines is a *sacrificium intellectus*. On the other hand, a compendium of doctrines about God is quite different from a personal faith in God.

obscured the real fundamentals of the Gospel which inspire trust, confidence, and even the assurance of personal salvation, it had to develop a whole series of surrogates intended to give the confidence and peace of mind which faith alone could no longer give. By so doing, the Roman Catholic system has fulfilled a real human need. Lutheran church historian Rudolf Sohm called Catholicism "the religion of the natural man," because it appeals strongly to man's natural religious sense. In this sense, Catholicism is more humanistic than Protestantism. But—according to the New Testament—the religion of the natural man is not adequate to bring him to salvation. For that evangelical faith alone is necessary—and sufficient.

(*ii*) *The practical result of a false trust.* The practical result of a false trust such as that described above and presented as an implication of the Roman Catholic theological system, is that wrong objects of trust become the most important ones. The church, the sacraments, the saints, the hierarchy, the priesthood, the liturgy—all these things assume too much importance not only in theory, but in practice as well. From an evangelical perspective, this is spiritually dangerous for the individual believer, because it can lead him away from the one thing that is needful to a host of other things which cannot bring his salvation. In today's theological situation it is also practically harmful for the church and for theology. Thus today we see Roman Catholics seriously discussing the communion liturgy, or the amount of attention which Christians ought to pay to Mary, with "Protestants" who believe that Jesus himself was a mere man whom his followers erroneously elevated to divine stature. Liberal Protestants have let intellectualism, "dependence," "ultimate concern" replace their concern with the central facts of redemptive history; Roman Catholics may let their preoccupation with peripheral or misleading facets of Christian life blind them to the central facts. But the result is the same: a non-evangelical religion which lacks the power of the Gospel.

Theological Conclusions

The basic conclusion of the orthodox or evangelical Protestant, then, must be that the "too much" of Roman Catholicism as a theological-ecclesiastical system is like the "too much" of the Judaizing

Christians whom Paul rebukes in Galatians. It turns the true Gospel into another Gospel, which in the last analysis is no Gospel at all. Of anyone who does this, Paul says, "Let him be accursed" (Galatians 1:8). Naturally the evangelical Protestant realizes that much binds him to the believing Roman Catholic. Their churches, despite generations of antagonism, do share common hopes and face common perils. But when he is asked to discuss the merits of Roman Catholicism as a theological system expressing the fundamental truths of the Gospel of Christ, no matter how gently, courteously and objectively he tries to do so, there will still be echoes of Galatians 1 in his comments. This is because evangelical Protestantism is meaningless unless justification comes solely and sufficiently "by faith alone." If this is right, then what is wrong with Roman Catholic theology is not just a certain extravagance, a certain proliferation of unnecessary theological variety, but a failure to grasp the one thing that is needful.

Of course there are countless Roman Catholics who do clearly see the one needful thing. But the system, as a system, bypasses the very heart of the Gospel. This, and not Latin in the Mass, the celibacy of priests, or even a more doctrinal thing like transubstantiation, is what the evangelical Protestant objects to in Roman Catholicism. And this is why neither the use of English for the Mass, nor the marriage of priests, nor the charity and hospitality of the Pope, nor any other change can reconcile him to the system. A liberal Protestant who does not believe in Christ as the divine and wholly adequate Saviour finds it easy to come to terms with an urbane and peaceable Catholicism especially when both are threatened by the same external enemies. An evangelical Protestant, on the other hand, can have a real spiritual fraternity with a Catholic when they realize that both honor and serve the same Saviour, but he cannot come to terms with the system. For any kind of Catholic, a liberal Protestant is a more companionable and agreeable dialogue partner, but for the believing Catholic, it is only the evangelical Protestant who can be a *Christian* dialogue partner.*

---

*To avoid the confusion so often inherent in the use of labels, let us reemphasize that "evangelical Protestant," as used here, does not mean a Protestant who belongs to a particular church or to a particular party, but one to whom the central truths of the Gospel, of the evangel, are in fact central and primary —and not education, social action, or any one of the host of other popular substitutes. In this sense of the word, no one can be a true Christian at all without being evangelical.

From this perspective the evangelical cannot deny that something is moving in Rome, but he cannot yet be sure that it is moving far enough, or even in the right direction, to restore the one thing that is necessary for every Christian individual and every Christian community. That remains a fundamental, dynamic, personal faith in Jesus Christ as the incarnate Son of God and as one's own Lord and Saviour. If the Roman Catholicism of an earlier day held a true doctrine about Christ but in practice failed to take the consequences and substituted a system for faith, today's Catholicism is in danger of abandoning not only its cumbersome system but its Christian foundations as well. This puts the concerned Protestant in a difficult position. From having been frightened of Catholicism as a monolithic, authoritarian structure which was capable of crushing him any time it thought it could get away with it, he now is horrified at the way the massive system and the substance behind it seem to be melting away under the attacks of secularist radicals inside and outside of the Roman church.

Previously the evangelical might claim, "I understand the Gospel more purely, more simply, better than the Roman Catholic, but at least he acknowledges the same basic facts." Today this common heritage of basic facts seems to have vanished with the new stance of official Roman Catholicism, leaving the evangelical Protestant isolated in a way he never felt himself to be before, so long as the great, dangerous, and hostile—but also orthodox—Roman church was still there. Today he can no longer claim so confidently that Roman Catholicism too acknowledges the same basic facts—he can only look for orthodox believers within a shifting Catholic doctrinal structure. Perhaps fifty years ago the conservative Protestant could have spitefully rejoiced at Catholicism's troubles. But today he can only see in them the tremendous power of the intellectual and spiritual convulsions of our day, which not only shake his little denomination or local congregation, but which seem capable of turning the vast Roman church inside out. In the early days of his revolt from Rome, Henry the VIII of England tied Catholics and Lutherans back to back and burned them at the same stake. In our age of revolt against reason, the modern world—or perhaps even the organized churches themselves—will soon be tying believing Protestants and Catholics back to back. Perhaps this will be the real ecumenism of the future.

2. Historical and Practical Objections to Roman Catholicism

For centuries Catholic theologians have worked to produce defenses against Protestant attacks based on Catholic history. Protestants charged, for example, that Peter never led the whole church, that the early church had no idea of papal primacy, that no one understood Matthew 16:18 in the traditional Roman Catholic way, that at least one legitimate pope did in fact err and teach clearly heretical doctrines, and was anathematized for it (Pope Honorius, d. 638). Roman Catholics, with considerable labor and sometimes with considerable imagination, have defended themselves and their church against these charges, feeling that if their church could be proved to have erred on a single major point, their position would collapse. The most famous Catholic theologian of Germany in the nineteenth century, Ignaz von Döllinger (1799-1890), a fervent anti-Protestant, sadly abandoned Roman Catholicism when papal infallibility was proclaimed in 1870, for he believed the church had abandoned factual consistency.

Today Protestants can still produce the historical arguments against Roman Catholicism. They are still formidable, as any Catholic scholar who has dealt with them knows. But they are all predicated on the assumption that Catholicism claims to be an internally true and self-consistent system. This was what the Catholic Döllinger claimed for his church. He felt forced to leave it when it committed itself to a position which he sincerely believed to be inconsistent with historical fact. But Döllingers are rare today. There are "Catholics" who can happily talk of the death of God, who support Marxist revolutions, preach the irrelevancy of the Ten Commandments, perform acts which Canon Law calls sacrilege, and who still consider themselves to be good Catholics, in fact to be better than their scandalized conservative brethren.

Under such circumstances, to repeat the historical arguments against Roman Catholicism is pointless. A Catholicism which can go happily on even if Bultmann convinces it that Christ never rose from the dead certainly will not be shaken by an argument that Pope Honorius taught heresy in the seventh century. For the believing

Catholic, who still wants internal consistency and who still thinks that Catholic doctrine must be a coherent and self-consistent whole, it may be enough to say that in the historical field there are massive objections to this belief.[3]

Leaving the history of doctrine, let us take a different example: persecution. The history of persecution is a delicate subject. Protestants believe that Catholics have used the power of the state, *as a matter of policy,* to spill the blood of religious dissidents—so much so that sixteenth-century Protestants considered the church of Rome to be the woman "drunk with the blood of the saints," of whom St. John speaks (Revelation 17:6).[4] Roman Catholics can of course point to examples of Protestant persecution (although Protestants tended to repress other non-conformists, such as Anabaptists and Quakers, more severely than they did Catholics). Then it can be argued that Protestant persecutions of Roman Catholics were less extensive because the Protestants had less power on their side and were reluctant to risk Catholic retaliation. Examples of Protestant discrimination can be brought forward, less serious than persecution, but still reprehensible. The discussion soon becomes a technical one, balancing statistics against historical probabilities and uncertainties against speculations, and hardly capable of giving us any real satisfaction.

Here the most relevant thing to do is not to charge that Catholics persecuted Protestants more severely and on a wider scale than Protestants persecuted Catholics—a charge for which much historical support can be produced but to which many objections can also be made. The point is that Protestants have a lively memory of Catholic persecutions when the Roman Catholic Church had the power and the opportunity. The memory of suffering endured is in any case more vivid and persistent than that of suffering inflicted on others. It is rather as though the pagan Roman Empire should suddenly have revived, with great power, in the seventh century. Would not the Christians have been apprehensive, remembering the persecutors from Nero to Diocletian? The fact that the Christian Emperors who succeeded Constantine the Great had treated the pagans badly would hardly have comforted seventh-century Christians faced with the prospect of a new pagan Empire. Built into Protestant self-consciousness is this strong memory of Catholic persecution. Perhaps it is exaggerated, perhaps it ought to be balanced with a confession of

Protestant wrong-doing, but it is still a fact, and one which influences Protestant attitudes towards Rome today. Where Protestant faith is strongest, there Protestant memories are longest. So it is precisely the Protestants who believe most—who could thus be the best spiritual co-belligerents of embattled orthodox Catholics—who are most apprehensive and suspicious of Rome.

The most serious aspect of the charge is the contention that Roman Catholicism has used religious persecution as a *deliberate and prolonged matter of policy*. Protestants cannot deny that they too have persecuted. Although Luther himself spoke out against the use of coercion in religious matters, even he eventually went along with some acts of repression. John Calvin brought about the trial and execution of Servetus for antitrinitarianism in 1553. Under Queen Elizabeth I, many Roman Catholics suffered the death penalty—although political considerations were often intertwined with religious ones. These are black marks on the record of Protestantism. But in no case did persecutions persist for a long time, nor have Protestants ever had easy consciences about them. They began to repent of them of their own accord. The Protestants of Geneva have erected an expiatory monument to Servetus—no help to Servetus, of course, but still a clear gesture of repentance. Protestants will admit that persecution is no longer a part of Roman Catholic policy,[5] but the policy and the sins of the past have never been very frankly faced and confessed. Thus there lingers the suspicion that given the right set of circumstances, Rome might do it again. Such a suspicion is probably highly unwarranted in the twentieth century, but it is not entirely without foundation. Protestants must continue to ask Rome, "Where are your expiatory monuments?"

3. Unity at the Price of Sanity?

The Catholic-Protestant rapprochement is proceeding at a rapid pace, but it takes strange turnings. The former Episcopal Bishop of California, James A. Pike, himself a convert from Roman Catholicism, has engaged in bitter and often unfair polemics against his former church, taking any platform available to him, including *Playboy* magazine. But Pike's successor as Bishop of California, Chauncey

Kilmer Meyers, has called upon Protestants to accept the Pope as the spiritual head of Christianity. Catholics naturally respond to Bishop Meyers better than to Bishop Pike. But in the present theological climate, Meyers' acceptance of the Pope may be on a par with Pike's visit to a medium.

Pike gained notoriety for his repudiation of all those traditional Christian doctrines which, he felt, modern man could not accept. He seemed to think, like his colleague Bishop Robinson and their German mentor Bultmann, that a man who looks at television cannot believe in the Trinity. Yet Pike not only looks at television, he can also use television to publicize his interest in spiritualism and the power of a medium to communicate with the dead. We know that Bishop Pike's personal life has been scored by personal tragedy, yet it would belittle him to suggest that he does not know what he is doing in this widely-publicized fascination with spiritualism. Pike simply is illustrating this: for a Christian leader who has abandoned the authority of the Bible and objective truth in Christianity, anything goes.

The Bible condemns any resort to witchcraft, and in the Old Testament to consult a medium (Heb. *ob,* having a familiar spirit) was punishable by death (Exodus 22:18, Deuteronomy 18:11). The German theologian Kurt Koch maintains that where objective, revealed Christian faith is in decline, a flood of superstition, magic, and witchcraft sweeps in to replace it. Bishop Pike's own theological rebellion and subsequent fascination with spiritualism are only a dramatic and widely-publicized example of this widespread phenomenon.[6] But what relationship is there between Bishop Pike's accepting the medium and Bishop Meyers' accepting the Pope? The point is that in the context of contemporary Protestant theology, accepting the Pope may mean exactly the same thing as accepting a medium: it may mean that the rational mind is at the end of its tether, and that the bishops are ready for any leap into the darkness. But this is a negation of traditional Catholicism as well as of orthodox Protestantism.

In the present theological situation, we must have the courage to negate, to tell people what it is that we do *not* mean. If Bishop Meyers had repudiated Pike's theological vagaries and spiritualism and had reaffirmed his own commitment to orthodox Christianity as objectively true, and *then* had spoken of the Pope as the spiritual head of the church, he would have said something important. He would have ceased to be a Protestant, but he would have been making sense. But in a climate in which one Episcopal bishop consults mediums, for another bishop to consult the Pope is not the answer to our ecclesiastical divisions. In order for our affirmations to mean anything, we must also have negations. The orthodox Protestant rejects Pike because Pike rejects biblical authority. But no more can he follow Pike's successor—unless he wants to surrender not merely his church polity, but his faith.

The Protestant who believes in a powerful, loving, divine-human Saviour, thereby denies certain things. In this context, it means that he will continue to deny some of the claims of the traditional—and of the modern—Roman Catholic Church. If he were to give up his theological opposition to the Roman system, he might make unity appear easy, but he would put it on the non-rational level—like Pike and the medium.

Thus, in the last analysis, evangelical Protestant opposition to Rome should please the serious, believing Catholic more than the easy cordiality of Protestant liberals. The evangelical Protestant resists easy unity because Christ has real authority for him. But can the serious Catholic call anyone a brother, "separated" or not, for whom Christ has little or no authority? Luther, Calvin and their reforming colleagues made grievous charges against Rome. They made them because they believed Christ's honor required it. Some of their letters have been answered; many have not. We must bring their charges up again not because we hate Rome, nor because we dislike the thought of reunion. We do not bring them up because we feel our own position to be irreproachable, nor in order to bolster our own self-satisfaction. We bring them up because the honor of Christ, as we have learned to know him, requires it. Perhaps we are too severe, perhaps too harsh—but our criticism is healthier than indiscriminate liberal approval.

The evangelical Protestant has learned some things from history. He should, for example, have learned to be honest and to be a gentleman in religious dialogue. But he should not have learned, like the liberal church, to forget the honor of Christ. He must state his convictions, and defend his principles, for only thus can he be of service to his Lord. And only thus—not incidentally, but logically—can he be of any use to those Catholics who love Christ more than they love the spirit of the twentieth century.

Notes

[1]Hermann Sasse, "Holy Church or Holy Writ? The meaning of the *Sola Scriptura* of the Reformation." *Interchange*, Supplementary Paper (Sydney, 1967), p. 4. Italics mine.

[2]Karl Heussi, *Kompendium der Kirchengeschichte*, 12th ed. (Tübingen, J. C. B. Mohr, 1960), p. 336.

[3]For a taste of the Protestant literature dealing with this subject, see Vittorio Subilia, *The Problem of Catholicism* (London: S.C.M., and Philadelphia: Westminster, 1964); Gerrit C. Berkouwer, *The Conflict with Rome* (Philadelphia: Presbyterian and Reformed, 1958), and Loraine Boettner, *Roman Catholicism* (Philadelphia: Presbyterian and Reformed, 1962; London: Banner of Truth, 1966). All of these books are more or less hostile, but each has considerable scholarly merit. The Catholic who wants to know something about the depth of Protestant objections to Roman Catholicism may consult them with profit.

[4]*The Bloody Theater or Martyrs' Mirror* (1660), translated by Joseph Sohm, gives a historically valuable and thoroughly horrible account of the religious persecution of the Anabaptists, largely at the hands of Catholic authorities (Scottsdale, Pennsylvania: Herald Press, 1951).

[5]Charges are frequently made that Roman Catholic persecutions of non-Catholics are not unknown in our own age. See Boettner, *Roman Catholicism*, pp. 479-525. Cf. Hervé Laurière, *Assassins au nom de Dieu* (Paris: La Vigie, 1951), and Edmond Paris, *Genocide in Satellite Croatia* (Chicago: Institute of Balkan Affairs, 1960). Protestants must beware of rashly making such charges. Catholics, by contrast, should recognize the fact that these charges do keep on arising and that much evidence is offered to substantiate them. They cannot simply be made to disappear with the wave of an ecumenical wand. A single such charge is enough to reawaken slumbering Protestant suspicions. Therefore they should be faced, not ignored.

[6]See Kurt Koch, *Christian Counseling and Occultism* (Grand Rapids: Kregel, 1965).

CHAPTER 9

· WHAT IS "MODERN THEOLOGY" AFTER? ·

For the time will come when they will not endure sound doctrine, but wanting to have their ears tickled, they will accumulate for themselves teachers in accordance to their own desires, and will turn away from the truth, and will turn aside to myths.

II TIMOTHY 4:3-4, (NASB)

At a meeting in Italian Switzerland in 1965 an African Christian—a man with a Yale Ph.D. and now a professor of English literature in his homeland—said in a kind of personal testimony: "One of the wonderful things about being a Christian is that while you aren't spared trouble, the Bible warns you in advance about it." The general warning which St. Paul gave to Timothy about doctrinal deviations has never been so well fulfilled as in our own generation. No doubt the orthodox of previous generations have despaired over their contemporaries who would not endure sound doctrine—and not without reason, for the history of the church is the history of heresies. Yet we can say that during most of the church's history, the standards of orthodoxy have been widely, if not universally, recognized. The ecumenical creeds, of which we have already spoken, the Apostles', Nicene, and Chalcedonian Creeds, have always been accepted throughout both the Eastern and Western branches of Christendom,[1] by both Catholics and Protestants, Lutherans and Reformed. Even today these creeds, supplemented by the Athanasian Creed in the Western Catholic and Protestant churches, are officially endorsed almost everywhere.

Yet now this formal adherence to the great doctrinal standards is crumbling. In some places, such as in the United Presbyterian Church in the United States of America, the official standards are being pushed into the background to make room for new confessions which are theologically vague. Elsewhere, for example in the Evangelical Church in Germany, the old statements of faith are still formally required of all ministers even though absolute doctrinal chaos reigns in the theological faculties and has begun to take over the parishes.[2] No one is as unpopular in Protestant circles as a man who represents historic orthodoxy competently; no one is as celebrated as a prominent churchman, be he bishop or professor, who thinks up a new and outrageous way to propound an old heresy. Official Christendom, not only Protestantism but also Catholicism, is indeed accumulating teachers in accordance with its own foolish whims, and it is increasingly turning to new mythologies as substitutes for reality. This development is being presented to an unwilling, puzzled, but gullible general church public as the result of twentieth-century progress, i.e. of "modern" theology.

One could legitimately complain that neither the methods nor the conclusions of "modern theology" are exactly modern, but that is beside the point. They are being marketed as new. That alone virtually proves them in the eyes of most mid-twentieth-century men and women. For the sake of truth we must say clearly that this expression, "modern theology," is a misnomer. Logically, to be "modern," theological ideas would have to be the product of our own "modern" age. Instead, the specific *doctrines* of "modern" theology can be found in Plato, in the pre-Christian Jewish philosopher Philo, in the early Gnostic heretics of the second century, in the pagan, anti-Christian polemicist Celsus, and in countless other pre-Christians, non-Christians, heretical Christians and anti-Christians. The specific *methods* of modern theology date back only to the mid-nineteenth century, but is the nineteenth century modern?[3] Whether it is justified or not, the movement has preempted the title "modern" just as effectively as the Communists have taken over the words "popular" and "people's." Therefore, in order to avoid constantly making reservations and continually using quotation marks, we shall henceforth speak of modern theology and mean by it what its adherents mean. But we shall do well always to place a mental question-mark between the words whenever we encounter the expression.

1. What is Modern Theology?

No emphasis on the troubled situation of the contemporary church or of the mid-twentieth-century Christian would be complete without an attempt to answer this question. In the United States and Great Britain there is not as yet any distinct and unified body of theological opinion which is bold enough to claim the title modern for itself alone. In the Anglo-American world, Protestant theology presents too broad a spectrum for any segment to attempt this. There is still a solid phalanx of evangelical orthodoxy as well as many irregular formations of liberal evangelicals, evangelical liberals, pious conservatives, liberal pietists, and even "old-fashioned" liberals. All of them live in the twentieth century, and in one way or another come to terms with it. In Germany, however, *moderne Theologie* is not merely a term to date the movement. It is a party, a war-cry, even a title of glory. The party it designates has all but taken over academic theology, increasingly controls church administration, and is making itself felt more and more emphatically on the parish level.

Why should we be interested in the doings of German theologians? We had better pay attention, for Germany's *moderne Theologie* is being imported into the United States at a fantastic, increasing rate. Some theologians have immigrated, among whom the late Paul Tillich is the best-known example. The works of modern German theology are translated into English and published in Britain and America almost before they are off the presses in Germany. Many American theologians have done much or all of their training there. Finally, important modern German theologians are frequently invited to the United States for lecture tours which often fall little short of triumphal processions. The United States at the moment may be behind Germany in theological modernity,[4] but it is rapidly catching up. Thus American Christians of every denomination have good cause to try to understand modern German theology.

It may even seem that this attempt at understanding modern theology comes late; in a certain sense that is true. Many of the great men of modern theology are already eighty years old, and others have passed from the scene at an equally great age. Martin Heidegger, the existentialist philosopher who has inspired so much of modern theology's approach to revelation, is an octogenarian, and began to make his mark in the 1920's. Yet, curiously enough, the significance of what modern theologians are doing to theology and the church only began to dawn on the general public in the 'sixties, when Bishop John Robinson popularized a melange of the ideas of Bultmann, Bonhoeffer, and Tillich in *Honest to God* (1963). Remarkably, it was the German version of Robinson's little best-seller, "God Is Different" (*Gott ist anders*), which really opened the eyes of Germans themselves to what their theologians were doing. As a result, it is only in the past few years that German writers have begun seriously trying to explain their own modern theology to the German public.

No better guide for the understanding of what modern theology thinks of itself can be found than the small booklet by Martin Voigt, "What Is Modern Theology's Goal?"[5] Voigt is an enthusiastic advocate of the movement. He carefully sets forth its attractive features, and minimizes its affronts to the conservatives, whom the Germans usually call "pietists." First and foremost, he sees modern theology as a result of scientific theological discoveries of recent decades. For him, modern theology is the logical, necessary consequence, for the intellectually honest Christian, of modern progress in biblical and comparative religious research. It is especially unfortunate, particularly for any understanding of what is at stake, that when modern theology is criticized, its critics often tacitly accept its claim to be the only *scientific* kind of theology, and present themselves as the defenders of practical Christianity, of "faith," or of piety. That this will automatically pre-dispose the uncommitted in favor of what is modern and scientific is obvious. That this surrender is neither necessary nor desirable, for the sake of objectivity as well as for the sake of truth, will become evident as we examine what Voigt calls "the three great discoveries of modern theology."

2. Discovery No. 1: The Humanity of the Bible

We have said that the history of the church is the history of heresies. It is also true that virtually every important heresy arose as a kind of a reaction to the failure of the orthodox, catholic church to do full justice to some important and legitimate aspect of Christian doctrine

or life. In fact, Christian theology itself began to develop as a reaction
to the Gnostic speculation which tried to *explain* the significance of
Christ in philosophical terms, instead of simply preaching repentance
and salvation. The cults which claim to produce healing miracles
arose to fill a real lack created by the church's widespread failure to
act on Christ's command, "Heal the sick" (Matthew 10:8). The mil-
lenialistic enthusiasm, with its visions of the approaching end of the
world, which appears from time to time, is explicable in part by the
church's tendency to downgrade the very important New Testament
teaching on the Second Coming of Christ. Such illustrations could
be multiplied. Seen from this perspective, modern theology's claim to
have rediscovered the humanity of the Bible, together with all its consequences for doctrine and the church, may be an understandable
reaction to an excessive emphasis by Protestant orthodoxy or by fundamentalism on the Bible's divinity.

When modern theology says that it has discovered the humanity
of the Bible, it means this in both senses of the word discover: it
claims (1) to have recognized it for the first time, and (2) to have uncovered it so that others can see it too. As far as (1) is concerned,
strictly speaking this claim cannot be true, for the Bible itself expressly
tells us about the human role in its making: *"Men* moved by the
Holy Spirit spoke from God" (II Peter 1:21, NASB). The only document to come directly from God's hands, if we may put it thus, was
the first set of the Tables of the Law, which Moses smashed when he
found the Israelites dancing around the golden calf on his descent
from Sinai (Exodus 32:15-16, 19). St. Luke, in the opening lines of
his Gospel, makes it clear that he did careful historical research; no
angel told him the story of Jesus (Luke 1:1-4).

This human participation is taken into account in the traditional
Protestant doctrine of inspiration, which teaches that the human
writers of the Bible kept their integrity as responsible human beings,
while the Holy Spirit preserved them from all error and directed
them to all that was necessary to fulfil his purposes. The writers' educational background, literary and linguistic skills, personal stylistic
traits, and so on, all had full opportunity to express themselves.
Orthodox doctrine has always officially recognized the mystery of the
joint human-divine origin of the Bible. The problem has arisen because Protestants, sometimes in conflict with the claims for tradition

made by Roman Catholicism, sometimes as a cheap—and ultimately ineffectual—way to squelch sceptical questions, have frequently stressed the divinity of the Bible and disregarded or neglected its human aspect. Modern theology can legitimately claim to have rediscovered the humanity of the Bible by contrast with such an uncritical bibliolatry. However, bibliolatry in this sense could arise only when Protestants ignored both what the Bible says about itself and their own officially confessed doctrines.[6]

With regard to (2), modern theology claims to have uncovered something which in one way or another, was being hidden by both traditional orthodoxy, with its alleged bibliolatry, and by old-fashioned liberalism, which failed to take the Bible really seriously. There is merit in this claim. The difficulty is that in taking credit for having drawn our attention once again to the humanity of the Bible, these theologians go on to prove its humanity in terms of alleged examples of unreliability, inaccuracy, and irreconcilable contradiction. This is an important allegation, and it must be considered from three perspectives: (1) are the examples really there, as charged? (2) did modern theology discover them, as claimed? (3) are errors essential if the Bible is to be truly human?

(a) *Are Errors Essential?* As the third question is the most fundamental, it should be answered first. We must begin by distinguishing between actual error, such as false statements of fact and real internal contradictions on the one hand, and lack of completeness on the other —just as one must distinguish between actual sin and lack of moral perfection in man. According to Genesis, before the fall Adam and Eve were free of sin, but they did not possess all moral perfections: they did not, evidently, possess the virtues of prudence or of fidelity. Likewise, we should never claim that the Bible offers us all possible information on every subject or even on the subjects it treats. For example, it cannot begin to offer us an exhaustive description of God. But it can—and it does, if the historic Christian faith is valid—offer as true, reliable, and adequate knowledge about him, knowledge which, as St. Paul tells us, is "able to give you the wisdom that leads to salvation" (II Timothy 3:15). If we do not confuse reliability and freedom from error with total comprehensive information, we can say that error—like sin—is not necessary to humanness.

Finitude—in the Bible's case, this means lack of total comprehensiveness—is a necessary human characteristic, but error is not. Each of us can—and does—make many error-free statements every day. For example, "I paid ten dollars and ninety-five cents for this hat." If we can, in a limited realm and using only our own ability, make a statement that is free from unreliability, inaccuracy, and internal contradiction without ceasing to be human, is it unthinkable for men to make reliable statements about God, if he is real and his Holy Spirit is assisting them? In part, modern theology's charge of errors in the Bible is based on its conviction that to err is human rather than the conviction of its humanity being based on discovering and proving actual errors. Part of the persuasive impact of this argument comes from the fact that all of us already realize that the Bible is in some sense a human book—it says so itself, as we have seen—and we unthinkingly accept the implication that, as it is human, therefore it must contain errors. The mistake lies in taking "to err is human" as a statement of an absolute equivalence: "Humanness is equivalent to making errors, everywhere and all the time." In this extreme form, we can discern the sub-Christian or *graceless* pattern of thought which underlies the conviction that if the Bible is human, it must err.

Orthodox Christianity sees error and falsehood, like sin, as results of a real, historic fall. They are *not* essential to human nature, but distort it and even ruin it. In our present world, after the fall, they are endemic in man, but they are part of his *condition, not* of his *nature.* Their real effects can really be overcome in individual, historic human lives as a result of the real redemption accomplished *for* eternity, but *in* space and time, by Jesus Christ. The historic fall was abandoned by the old liberal theologians with whom most of the modern theologians first studied. (In this respect, liberal theology evinced the same optimistic confidence in the goodness, i.e. unfallenness, of man as liberal political philosophies, and has run into the same problem: man does not behave as though he were naturally good and unfallen.) At this point, orthodox and modern theology, in distinction to liberal theology, read the evidence the same way: both recognize the lostness of man. But orthodox theology, believing in a God who acts in real history, and to whom man is really responsible for *his* actions in history, says that the lostness is not natural, not part of man's nature, and that it can be overcome by grace; i.e. by the renewed action of God in history, *without destroying man's integrity as man.*

Intoxicated by its enthusiasm for man and his progress, nineteenth-century liberal theology lost the concept of a God who actually acts in history. In this it followed its intellectual forebears, the Deists and rationalists of the eighteenth century. They too misunderstood man's nature, thinking of him as naturally good if not corrupted by his environment in society. (The patron saint of this school of thought is Jean-Jacques Rousseau.) Modern theology has come to a greater realism about man. It had to do so, after two world wars, or—as some modern theologians like to put it—after Auschwitz. But it still operates on the Deistic basis of a *closed materialistic universe,* in which God, if he exists, never acts.[7] Consequently its failure to be able to accept the idea of a reliable Bible *could* result *entirely* from its prior rejection of the idea of any kind of effective grace. In a history in which God, by definition, cannot act, i.e. in which grace is at most an idea, not a reality, man must be the way he is, i.e. erroneous, sinful, and lost, *by nature*—and he can never really *be saved* by a living Christ. He can only, at best, come to a better and nobler *self-understanding* through an encounter with the Christian message, the *kerygma.* Modern theology does not proclaim a new creation, but a new comprehension.

It is remarkable how close modern theology and orthodoxy are where the facts of man's situation are concerned. But orthodoxy calls it his *condition,* resulting from sin and capable of being changed by grace, while modern theology sees it as his *nature,* to be accepted and nobly faced. The application of this equation between error and humanness to the Bible by modern theology *might* be a result of scientific inquiry. In some cases, it may be. In the final analysis, only the individuals concerned and God can say. But it ought to give us cause for suspicion when we recognize that this equation and its application are logically *inevitable* for those whose philosophical presuppositions leave no room for a historic fall nor for a God who acts in history. And such a presupposition is the common and fundamental starting-point for all modern theologians.[8] Even if their historical and textual research did not fairly convince them that we have a fallible Bible, they would be forced to conclude this from their general philosophical outlook, which denies both a real Fall and effective grace. In other words, given the world as it really is, if there is no real Fall, then everything is fallible. We must now ask ourselves: did modern theology discover the "errors"?

(b) *Who Discovered the Errors?* Voigt, to support his view that modern theology has discovered the humanity of the Bible, attributes the uncovering of errors in it to the "modern historical research which began to flourish in the nineteenth century."[9] On the one hand, it is true that nineteenth-century scholarship put its finger on a large number of problematical passages in the Bible which challenge the concept of its inerrancy. On the other hand, it is surprising how long Christians have known about most if not all of them. "The alleged factual errors and internal contradictions in Scripture which are currently cited to demonstrate the impossibly archaic nature of the inerrancy view are themselves impossibly archaic in a high proportion of instances."[10] Explanations of them have been available for centuries. Whether or not the explanations are accepted as convincing or whether one finds the evidence for errors and contradictions too strong usually depends on other factors besides the evidence and the arguments. In any case it is clear that anyone who rejects the concept of effective divine intervention in history will opt for the errors and contradictions. Modern theologians have a different set of reasons *why* they believe in the fallibility of the Bible, but the examples they cite, for the most part, were discovered long before our time.[11]

(c) *Are the Examples Really There?* From what has just been said, it is evident that other factors besides the actual evidence can and often do influence the conclusion one reaches about the trustworthiness and authority of the Bible. Surely no one can logically accept the full trustworthiness and authority of Scripture without taking the consequences and being a believing Christian. In other words, believing the Bible and trusting its contents is difficult to separate from Christian faith as such. If we have it however, Christian faith is not entirely the result of the evidence we can assemble for it. The grace of God must play an essential part in winning our hearts and minds to faith (John 6:44). And precisely this divine intervention which is an essential part of historic Christian doctrine and a necessary condition of personal Christian faith is unacceptable on principle to modern theology.

Nevertheless, because the evidence alone is insufficient to create faith, we are not to disregard evidence: that again is a "modern" solution. Voigt, speaking for modern theology, affirms that to ask for verification of God's claims and demands is "to place his very divinity at stake."[12] This impressively humble and pious-sounding phrase is deceptive. The historic Christian conviction, from the earliest times, has been that God *does* authenticate his claims by evidence (cf. Luke 1:3-4, John 20:30-31). One could really say that that is precisely what the Bible is all about. The evidence is never so compelling as to destroy man's freedom to reject it, but it is always sufficient so that faith need not and should not violate man's intellectual honesty. What is at stake, if we dare not ask for verification of the *kerygma*, is not God's divinity but our *humanity*. If we dare not ask, we must surrender both our responsibility and our intelligence. "Freedom" remains—freedom to "decide." But a decision made without the possibility of intellectual questioning and verification is not a fully human decision: it is a blind leap. It is this kind of decision without evidence, not the Christian's submission to the authority of Scripture after he has examined the evidence, which is the real *sacrificium intellectus*.

Now how do matters stand as regards the evidence for the alleged errors and internal contradictions on which the humanity of the Bible is based, in the modern theological sense of humanity? This is not the place for a full discussion of this important issue which has been ably and amply treated by other and better-qualified authors. We must be content with two rather programatic statements of fact: (1) On the basis of the best available evidence, it is easier to believe in the complete trustworthiness of the Bible today than at any time in the past century. (2) People who claim to be finding errors on scientific grounds almost always demonstrate a degree of preconceived opinion which makes their objectivity doubtful.

A hundred and fifty years ago we knew virtually nothing about the ancient Near East, except what the Bible itself reported. As our accurate knowledge of biblical times has advanced, opinions downgrading the authority of the Bible have had to be abandoned in case after case. Werner Keller has presented this in popular form in *The Bible as History*,[13] and more scholarly treatments are readily available. The work of Kenneth A. Kitchen of the University of Liverpool shows how many of the "results" of nineteenth- and twentieth-century biblical criticism, tending to minimize the reliability of the Old Testament, have themselves been refuted by genuine historical research on the basis of archaeological discoveries.[14]

Because at the beginning of the development of historical-critical Bible scholarship, very few other sources were available from the ancient Near East, its pioneers had to work largely on the basis of judicious guessing and of intuitive analysis of the Bible itself. From this were derived theories concerning the origin, development, and original function of the Bible documents. Each new scholar built upon the work of his predecessors. As a result biblical scholarship has developed a powerful tradition of its own. Now, in the twentieth century, as archaeologists have discovered document after document, undoubtedly genuine and contemporary with the biblical records themselves, these critical theories ought to be radically revised. But in fact they are not being radically revised by many theologians. Why not? The answer is in part that a theologian's prestige is involved in the surrender of positions to which he has confidently committed himself. If even a natural scientist often has trouble abandoning a pet theory when the experimental evidence is against him, we must not be surprised at a greater reluctance among theologians, where the evidence is seldom as conclusive as that from the laboratory. In part, the answer lies in the fact that teachers are often propagandists for a particular point of view. Such teachers are at best not interested in evidence which contradicts them; at worst, they conceal or misrepresent it.[15]

How one resolves the question of an erroneous vs. an inerrant Bible, therefore, is not merely a question of the evidence: it is also, to a large extent, a question of one's predisposition. The conservative critics of modern theology cannot conclusively refute its every attack, but they have provided sufficient contrary evidence (1) to make it perfectly plain that its objectivity is open to question and, (2) to place it under suspicion of being in part propaganda and not pure science. No better clue could be given than the reaction of many modern theologians when the conservatives bring evidence against their historical arguments: although they claim to base their convictions on research, when they are challenged they take refuge in faith (as they define it), saying, "Faith is not interested in historical proofs!"[16]

A final criticism of the objectivity of modern theology lies in the degree to which it has embraced the existentialist philosophy of Martin Heidegger. (Heidegger is admittedly a major influence on modern German existentialist theology.) "It is worth remarking, in view of the common repudiation by traditional Protestant theologians of *all* systems of philosophy as seductive artifacts of fallen man, that Bultmann is committed to the particular philosophical system of Heidegger every bit as much as the most doctrinaire textbook Thomist could be to the Aristotelianism of Aquinas."[17] Apparently it took a non-Christian, non-theologian, the Jewish philosopher Hans Jonas, to ask the obvious question: "Don't you see what you are dealing with? Don't you sense the deeply pagan character of Heidegger's thought?"[18] A theology which is based on a deeply pagan philosophy can hardly give an objective restatement of the real meaning of Christianity.

As far then, as the humanity of the Bible is concerned, the historic Christian faith says to modern theologians: it is human, indeed —and says so itself—just as Jesus Christ himself is human. But it is a humanity which corresponds to God's purpose and is permeated by his grace. Error is no more necessary to the humanity of the Bible than sin is to Christ's true humanity. Although you cannot have the credit for discovering the humanity of the Bible, I owe you thanks for rediscovering it and perhaps for rescuing it from my occasional lapses into uncritical bibliolatry. But even more dangerous than my tendency towards a one-sided divinization of the Bible is your surrender to a graceless view of man, your self-imposed exile in a world where God cannot act. In such a world, nothing has meaning, not even the theology you so laboriously work out to meet its needs. If you have freed my adherents from some outmoded conceptions of God, I must be grateful. But I cannot but try to free you from your bondage to a world where God is a philosophical fiction. It is your closed world which is the fiction, and it is a fiction from which you must be liberated—lest by it you forever enchain yourselves, and drag others to destruction with you.

3. *Discovery No. 2: The Literary Forms in the Bible*

Modern theologians have studied the text of the Bible with an incredible zeal for every detail. This zeal would be more logical if the Bible were in fact mechanically dictated by God, right down to every Hebrew vowel-point. This remarkable phenomenon itself attests, in a way, the divinity of Scripture, which continues to exert such a compelling fascination. Theologians who bitterly deny that a single word is divinely inspired in the traditional sense nevertheless are so fascinated by it that they will spend six decades, like Rudolf Bultmann, meticulously studying every word. There is a kind of bitter irony in this. Some men devote a lifetime to analyzing, evaluating, and criticizing the words and the Word, setting themselves up in a position of supreme authority over Scripture. Often they can speak in tones of disarming humility and piety, but at other times they reveal an almost incomprehensible arrogance in the way they denigrate Christ, his apostles, and their words.[19]

A fact which ought to cause some reflection is that the originator of modern form criticism (*Formgeschichte*) was Nietzsche's friend, F. C. Overbeck (1837-1905).[20] Overbeck, a professor of theology at Basel, was a complete unbeliever and an anti-Christian. He opposed the reigning optimistic liberalism of the theology of his day with an attitude of morose and atheistic scepticism. Those who have followed his insights as the lodestar for their understanding of the New Testament, i.e. the modern theologians, oppose old fashioned liberalism in the name of "faith." But as they do so they find themselves in the company of the death-of-God men—just as Overbeck was a friend and admirer of Nietzsche. Perhaps the historical connections of modern radical Bible criticism to Overbeck, Overbeck's relationship to Nietzsche, and the relationship of modern theologians like John Robinson to Paul van Buren and of both of them to the prophets of the death of God are not coincidences. Lest it be thought that making such a remark on the *results* of radical form criticism before discussing its method, purpose, and accomplishments, is intended to prejudice the reader, let it be said that these linguistic, stylistic, semantic, and other considerations are often so difficult to understand, even for the specialist, that a preliminary glance at the destination our critics reach and at the company in which they travel may be of great help in understanding precisely what it is that they are doing.

Basically, the work of the form critics is an attempt to take a portion of the Bible and (1) identify its literary *genre*, whether it be a chronicle, a treaty, a hymn, part of a service of worship, part of a sermon, or something else. Sometimes the Bible clearly identifies passages as one of the above; at other times there is other good evidence for giving a text one label or another. In many cases the identification must be based on the scholar's guess-work, hunch, or preconceptions. Having thus classified a passage, the critic then (2) establishes its *Sitz im Leben* ("seat-in-life," i.e. the purpose it was originally intended to serve when it was composed). Such inquiry should, in theory, help the Bible texts to speak for themselves, and free them from the tradition-bound standard interpretations they have picked up over the centuries of church history. In the hands of a scholar who has submitted himself to the authority of Scripture, such inquiry can be very fruitful. In the hands of an avowed unbeliever like Overbeck, it is a different matter. When a scholar (as is often the case with students of theology) is wrestling with the tremendous problem of obedience to God and the rebellious strivings of his own self-will, such methods, and the encouragement they give to sit in judgment on the Bible and on the Christ it proclaims, may be a deadly stimulus. They may be just what is needed to lead him to assert his "freedom," by which is really meant that rash pride and self-love which ultimately can put him in bondage forever.

The work of the form critics is regarded by their disciples as giving unique insights into the meaning of biblical passages, especially New Testament passages, by discovering their original *Sitz im Leben*. The positive value of these methods, fairly applied, cannot be gainsaid. The difficulty arises when possibly valid evaluations of the literary genre of a passage are made the basis for sweeping and often invalid value-judgments of its content. Form criticism, for example, has provided valuable evidence against the older source-critical theories, which sought to trace the present Gospels back to a conflation of Mark and other written sources, now lost. By identifying certain passages as rooted in the worship of the first Christians, the form critic cut the ground from under the source critic's attempt to give them a definite place in a hypothetical lost source. In addition, form criticism has provided us with evidence to show that we can never go back far enough behind the present New Testament documents to arrive at a Jesus who is not supernatural. "Thus, Form Criticism," writes Professor F. F. Bruce of the University of Manchester, "has

added its contribution to the overthrow of the hope once fondly held
[by nineteenth-century liberal Protestants] that by getting back to
the most primitive stage of the gospel tradition, we might recover a
purely human Jesus, who simply taught the fatherhood of God and
the brotherhood of man."[21] Having all this to its credit, however,
form criticism became a tool to relativize and discredit the actual
content and message of the New Testament.

The most significant conclusion of the form critics is that much of
the New Testament has proclamation, the winning of disciples, as
its primary purpose. As far as it goes, this is not wrong. St. John tells
us of his Gospel, for example: "Many other signs Jesus performed
also in the presence of the disciples, which are not written in this
book; but these have been written, that you may believe that Jesus
is the Christ, the Son of God; and that believing you may have life
in his name" (John 20:30-31). The difficulty arises when the modern theologians tell us that because there is an evangelistic intent, the
Gospels cannot contain true history. Here the German distinction
between *Geschichte* and *Historie* assumes great importance. *Geschichte* means meaningful events; *Historie* means occurrences which
can be verified by the work of historians. In English we usually distinguish between history and chronicle. History tells the events as
they happened, evaluates and interprets them; chronicle simply gives
what happened in its chronological order. Somehow in the minds of
many modern theologians the awareness that an event has real significance and evokes an emotional response or a decision of the will,
making it *Geschichte,* takes it right out of the realm of *Historie.* Historians can no longer discuss it in the language of their craft: it must
be left to theologians and the language of "faith."[22]

Thus the ordinary believer is confronted with a situation in which
the modern theologian seems to be calling for a higher piety than his.
The Resurrection of Christ is too great to be merely *historical*: it
must "break the frame of history." The difficulty is that this argument
misses or destroys the major point of revealed, biblical religion: the
God of Eternity and Infinity does act in human time and in human
space. To say that because it is more than historical it is not historical
is to do as the ancient Docetists did with Jesus: affirming him to be
more than a mere man, they said that he was not a man at all; he

became only a phantom. Of course the Resurrection of Christ must be more than *mere* history, like the account of Julius Caesar crossing the Rubicon. But it does not thereby cease to be true history.

The tendency of the form critics to turn an examination of forms into a repudiation of the content will not surprise anyone who has ever heard Bultmann's oft-repeated dictum: The Resurrection cannot be historical, *because dead men do not rise.* Form criticism, although sparked by an unbeliever, can be a valuable tool in examining the Bible, but only as long as one does not start with a principle like Bultmann's, which makes any alleged attempt to get at the "real meaning of the Resurrection narratives" a sick joke: "Dead men do not rise." Here too, then, modern theology shows itself to be part genuine insight, part unscientific and anti-Christian prejudice. The detailed problems raised by the form critics can be answered in detail, and satisfactorily, *if and only if* one does not begin by assuming that the Gospels cannot be true as they stand and seeking to find an alternate theory to replace the conviction of their truth. Here we must content ourselves with two observations: (1) Discussions about the *Sitz im Leben* of ancient texts by modern men cannot tell us, in the last analysis, not to trust the plain statements of ancient men who were willing to die to witness to the truthfulness of what they report. (2) Form criticism, like every other theological tool, becomes a deadly deceiver in the hands of those who, whether innocently or maliciously, operate on the basis of philosophical presuppositions disguised as scientific principles.

4. Discovery No. 3: Dialectical Theology as the Basic Content of the Bible

Here we are dealing with a proposition which would be almost ludicrous if it were not so serious. Having followed the methods, in discoveries 1 and 2, of men like Bultmann, we arrive at dialectical theology, i.e. the system of Karl Barth, one of Bultmann's bitterest adversaries. By following Bultmann and arriving at Barth, Voigt shows that he himself is a typical representative (or victim) of the modern mentality as represented in theology. He presents it not as a synthesis or reconciliation of opposites, but as a perfectly natural progression. Lest the reader think that Voigt is an inept or eccentric representative, let him recall that Bishop Robinson built his best-selling *Honest to God* out of the ideas of Bonhoeffer and of Tillich, two men whose basic convictions contradict each other. For modern theology, as for the modern mentality, formal contradictions are unimportant: formally meaningless language can be canonized.[23] By claiming Barth's great program of dialectical theology for modern theology, Voigt unwittingly shows his own captivity to non-rational thinking. On the other hand, in the process, he points up some fateful similarities in the convictions of Barth and his detested adversaries. By so doing, he reveals that Barth too has swallowed some of the strong brew of modern unreason, and that he is not as far from modern theology as he himself would like to be.[24]

(a) *What Is Dialectical Theology?* This question is complex, and for a full answer one must read the special literature. In brief, however, it is a humanly and theologically motivated reaction to nineteenth-century theological liberalism. The theology of the nineteenth century, with its optimistic faith in continuing human progress, saw no need of any such things as the revelation or the grace of a transcendent God. This optimistic immanentism was dealt a fatal blow by the experience of World War I, which destroyed the stability of Europe. At the same time, scholars like Albert Schweitzer and the early form critics were cutting the ground from under liberalism's simplified picture of a Jesus who taught the fatherhood of God and the brotherhood of man. They made it clear that the real Jesus of history had presented himself just as the Bible says, as the Son of God who would come in the clouds of heaven to judge the living and the dead.

This rediscovery of the eschatological element in Jesus' teaching, of the fact that he will come again as Judge as well as Saviour, was eminently suited to a war-weary world waking up to the criminal folly and determined perversity which comes so easily even to modern man. Barth reemphasized the sovereignty, holiness, and transcendence of God. God does not present himself to man in the Bible for man's evaluation, but in his Word he judges man.

In 1919, when Barth published his epoch-making *Commentary on Romans,* the emphasis on God's *otherness,* his transcendence, was a necessary and healthy note in a world sick to death of the things that were immanent in it, in man and his institutions. With Barth, men learned again to read the Bible not with the urbane detachment of a liberal professor, but with the awestruck heart of a Luther, who said, "When you hear the voice of God commanding, you tremble— and obey." In the pages of the Bible, as nowhere else, one encounters the commanding, challenging, judging, and redeeming Word of God himself.

(b) *The Weakness of Dialectical Theology.* The necessity of the revolt led by Barth was clear. Unfortunately, like many revolutions, it destroyed existing evils but did not build something better in their place. On principle, Barth's dialectical theology was too much a reaction. You can only tell a man that God cancels out his human attempts at righteousness so often, and then the man must begin to ask, "So what?" To that question dialectical theology, with its vision of God as *totally other,* had no satisfactory answer. In his approach to the Bible, Barth insisted that while it *becomes* God's Word to you in the existential situation of encounter, it is not God's Word as it stands.

As a result of the negative and reactionary aspect of his theology, Barth was doomed to lose the initiative to others. His reaction, his criticism of liberal theology, was a crying necessity in the early postwar era, but it could not satisfy people indefinitely. Barth himself began the construction of a new system, the monumental *Church Dogmatics,* which he never completed. But the world could not wait. New and strident voices were arising, voices which ultimately would do away with faith in the sovereign personal God and the divine Redeemer-Son whom Barth proclaimed, relegating them to the world of myth. No one would deplore this more than Barth, but with his lack of confidence in a *trustworthy* as well as authoritative Bible, he had no ground on which to stand to oppose them. It is no accident that his student Paul van Buren is now one of the most radical of modern theologians.

Voigt sees Barth and the really modern theologians as coinciding in their realization of the non-verifiability of God's claims on man— and in this he has put his finger on the sorest point in all of dialectical theology. Barth in fact believed in the Holy Trinity, the incarnation, virgin birth, atonement, resurrection, and second coming of Christ. Bultmann and his adherents do not. That is a vast difference.

But Barth believed that man has no right to question God or ask him to authenticate those challenging texts which claim to be his voice speaking to man. In his feeling that such a question jeopardizes God's divinity, Barth came around again to the humanity of the Bible, in modern theology's sense. But a God who will not let us ask him to show us that he is really there and is really God is a God who will not let man be man. If that is the God of dialectical theology, it is not the God of the Bible.

5. Conclusions

According to Voigt, modern theology, building on two partially valid discoveries, or rediscoveries, as the case may be, eventuates in the conclusion that dialectical theology is the central message of the Bible, which is false. Fundamentally, modern theology denies the historicity of the great biblical events, claiming that they never happened, but wanting to keep their meaning, their message, their challenge to decision. A dialectical theologian like Barth believes that they happened, but he denies their *Historizität* (historical verifiability). He does this to preserve the glory of God from debasing contact with man and matter. Barth's motive is nobler, but his result in too many cases is the same, just as Voigt shows: God is removed through an infinity of space and an eternity, and we can only hear an unverifiable voice in an erroneous Scripture calling on us to believe, to hope, and to obey. It is obvious that the figure of Barth, with his profound sense of awe before the majesty of God, and his deep reverence for Christ, is much more appealing than those of the arrogant modern theologians who correct Jesus and dismiss God. But we must be aware that Barth too, despite his attractiveness, contains no real solution, but gives us another version of an inaccessible God whom we may fear but can only trust irrationally, and thus ultimately inhumanly and falsely.

Thus despite their real differences, both modern and dialectical theology deny what is fundamental to biblical religion: that God acts in space and time, in real history, that he has, in fact, involved himself with man and matter. Philosophers have always found this to be demeaning to God, but God—and this is meant seriously and reverently—was big enough to do it, because he loves us. In the words of St. Irenaeus, "The Son of God became a Son of Man that sons of men might become the sons of God." That is the message of the Bible, that, and that it happened in our history—the nails in the cross of Christ were real—they could have nailed us. The stone rolled away from his tomb on Easter was real—it could have crushed us. The One who rose from the tomb is real, and alive, and he can save us. He can also judge us, and will or, as he says of whoever rejects him, "The word I spoke will judge him at the last day" (John 12:48).

The "modern mind" of the nineteenth century rejected those claims, and tried to prove them false. The dialectical theology of the twentieth century accepted them, but gave up every claim to test their truthfulness. The modern theology of today rejects them again, but not because of disproving them. Despite frequent claims to historical proofs, it is basically true that for modern theology, "faith is not interested in history." The confident "modern mind" of the turn of the century was shocked by and was repudiated by dialectical theology, but it was not defeated. Its optimism is gone, and its bourgeois morality, but its arrogance, its claim to totality is still there— and in the church we call it modern theology.

Notes

[1]The Creed of Chalcedon (451) was not accepted by the small branches of the church known as Monophysites. The efforts of the Roman Empire to impose the official creed of 451 by force contributed to unrest in Syria and Egypt which in turn facilitated the Moslem conquest of those lands. Recent study and discussion seems to show that the faith of the Monophysites (who confessed *one divine nature* in Jesus Christ as opposed to the orthodox doctrines of *two natures, divine and human*) was not so different in substance from what the orthodox meant by the formula adopted at Chalcedon. Awakening nationalism played a major role in these controversies; Syrians and Egyptians used the Monophysite movement to protest against the political supremacy of the orthodox Latins and Greeks at Constantinople.

[2]The belligerent German evangelical Dr. Gerhard Bergmann documents this

thoroughly in his new book, "Church at the Crossroads: Faith or Error" (*Kirche am Scheideweg. Glaube oder Irrglaube*. Gladbeck: Schriftenmissions-Verlag, 1967). An editor of the German news magazine *Der Spiegel*, Werner Harenberg, has devoted a whole volume to citing the mutually contradictory opinions of modern German theologians (*Jesus und die Kirchen. Bibelkritik und Bekenntnis*. Stuttgart: Kreuz-Verlag, 1966). Harenberg supports the *Spiegel's* general policy. This magazine, the most influential serious magazine in West Germany, consistently attempts to discredit all the traditional sources of order and authority in society, especially the German federal government, the Christian Democratic Party, and both major German churches. Nevertheless, it must be admitted that while Harenberg writes deliberately to discredit the Evangelical Church in Germany, his facts and quotations are accurate. NB. British and American usage of "evangelical" to refer to orthodox Protestantism and to emphasize the importance of individual faith and personal commitment must not be confused with the German designation "Evangelical" (*evangelisch*) which in practice means nothing more than Protestant in the most general sense.

[3]For a consideration of some of the methods of modern theology as applied to the Old Testament, see Kenneth A. Kitchen, *Ancient Orient and Old Testament* (London: Tyndale Press, and Chicago: Inter-Varsity, 1966).

[4]We should observe that many American radicals are not real *theologians* in the German sense, inasmuch as they do not develop their thinking on the basis of the biblical documents and accepted theological methodology. Altizer, for example, gives the works of Hegel, Nietzsche, and William Blake as the "sources" for his new atheistic Christianity. Even the most radical German theologians are too methodical to buy such a procedure. Consequently men like Altizer, despite their celebrity in America, are all but ignored by the German university professors whom they honor as their mentors.

[5]*Was will die moderne Theologie?* (Gelnhausen: Burckhardthaus Verlag, 1966). Quotations from this work used by permission. American readers can get an impression of what is going on in German theology, and of what is being imported into America by consulting the American translations of the important periodical, *Zeitschrift für Theologie und Kirche*, published by Gerhard Ebeling, one of the foremost post-Bultmannites: James M. Robinson, et al., editors, *Journal for Theology and the Church*, Volumes I, ff. (New York: Harper Torchbooks, 1965ff.).

[6]The classic work on this subject is from the pen of the Princeton theologian Benjamin B. Warfield: *Revelation and Inspiration*. The original Oxford University Press edition, now out of print, has been republished under the title *The Inspiration and Authority of the Bible* (Philadelphia: Presbyterian and Reformed, 1948). James I. Packer also gives it in *"Fundamentalism" and the Word of God* (London: Tyndale, and Grand Rapids: Eerdmans, 1958), and in *God Has Spoken* (London: Hodder and Stoughton, and Philadelphia: Westminster, 1965). See also John W. Montgomery, *Crisis in Lutheran Theology*, Vol. I (Grand Rapids: Baker, 1967), pp. 15-47.

[7]A tragic irony of modern theology is that it seems to be mired in an out-moded scientific world-view while claiming to be coming to terms with modern science. It is actually stuck back with nineteenth-century and early twentieth-century science (which may be quite understandable, inasmuch as the architects of modern theology got their exposure to the natural sciences at the turn of the century and then abandoned them for theology.

[8]Bonhoeffer, for example, speaks of the *powerlessness of God*. Bultmann makes his views abundantly clear: for him, the very concept of God acting in history is myth, as such incomprehensible to modern man, and to be rejected. For Tillich, God was effectively beyond all access, as "the God beyond God." Bishop Robinson combines all these elements in *Honest to God*, chapters 2 and 3. All of them have this in common: God disappears as a person who can act. Even Karl Barth, a conservative on doctrine and a critic of these modern theologians, seems to share something of the dangerous twentieth-century tendency to remove God from history, from anything with which we can have direct contact, by making him the "totally other." Where the personal God of history goes out, the impersonal god of pantheism eventually comes in, usually by way of a contentless mysticism stressing experience and rejecting doctrine. The modern example *par excellence* is the cult of L.S.D., meaningfulness without meaning.

[9]Voigt, *Moderne Theologie*, p. 8.

[10]Montgomery, *Crisis in Lutheran Theology*, Vol. I, p. 19.

[11]The antiquity of the charges as well as of their refutations can be seen in the Protestant classic by John W. Haley, *An Examination of the Alleged Discrepancies of the Bible* (Andover, 1874), reprinted in 1958 (Grand Rapids: Baker).

[12]Voigt, *Moderne Theologie*, p. 26.

[13]Werner Keller, *The Bible as History* (New York: William Morrow, 1956).

[14]For the general picture of the revisions which modern discovery should encourage modern theology to make in its major theories, see Carl F. H. Henry (editor), *Revelation and the Bible* (Grand Rapids: Baker, 1958), especially the articles by N. H. Ridderbos, "Reversals of Old Testament Criticism," pp. 333-350, and M. C. Tenney, "Reversals of New Testament Criticism," pp. 351-367. In addition to Kitchen's excellent book already cited (f.n. 3 above), one should consult his article, "Historical Method and Early Hebrew Tradition," *Tyndale Bulletin* (London) Vol. XVII (1966), pp. 63-97. Kitchen calls the work of Otto Eissfeldt, one of the most famous Old Testament scholars, "An able summary of a mass of speculation, but not history in any normal sense, while the contribution of external controls has been almost entirely dispensed with" (p. 64).

[15]In one of his famous courses in the late 1950's when he was still at Harvard, an overview of Western intellectual history, Arthur M. Schlesinger, Jr. used to interpret early Christianity as a perversion of Christ's teaching by Hellenistic philosophy. This view was *de rigeur* before World War I among liberal scholars such as Harnack (1851-1930), and involved the assumption

that St. John's Gospel was a second-century document because of its Hellenistic philosophical language. This language "proved" how much Hellenistic speculation had infected Christianity. But by the 1950's the discovery of the Dead Sea Scrolls had conclusively shown the complete Jewishness of John's language. Nevertheless Schlesinger did not revise his interpretation to fit the facts. Of course, he is not a professional theologian, but such neglect is not praiseworthy.

[16]Voigt, *Moderne Theologie*, p. 27.

[17]Eric L. Mascall, *The Secularisation of Christianity* (London: Darton, 1965; New York: Holt, 1966), p. 9.

[18]Hans Jonas, "Heidegger und die Theologie," *Evangelische Theologie* Vol. XXIV, No. 12 (December, 1964), p. 630; the English original, in *The Review of Metaphysics* for December, 1964, was not available to me.

[19]Bergmann gives an impressive and depressing number of examples of such theological arrogance in his work cited above (f.n. 2).

[20]See the article on Overbeck by P. Vielhauer in *Die Religion in Geschichte und Gegenwart*, 3rd edition (Tübingen: Mohr, 1960), Vol. IV, col. 1750-1751.

[21]F. F. Bruce, *The New Testament Documents* (London: Inter-Varsity, and Grand Rapids: Eerdmans, 5th ed. 1960) p. 33. On pp. 31ff., Professor Bruce, a classical historian turned biblical scholar, gives a short discussion of form criticism.

[22]We must write "faith" because when modern theology uses the term, it means something quite different from what historic Christianity means. See § 4 of this chapter.

[23]One of the leading extreme modern theologians writing in English, Paul van Buren, attacks orthodox theology on the grounds that, by the criteria of linguistic analysis, it makes meaningless statements (*The Secular Meaning of the Gospel*. London: S.C.M., 1963, pp. 1-7 and following). However, as Eric Mascall shows in *The Secularisation of Christianity*, pp. 40-105, van Buren's own language is even more meaningless. Of course the variety of Christianity which van Buren takes under fire is less the old orthodoxy than the neo-orthodoxy begun by Barth, which denies that religious truth can be verified. J. W. Montgomery examines the meaningfulness of the language of modern theology in *Crisis in Lutheran Theology*, pp. 25-44.

[24]Karl Barth, who died on December 9, 1968 in Basel, is a hard man to analyse. He is fervently attacked as a hopeless conservative by modern theologians, and his monumental writings often lie unread. Yet as Voigt suggests, Barth has more in common with modern theology than he likes to admit. The problem is this: a man who believes as Barth believes may be a sound Christian in his own life, but he is incapable of communicating the truth of historic Christianity to the next generation. Paul van Buren, a figure in God-is-dead-theology, did his doctorate under Barth. For a sympathetic but careful evangelical evaluation of Barth, see Colin Brown, *Karl Barth and the Christian Message* (London: Tyndale and Chicago: Inter-Varsity, 1967). Brown gives helpful advice for further reading on pp. 154-159.

Chapter 10

· ALTERNATIVES TO
BIBLICAL AUTHORITY ·

Then goeth he, and taketh to him seven other spirits more wicked than himself; and they enter in, and dwell there, and the last state of that man is worse than the first.

Luke 11:26

Our secular theologians tell us that Jesus' story about the man whose evil spirit left him, only to return later with seven others more wicked than himself, belongs to the realm of myth. There are some very good reasons for not consigning the views Jesus held on evil spirits to mythology, but quite apart from its theological implications, his story has a very practical one. Getting rid of one guest —or master—you do not like does no good if the vacancy is quickly filled by worse ones. This is something that does not happen only in biblical parables. It happens in life, both to individuals and to societies.

Revelation and Reason

No thoughtful Christian would accept a parallel between an authoritative revelation as Christianity has it in the Bible and the evil spirit of Jesus' story. For the Christian, an authoritative, understandable revelation is a precious treasure, not a hard master. Unfortunately, as Western culture has moved farther and farther from its Christian base, all too many Christians have swallowed the pervasive suggestion that biblical authority is somehow oppressive and a constraint on human freedom. Objectively speaking, such a suggestion is false. To accept it is to abandon the whole biblical message, which is convinced that it is precisely the authority of God and of his Word which makes human freedom possible. Even without accepting the biblical position on its own authority, we can see that the widespread conviction that an authoritative revelation is a threat to freedom has opened the gates to far worse threats.

However we may wish to evaluate America's goals and strategy in World War II, one thing is abundantly clear: an excessive preoccupation with the threat represented by Nazi Germany (and, to a lesser extent, by Japan) virtually blinded us to the possibility of other threats. The result was that anti-democratic tyranny controls more of the world after World War II than it did before. The specifically Nazi evil of genocide has been banned, it is true—although even with respect to genocide, suspicious-looking parallels are cropping up here and there.

The only parallel which should be drawn between biblical authority and the Nazi menace of the 1930's and '40's is to say that many educators, sociologists, and clergymen seem to look upon biblical authority as the political leaders of the 1940's looked on Nazism. It is seen as *the* barrier to peace, happiness, and prosperity for modern man. We would not call the spirit of biblical authority an evil spirit, but we will admit that when it is banished, seven or more really evil ones have free entry into the house of our intellect.

(a) *Authoritative Revelation and a Definite Content.* Christianity, like the religion of Israel before it, was grounded on the fundamental concept of an authoritative revelation expressed in ordinary, understandable, human language. No early Jew or Christian would have dreamed that God told man everything about Himself in the Bible, nor would he have claimed a perfect understanding of everything in it. But the church, like Israel, knew that the words of the Bible are God's words, to be believed, learned, obeyed, and trusted. In fact, even modern, hypercritical biblical scholarship bears a kind of strange testimony to the divine origin of the content—the words—of the Bible by its intense preoccupation with them. One of the great goals of "liberal," rationalistic biblical criticism, which it thinks it has fully achieved, was to destroy the concept that the words of the Bible are directly inspired and stand in a definite relationship to what God wants to say to us. However, to achieve this doubtful triumph, it has studied the *words* of the Bible with a detailed fascination which would be reasonable only if they were actually uttered by God, but not if they were nothing more than the literary precipitate of a nomadic people's religious exaltation.

A major tactic in the rationalistic attack on historic Christianity has been to attack the details while claiming to respect the substance, to challenge the *content* while claiming to revere the *authority* of Christian revelation. To a certain limited degree, this tactic appears justified, even to the most orthodox Christian, because undoubtedly there are problems of detail in the transmission of the biblical texts as well as with certain traditional interpretations of them. But once it progresses beyond a certain elementary level, an attack on details inevitably imperils the substance; a challenge to the specific, definite content of revelation is a challenge to its authority.

The link between a definite content and binding authority is obvious in one direction: if certain texts, propositions, commands, promises come, in their definite content, from God, they obviously have an authority which we must recognize by accepting, believing, obeying, and trusting them. But coming from the other direction, it is often felt that we can have a kind of Authority without a definite content, a "Word of God" without any definite words of God. At first glance, such a feeling may appear more reverent and humble than the orthodox position, which seems to bind the almighty God to paltry human words. We should humbly bow before the Voice of God, but we must not presume to claim that we know what the Voice is saying. Such apparent reverence is only a cloak for human self-assertion, for if God has not said anything definite and understandable (which means identifiable *words* of God making up the Word of God), then we have no definite obligations to him. We can act in accordance with our own judgment or inclinations.

Ultimately, no matter how much we talk about the Word of God and its authority, about recognizing God's infinity and our finiteness, or use any other such language which seems to preserve a fitting reverence for him, unless we are willing to recognize his authority in the details of the content of revelation, we cannot have his authority at all. We end at best with something as vague as Schleiermacher's absolute dependence or Rudolf Otto's sense of awe, or with the even less Christian reverence for life of Schweitzer or ultimate concern of Paul Tillich. No matter how willingly man may incline himself before the Idea of the Holy or the Mystery of the Universe, if he never recognizes a specific word from God as authoritative, he remains his own authority in everything specific. That is to say, he is a law unto himself unless in specific situations he is willing to submit himself to a definite law of God.

(b) *Definite Content* vs. *Acclamation and Development.* Attacks on the details of biblical revelation (apart from a few special and technical considerations not treated here) generally do not arise out of intellectual difficulties with the details themselves, but from a prior decision in favor of a rival philosophical, moral, or religious principle. In other words, we do not reject certain details of biblical revelation because we find them to be false, but we find them to be false because we have already rejected them. Among the most characteristic prior reasons for finding fault with specific details of biblical revelation is a shift of allegiance from the concepts of divine authority and absolute, eternal truth to those of relative authority and relative truth.

The intellectual, theological situation has been complicated—as is always the case with the complex creature man—by confusion and interaction between the spheres of God's authority, religious authority, and political authority. The claim of biblical authority upon our understanding and obedience is quite different in principle from that of any political authority to maintain a certain governmental and social structure. The one really *is* based on divine right, the other largely on traditional and other secondary factors. However in practice the claims of the church or the churches, the Bible, and of traditional theology have often been thoroughly intermingled and confused with mere conservatism, traditionalism, and the defense of established privileges and vested interests. The political revolutionaries sought to replace the real or imagined stability of the ancient imperial and monarchial structures with a flexibility and movement which would permit progress. A similar confidence that change means improvement and that the voice of the majority is the voice of truth has contaminated theological discussions, where it is completely out of place.

Theology is just as much a victim of the prejudice that change means improvement as is the social order, and this prejudice is even more dangerous in theology than in politics. If there ever was an authoritative revelation, then change from it means degeneration, not improvement. The theologian's aim should be to conserve the precious heritage of an authoritative, reliable divine revelation, and to apply it meaningfully to his own people and age. Of course pure conservatism in theology can be deadening, and has often been so in the history of Christianity. Christian faith is like breath: if you hold it, you die. But the fact that one must breathe in and out several times a minute does not mean that the air must be different from minute to minute. Quite the contrary is true: the air must be the same from moment to moment, with virtually identical constituent elements necessary. Theology must be fresh if the church and the individual Christian are to live, but it must not be different. Once the popular and uncritical prejudice in favor of change has been allowed to seep over into theology, it is perfectly obvious that the concept of an authoritative revelation, of a faith once delivered, must go. In general, it is the content or contents of revelation which are attacked first and most vehemently, not its authority. Its authority may be defended, even exalted. In fact, one is frequently told that the contents *must* be attacked (corrected, brought up to date), precisely in order to safeguard the authority of the Bible or of the church. But once the principle of change for the sake of change has been accepted in the realm of theology, then it is only a matter of time before the whole deposit of faith, including even the most essential elements, has disintegrated and disappeared. In eighteenth-century theology, the detailed attacks began; in mid-twentieth-century theology, the substance is gone. We speak of "theology after the death of God."

Dietrich Bonhoeffer is famous for his plea for "religionless Christianity," which has been interpreted by his devotees as a program to preserve some kind of an "essence" of Christianity while dispensing with all of its definite and specific parts, which are relegated to the realm of the religious. Whether or not Bonhoeffer has been fairly interpreted by those who have come after him,* his desire to free Christianity of its religious elements was based on his conviction that

---

*It is difficult to pass judgment on Bonhoeffer, whose life was cut short by a Nazi execution. He has become a hero to the "death of God" and secular theologians. For an analysis and criticism of "religionless Christianity," see Leon Morris, *Religionless Christianity?* (Chicago: Inter-Varsity, 1964).

man has made basic changes and thus requires a changed religion—
or actually, not a religion at all, but a religionless Christianity. Thus
the progress which man has made, or thinks he has made, becomes
the standard by which to correct the words once uttered by God. To
make man's real or supposed progress the standard for judging the
revelation of God is either to say that there is no God—which Bonhoeffer was unwilling to say—or that he does not reveal himself or
act in any definite way. This is precisely what Bonhoeffer has led
to, if he did not himself believe it. His concept of the "powerlessness
of God" to act in real history—so absolutely contrary to the biblical
picture of him—leads us to suspect that Bonhoeffer really did turn
his back on an authoritative revelation, to place his confidence in "the
world come of age." The term is Bonhoeffer's, but the idea is much
older.

The eighteenth-century German dramatist and critic, G. E. Lessing, in his *On the Education of the Human Race,* put forward the
theory that revelation was a necessary aid to man in his early years,
but that as the race advanced, it could do away with divine revelation
and rely on its maturing reason. It is no accident that Lessing published and defended the work of Samuel Reimarus after the latter's
death. Reimarus was one of the first theologians to attempt to reduce
the stature of Christ without explicitly repudiating Christianity. In
this, he set a pattern which has now become all but universal among
academic theologians.

Reimarus, like so many of those who have come after him, denied
the accuracy of the content of the biblical revelation about Christ,
but wanted to preserve his moral authority. He was to become a kind
of constitutional monarch, ruling men not on the basis of any inherent
authority of his own, but on the basis of a kind of social contract
made with him by reasonable human beings. Man was not to respect
Christ as the divine Son of God, but was to concede to him the honor
due him because of his moral excellence. Here the eighteenth century's confidence in man's inevitable moral progress and in the right-
ness of a majority decision coalesce. Lessing thought that primitive
man had to be cowed into submission to Christ by vesting him with
the authority of God, while modern (i.e. eighteenth-century) man
would willingly concede to him a high moral authority, as it were, by
acclamation.

In practice, this substitution might seem to have no harmful effects. Indeed, it can be argued that obedience based on a reasonable respect is better than that based on fear. But in this case this "reasonable respect" involves a basic misunderstanding of who Christ really is. It is a substitution of our image of him for his reality. Since a true knowledge of Christ is a necessary condition for eternal life according to his own teaching (John 17:3), this substitution has very serious consequences. Jesus himself said and did enough in the New Testament to convince us that we should love, trust, and respect him, not fear him. But it is precisely for what he is, as the New Testament portrays him, that we are to love, trust, and respect him—not for our own evaluation of him as a moral paragon. Finally, the desire to respect Jesus' authority in general without accepting it on anything particular has no practical value. The Christ who is merely the Good and Gentle Master, and not the Lord of Glory, can soon be pressed into the service of any ideal and of any morality whatsoever.

In one important respect, the revolt of the eighteenth and subsequent centuries against an authoritative revelation with a definite content is justified. The human mind can never be truly free, in one specialized sense of the word free, if there really is such a thing as an authoritative word with content spoken by a real God. If the highest good for man consists in unbounded freedom, then contentful revelation must go, because any content whatsoever would communicate something to be believed and to be obeyed, thus establishing an authority for us and limiting our absolute freedom. Again we have come back to the conflict between freedom and authority. If the Christian is right in recognizing the authority of God in the Bible, he cannot abandon it in quest of any concept of freedom. But we must not allow the problem to be expressed in terms of this fundamentally misleading opposition. We must go back and ask what freedom really is. In so doing, we will see that there is a good case for believing that true freedom, rather than being challenged by biblical authority, is established by it, and that the freedom one can gain by rejection of biblical authority is a false freedom, which leads to new and terrible tyrannies.

Two Different Conceptions of Freedom

The apparent conflict between an authoritative revelation and human freedom results from a failure to distinguish between two different concepts of freedom. For the sake of clarity, we shall refer to them as *Christian freedom* and *secular freedom*. By secular freedom we mean a concept of freedom which defines itself entirely within the temporal horizon of this material world in which we live.

Orthodox Christianity gives an important place to the concept of freedom. Jesus, citing Isaiah, spoke of himself as "proclaiming freedom" (Luke 4:18,21), and promised to make his followers "free indeed" (John 8:36). Christian freedom is a major emphasis in the teaching of St. Paul, and runs through the history of Christian theology. It is only especially prominent in Luther. Unfortunately when biblical authority is attacked in the name of freedom, conservative Christians often fly to defend authority without pausing to examine the attackers' credentials to speak for freedom. They fail to recognize that the attack on biblical authority is not for the sake of freedom *per se*, but for a particular concept of freedom, *viz.* secular freedom. When a conservative Christian chooses to defend biblical authority, he does well, but when he lets his opponents brand the argument as one between freedom and authority, he commits a double error, tactical and terminological. Defending authority against freedom is bound to be unpopular in any generation. Not only is this wrong tactics, it is wrong terminology, because secular freedom, according to the Christian conception, is a delusion, and ought never to be accepted, neither as a reason for opposing biblical authority, nor as a valid concept of freedom.

The historic, biblical Christian, who believes in the personal God of the Bible, honors him as his Creator, loves him as his Redeemer, and stands in awe of him as his Judge. He knows that he is called to be the servant of this God. To say servant alone does not fully correspond to the biblical vision of Christian man, who is not merely God's servant but also his child and his heir, but the Christian's relationship to God definitely and clearly includes the aspect of *service*, and this implies obedience. To this extent, then, the Christian is limited in his freedom, if by freedom we understand the absence of every restraint. On the other hand, we must not fail to see that secular man, who trumpets his freedom over against the Christian's subjugation to biblical authority, is not so confident that he is free once he is away from the Christian-secularist debate.

All too often the Christian, conscious of his own obligations and of the difficulty he has in fulfilling them, accepts the misleading picture of himself as fundamentally a servant and of the secular man as fundamentally free. Not only Christian theology should tell him that this is false: his powers of observation should do the same thing. The secular man would like to contrast the Christian's servitude with his own absolute freedom, which would consist in his having no master over him. If there were in fact no such master, the secular man would indeed be free, and the Christian in bonds, however easy his bonds and generous his master. But to accept this picture of freedom is to misread the facts. The Christian does not look upon himself as a strong, independent being, master of his world, free to act independently or to render voluntary obedience where he sees fit. Lessing and Reimarus, in the particular atmosphere of the eighteenth-century Enlightenment, might believe that; it is harder for us today. Today it is far easier for us to recognize man as the plaything of gigantic forces over which he has no control. Jesus' picture of the man who lost one evil spirit only to have him return with seven worse ones must seem much more plausible to us than it did to Lessing. The world is full of many masters seeking to enslave man, but there is One who wants man to be not only his servant, but his child and heir. Service to this Master is really freedom; "freedom" from him means to become the spoil of the others.

The secularist's confident posture of freedom is asserted over against the Christian view of authority, but within his own circle, he continually confesses—or proclaims—his lack of real freedom. And how can he really claim to be free, when his anthropology, his psychology, his cosmology all deny it? Prevailing theories of human evolution make the decisions of individuals, if not unreal, at least irrelevant in the light of inevitable evolutionary progress. Rival schools of psychology, both Freudian and behavioristic, deny man's freedom to make either good or evil choices: everything he does is determined by antecedent factors over which he has no control. The evolutionary optimism of Teilhard de Chardin is *religious* but not Christian or biblical—which is why it can be greeted with such optimism by an optimistic, evolutionary humanist like Sir Julian Huxley. Disinterested in revelation, Teilhard's theory acknowledges no authority other than inevitable progress, and although he equates this with the God of revelation and with Christ, this equation is virtually meaningless. Without an authoritative revelation, there is no such thing as a binding theological or moral judgment. And without the possibility of judgment, of a definitive and valid difference between the moral value of actions, there is no real freedom. Even our new and awesome power to destroy all mankind becomes irrelevant in the light of the popular theory that ours is but one of countless civilizations in the universe.

Modern secular man proclaims his unfreedom when he wants to shirk personal responsibility for some course of action, but he is not happy with his lack of freedom. Much modern music, art and literature exposes modern man's deep feeling of being trapped forever, a helpless prisoner in a blind universe. Another artistic current celebrates a kind of total freedom—the kind that eventuates first in the chaos and then the terrible bondage of drugs. When the secularists are left to themselves, they are well enough aware of their lack of freedom. Those who optimistically assert human freedom in a secular context are more often than not the products of a Christian background and have not been secularist long enough to sense what truly secular men know all too well.

We can be grateful to the extreme advocates of a secular freedom for the fact that they so clearly show the hollowness of the secular vision of freedom. The philosopher Herbert Marcuse, an idol of the new anarchist left in Germany (who has also influenced certain American "death of God" theologians), advocates the use of narcotics as an expression of total freedom and total protest. Compared to Marcuse, whose "freedom" implies slavery to drugs, even the radical Commune II of West Berlin is more reasonable. The Commune wants to rebel against the "tyranny" of bourgeois society in favor of Mao Tse-tung, but at least Mao's dominance is that of a human mind: the dominance to which Marcuse would open the door is mindless. There certainly are *some* secularistic advocates of freedom who would also resist Mao or bondage to drugs, but the fact that so many of them would not casts a dark shadow over the credibility of this secular vision of freedom.

The Christian must defend authority, but not against *freedom*. He defends it against *secular* freedom, because secular freedom is a fraud in which even the secularists never believe for long. The Christian defends biblical authority precisely because it gives him true freedom. The Christian concept of freedom is not that it consists in a total absence of every master, but in having a good and loving master. The Bible does not portray man as having a choice between dependence on God and independence, but between the service of sonship and the servitude of slavery.

The difference between Christian freedom and the fraud of secular freedom is that the true God is big enough to want children, while the "god of this world" wants only slaves. According to its own theory, secular freedom is service to no one, but in fact it easily becomes service to harsh and hateful ones. Christian doctrine tells us that this enslavement to tyrannical masters is the *inevitable* result of rebellion against the loving Father, but even without Christian doctrine we can observe that it takes place with great regularity.

The authority of biblical revelation limits man, it is true. Being in part propositional in form, using ordinary language and giving some clear commands and prohibitions, biblical revelation shows man certain limits within which he must keep. But within these limits he achieves a fulfillment impossible anywhere else, coming to enjoy what St. Paul calls "the glorious liberty of the children of God" (Romans 8:21). There is no reason for the Christian to be ashamed of this view of freedom—neither on its own merits, nor by comparison with the spurious freedom of secular man.

The propositional aspect of biblical revelation, i.e. the fact that it makes statements which are intended to be taken as statements of fact, is crucial. Revelation tells us who we are by pointing out to us our *limits,* defining us as creatures over against God the Creator, and as rebellious creatures over against the just Judge. If there were not this propositional, definite, and understandable aspect to biblical revelation, the limits would not be limits, and we could understand neither the fact that we are creatures nor the promise that we can be God's children. Cutting away the definite, propositional nature of biblical revelation only apparently increases our freedom. If we claim the freedom to disregard the explicit nature of God's commands on the grounds that they are historically conditioned, disregarding all that displeases us, we have no right to regard his promises as true, simply because they please us more than the commands. The two are too closely tied. Freedom to disobey the commands of God is a poor exchange for the loss of the glorious liberty of the children of God. We should beware of every attempt to generalize the specific commandments and injunctions of the Bible into vague general principles. Naturally they have principles behind them, but in many clear cases it is the specificness of the commandments which protects the principles. For example, the German theologian Rudolf Bultmann defines sin as "unwillingness to accept the fact that one is a creature." This definition has a considerable amount of truth in it, but it is precisely by disregarding explicit words of God that we clearly demonstrate our unwillingness to accept our creatureliness. Bultmann has thrown out explicit, binding revelation, claiming to preserve the substance with his general definitions. But the general definitions are meaningless without the specific cases which either fulfil or violate them, and these we can have only if we accept revelation as definite and specific. The loss of definiteness does not increase our freedom, but diminishes it, for it destroys our confident relationship to the Good Master and leaves us easy victims for a host of bad ones.

The Harsh Masters

To reject biblical authority *necessarily* results in our subjugation by a far harsher master, if the Bible is true. The fact that this biblical prediction is so often borne out in practice does not prove the authority of the Bible, but it ought to encourage us to take it seriously. Recent and contemporary history offers us countless examples of the bondage into which man plunges himself when he rejects the definite authority of God. German philosophers and theologians at the turn of the century thought that they were freeing Germany from the rule of Christianity. However, in destroying the moral structure of Christianity in Germany, they paved the way for Germany's insane slavery to Adolf Hitler. At the moment we in the United

States are claiming, ever more loudly, the "freedom" to disregard Christian moral teachings in many areas, especially in the area of sex. Who is to guarantee us that our boldly won "freedom" from traditional Christian morality will not result in a chaos from which we will beg a new tyrant to rescue us? The chaos is already beginning to develop, and more than one candidate for the role of tyrant "saviour" is already grooming himself on the sidelines.

The alternatives to guidance by authoritative biblical revelation are many. As we lose the structure which Christianity has provided, we also lose the ability to distinguish between the good, the bad, and even the horrible among the many masters who rise to claim our allegiance. The fact that Germany could fall to Nazism or that a philosopher can "crusade" for narcotics in the name of freedom is not an unfortunate cloud on the horizon. It is part of a general storm which inevitably results from the loss of a clear structure of values. Other cultures may have a more or less successful non-Christian basis for their values; individuals in our Christianized culture may also have a different but effective basis for personal morality. If Christianity is true at all, it is true for the non-Christian as well as for the Christian, but it is precisely within the context of a society that has been Christianized that the loss of the Christian structure is most devastatingly evident.

To cite examples of all the various types of harsh masters who beckon to us would be an endless task. The allegation that it is very difficult for "free" secular man to recognize a tyrant can be sufficiently well illustrated with reference to certain intellectuals' flirtations with Mao, or with drugs, but the clearest evidence of all, in our scientific age, is given by their flirtations with witchcraft, spiritualism, and the occult.

A certain amount of interest has been raised in our country by word of the revival of witchcraft in England, where according to some reports there are many thousand practitioners of this "ancient religion." Americans have also been treated, from time to time, with news of a cult of Satan-worshippers in California. These phenomena are not jokes; they have sinister implications. In a well-documented study, German theologian Kurt Koch has described the tremendous fascination which exists in Germany today for the world of evil spirits and magic. Without attempting to prove the reality of the spirits with which his subjects claim to be in contact (although he does not discount it), Koch gives a mass of evidence for the reality and disastrous nature of the consequences of this fascination for the mental health of those involved in it.[1] Kurt Hutten, director of the Protestant Center for Philosophical Questions in Stuttgart, Germany, has amassed a great body of information to substantiate his claim that superstition is increasing, not decreasing, as Christian faith loses its hold in modern Europe.

We have already referred to the former Episcopal Bishop of California, James A. Pike. Once hailed as a spokesman for a new kind of Christianity emancipated from the fetters of traditionalism, he has more recently embarrassed his admirers with his open enthusiasm for spiritualism. From within our Christian structure of truth, which is shaped by a revelation we acknowledge as true and authoritative, we can make distinctions between the human tyranny of a Mao, the mindless tyranny of drugs, and the demonic tyranny of occultism. For those who deliberately reject it, however, what St. Paul said holds true: professing themselves to be wise, they become fools (Romans 1:22).

There are indeed many alternatives to the authoritative biblical revelation and the internally consistent world-view which accompanies it. Unfortunately, the empirical evidence confirms the biblical warning: those who repudiate the knowledge of God end by not understanding anything, and by subjecting themselves, in one way or another, to the power of darkness. History and contemporary life offer us manifold examples, from Lord Russell to Bishop Pike, to see the melancholy but true fulfillment of Jesus' words, "The last state of that man is worse than the first."

Note

[1]*Christian Counseling and Occultism* (Grand Rapids: Kregel, 1965).

Chapter 11

· THEOLOGY AND THE
TOTAL CULTURE ·

If ye were of the world, the world would love its own.

John 15:19

The Roman Catholic Church must beware of contamination by radical unbelief disguised as Protestant scholarship. Protestantism must beware of unreformed Romanist expansionism disguised as polite ecumenicity. Individual Christians must beware of relativist brainwashing in their own congregations. Congregations must take care lest "progressive" elements in the World Council of Churches turn their denominations into political action groups to work together for a vision of a revolutionary, Marxo-Christian secular city. No nation as it exists today may presume to call itself a Christian nation, yet no nation dare cut itself off from its Christian heritage without risking the destruction of its own moral order and the punitive anger of God.

What can anyone, theologian, church leader, or individual Christian do in such a situation, with pitfalls on every side, dangers from above and tremors from below? Is there any solid ground? Is anyone or anything orthodox enough to satisfy the conservative, biblical, historical Protestant? Is anyone catholic enough to satisfy the *Christian* ecumenist? Is anyone sufficiently coherent, in the wonderland of twentieth-century religion, to satisfy the *rationally thinking* Christian?

There is—of this we can be confident—a solid, reliable core of Christian doctrine, common to all the major branches of Christendom, which we can call *basic,* or in C. S. Lewis' words, *mere* Christianity.[1] All the major churches, to the extent that they actually mean their creeds, possess this core in a formal sense. It is this common possession of real essentials which makes ecumenism thinkable for the orthodox Christian (although the extent to which a common faith in the essentials characterizes current ecumenism is quite another matter). Unfortunately formal adherence to the major creeds, even where it still exists, is inadequate to guarantee the preservation of the substance of historic Christianity in the total intellectual and cultural climate of our age.

There are two reasons for this. First, although the fourth- and fifth-century creeds and the sixteenth- and seventeenth-century confessions set forth truths which are as essential today as they were when they were first pronounced, these documents were drawn up to meet particular challenges, and the threats today lie on a different level. The Arians, against whom the Nicene Creed of 325 (amplified in 381) was drawn up, had so much in common with the orthodox or Athanasian party that it could be said that the quarrel was over an iota. (The orthodox said that Jesus Christ was *homoousios* with the Father, of the same nature; the Arians said that he was *homoiousios,* of a similar nature.) Of course the iota, the difference between *homos* and *homoios,* between *the same* and *alike,* is momentous. It means a great deal whether Jesus Christ is God made man, or was merely a good man who resembled God. Jesus' relationship to God the Father is crucial for Christian doctrine and theology, but at least the Arians agreed with the orthodox about the reality of the personal God and about the fact that God acts in history. Today we must go back behind statements of faith such as the Nicene Creed to recover basic constituents of the Christian understanding of God, the world, and man. Therefore in Chapter 6 a list of basic Christian doctrines was given which is not identical with the ancient creeds or with the confessions of the great denominations. And this brings us to the second reason why formal adherence to the major creeds is insufficient. They not only started with an assumed consensus on some doctrinal matters, which the fourth century did not need to state explicitly but we do, but they also presupposed that words mean something, that such a thing as contradiction exists, and that a formal confession of faith also involves a moral and an intellectual commitment.

Just as the Apostles' Creed was formulated against a particular heresy and does not explicitly speak of the Atonement or of individual conversion, and as the great sixteenth- and seventeenth-century confessions say nothing about some questions which are vital today, the list of doctrines given in Chapter 6 will probably not correspond to the needs of a subsequent generation. *But to recognize the legitimate variety of doctrinal emphasis which may be appropriate to a particular age and intellectual climate is never to say that Christian truth is relative to our age.* In the mid-twentieth century much more is necessary than merely to repeat the Apostles' Creed in a liturgical setting. But having said this, let us be perfectly clear about the fact that we too must confess and mean what the Apostles confessed and what the creed which bears their name[2] preserves—and not as "a testimony to the faith of the church," but as our own understood and felt commitment.[3]

The problem of the Christian in the last third of the twentieth century is often called a problem of communication, but this is true only in the second place. In the first place, it is a problem of content: before we begin to try to "communicate Christianity," we must be sure of the content. We must be sure that our content is identical to that of historic Christianity, or we have nothing worthwhile to communicate; and we must understand the content ourselves, or the most advanced techniques in the world will only enable us to spread confusion more efficiently.

1. The Total Culture and Our Understanding of Christianity

The late Paul Tillich virtually created a whole new language in his effort to make religion relevant to modern man. Billy Graham, by contrast, recommends teaching modern men to understand the old language. Because Tillich taught something quite different from historic Christianity, one may question whether he actually really helped the people whom he succeeded in interesting in his system. Whenever Graham preaches, using the historic concepts, many people respond. But when one considers the climate from which they come, one must ask how many of those who make "decisions" have even begun to understand what is meant by it. The modern intellectual climate has not only produced celebrated "theologians" who openly teach atheism. It also produces people who, with the best of intentions, publicly commit themselves to the ancient language of the historic faith without ever really coming to terms with its substance. Somewhere between the truth which the evangelist proclaims and the sincerity with which people often respond, something intervenes which prevents many of them from ever arriving at what they are seeking. This something we could call the mentality of the mid-twentieth-century man, but since it is not so much a characteristic of the individual as of the whole intellectual climate, we shall call it the *total culture.*

(a) *The Lost Christian Consensus.* When the great nineteenth-century evangelist Dwight L. Moody went among the Union troops in the War between the States, men would often beg him, "Tell me what I must do to be saved." Such men were precisely *not* convinced Christians, but the question reveals an awareness of the fundamental predicament of man as the Bible portrays him: apart from God, lost, and incapable of saving himself. Moody could speak to such men in simple, clear language, and they could understand him. When the twentieth-century evangelist Billy Graham says the same thing, a large percentage of his hearers is simply incapable of grasping his message—and this percentage must include many who are sufficiently moved by him to "come forward."

The central fact of our mid-twentieth century mentality is the complete lack of a coherent framework within which people can give order to the various segments which make up their lives and their personal relationships. A man may have many meaningful areas in his life: his work, his relationship to his wife—even his religious observance. But there is no overall framework which holds the different pieces together and makes the whole make sense. The triumph of the forces of evil in our generation is not the causing of such things as Auschwitz and Hiroshima,[4] but the destroying, for most twentieth-century people, of any overall framework, and of the very concept that such a framework is possible or desirable. This lack becomes painfully clear in the attempt to make the Christian message meaningful to modern men and women.

The depth of this problem is not at once evident. Leighton Ford, Billy Graham's brother-in-law and associate, affirms that many people are waiting to hear the simple message he brings and that they respond to it eagerly.[5] This is undoubtedly true. On the other hand, Dietrich Bonhoeffer has said harsh things about the evangelists who must first convince modern man, who according to Bonhoeffer is mature, self-reliant, and confident, that he is *lost* before trying to persuade him to be *saved*. Many theologians have taken Bonhoeffer's despondent lines from a Nazi prison of the 1940's as an authoritative injunction against preaching salvation in the 1960's,[6] but Bonhoeffer's estimate seems to have been wrong. The problem is not that people will not listen to an evangelist like Graham. Large numbers of them gladly listen to him. It is not even that they will not respond. Substantial numbers do. It is that even when they have listened, and even when they have responded, they still may not understand. In many cases *they cannot understand*, because even when changing their formal loyalties, and accepting the language of evangelism, or of Catholic spirituality, they still remain prisoners of the total culture. Instead of being transformed by the Gospel and thereby liberated from the tyranny of their environment, they transform the Gospel so that it says the same thing as the total culture.

The problem is precisely *not* what Bonhoeffer, surrounded by the blood and madness of Nazism, said it was: that modern man has no felt religious need. The trouble is that he still *feels* the need, and that he feels it as religious, but that he lacks the framework for distinguishing between one religious answer and another, or even for realizing that he should distinguish. There are plenty of people who feel lost, meaningless, unfulfilled, but for many of them the necessary intellectual framework, on which the evangelist builds his appeal, is simply not there. With a part of the audience, it is there; when they make "a decision for Christ" they understand what they are doing. With another, larger part the foundation is not there. They may not even understand who God is supposed to be, according to the Bible, not to mention actually believe in him.

This does not stop such people from coming forward, from "committing their lives to Christ," any more than it prevents them from taking L.S.D. to have a religious experience. Such people are genuine twentieth-century men and women. What distinguishes them from Dwight Moody's audiences of the previous century is not that they do not have any religious longings, nor that they do not sense their lostness. The difference—and it is a fundamental one—is that they do not know how to evaluate their lostness. They have no meaningful conceptual framework into which to fit it.

Thus the problem is not, as Bonhoeffer sighed and Robinson primly repeats, that modern man no longer has any religious sense, and is confident of his own secular maturity. On the contrary, here Paul Tillich, with his belief that man is fundamentally religious, was right. As the organized, main-line churches, led by up-to-date theologians like Bishop Robinson, cease to provide any *religious* solutions, modern man does not heave the grateful sigh they expect and pay his tithe with new enthusiasm. Instead, he turns to a thousand other equally *religious*, but far less scientifically, historically, *modernly* creditable solutions than that of historic Christianity—to tailor-made, Westernized Hinduism or Buddhism, to the religion of L.S.D. and psychedelic happenings, to myriad superstitions and even to the world of the occult. Modern man is no more immune than the ancient Hebrews to the biblical principle that the alternative to worshipping the true God is to worship idols—or demons.

We tend to react with tolerant amusement to reports on the number of self-professed witches in England, or to the rise of a cult of Satan-worshippers in Los Angeles. But these things are not amusing. Nor are they some kind of accidental throwback to a pre-scientific age, something that will disappear as science and education continue their triumphant march. They are part and parcel of the "world come of age." The fact is that science is no defense against superstition, nor even against belief in spiritualism, traffic with demons and the occult. Bishop Pike's famous flirtation with spiritualism is not an isolated incident to be explained in terms of the personal tragedies which have befallen him: it really belongs to the story of "mature" twentieth-century man. In 1965 there was for a time a spiritualist circle at Harvard University; until it became abundantly clear what it was, this circle was able to use a Ford Foundation grant for Harvard cultural events to provide the participants a private dinner before each seance. Science is no defense against superstition—and worse.[7]

The problem is thus not that modern man is not open to anything but scientific, rationalist solutions to the problem of life. This is what the Communists would like him to be like, but their own experience shows that this view is false. The problem is rather that the framework within which one can speak the Christian answer meaningfully has been virtually destroyed. The Christian answer is not rationalistic, but it is *reasonable* and depends on the possibility of real truth. Only a minority of twentieth-century men and women still think in terms of reason and real truth, where contradictory alternatives are mutually exclusive.

These "reactionaries" may be largely members of the middle class. It is no accident that Christianity is still most vital amid the much-abused middle-class: in part this is just the persistence of a cultural habit, but in part it results from the fact that the middle class has hung on to the concepts of a dichotomy between true and false, beween right and wrong, longer than either the upper class of the *dolce vita* or the lower class divided between proletarian despair and newly prosperous cynicism. As we have said in Chapter 3, the question of truth is vital to real Christianity.[8] But even the old middle-class is no longer a bastion for Christianity; it is disappearing or changing; the church must look beyond it.

In a world in which questions of truth assume a constantly declining importance, the number of people who can understand the evangelist's appeal is shrinking. Theology and religion are part of the total culture, and where the culture loses its awareness of objective truth, historic Christianity is possible only in either withdrawal from the total culture or in conscious, precise, and informed rebellion against it. The solution of withdrawal has been tried in the past—in Eastern Orthodoxy and Roman Catholicism, it is the way of monasticism, among Protestants it is the way of the radical separatists, the "plain people," Amish, Old Order Mennonites, and others like them. Quite aside from the fact that the policy puts obstacles in the way of the Christian duty to witness, it simply cannot work today. The total culture blankets the Amish settlement and pierces the monastery wall. *Only deliberate, precise, and informed rebellion is left.*

That the total culture does not influence only theology should be apparent. In the political and military sphere, it has made itself felt in the same way. We no longer feel much need to choose between mutually exclusive alternatives. Everything must be resolved by consensus, accommodation, mutual absorption of opposites. If there had been a nineteenth-century equivalent of Jomo Kenyatta and if he and his Mau Mau were really guilty of the crimes with which they have been charged, the leaders of nineteenth-century England could never have sat down at the same table with him. For twentieth-century England he is a revered Commonwealth leader, a man of moderation, a shining hope for African stability, although the old charges have not been refuted. Perhaps the attitude of post-World War II England is far more realistic, and better, in the long run, for Africa and the world. The fact which interests us here is that in the nineteenth century such a thing could not have been accepted. Had it been done out of political necessity (the nineteenth century also had its realists), it would have been branded an immoral act of expediency —perhaps tolerated, but certainly recognized for what it was.

Closer to home, the American attitudes towards the Vietnam war *all* represent, with the exception of the consistent militarists on the one side and of the convinced religious pacifists on the other, the same inability to make a choice between mutually exclusive alternatives. The government was unable to identify the enemy as an enemy with sufficient clarity to declare war—or to yield. Instead, it plays costly war games with the blood of Americans and Vietnamese. The so-called doves now appear to have won their battle to force the United States to yield to the Hanoi government and the N.L.F. Whether the new Nixon administration will be able to salvage peace with honor out of a dismally fouled-up situation seems doubtful. Regardless of whether we should ever have gotten involved in the war or whether we should have gotten out much sooner, there is no question that the domestic agitation for peace in Vietnam at any price has played into the hands of our external enemies. Those enemies, as events in Czechoslovakia in August, 1968 showed, are not so devoted to peace and non-intervention as many of our peace-at-any-price enthusiasts would have us believe.[9]

It would not be so bad if the "doves" had merely called upon us to admit defeat, and to pull out. Hannibal had to evacuate Italy, Napoleon had to retreat from Russia. Time and chance happen to them all (Ecclesiastes 9:11). It would be sad, dishonorable, perhaps, to betray the blood already shed there and the promises we have made, but no one can always avoid defeat. Instead, they told us that the N.L.F.—our enemy of so many years—would actually fulfill our hopes for Vietnam. That way lies madness—and it is the way of the twentieth century: the century of the automobile and supersonic flight, of the United Nations and Vatican II, of the hydrogen bomb and Auschwitz, of the ecumenical movement and "Black Power," of Ian Smith and Mau Mau. In short, it is the way of the century of un-reconcilable contradictions, in which we are asked to accept them all.

It is characteristic of our age that in religion, too, the framework of rational discourse is shattered. The pattern of sixteenth-century "religious dialogue" may have been ugly—councils and condemna-tions, anathemas and burnings: the demand, enforced by the sword and the stake, to make a choice. But dialogue in the twentieth cen-tury stands under the sign of pharmacology, not canon law: it is no accident that twentieth-century religious dialogue finds it so easy to pass from the bread and wine of an inter-denominational communion *agápē* to marijuana and L.S.D. There are no distinctions, no alterna-tives, no choices for us to make in our century: we take them all. The old consensus is gone, and with it our possibility of understand-ing theology without deliberately rebelling against the pattern im-posed on us by modern thought. Bishop Robinson spoke of "breaking the mould." He meant old-fashioned theological language. But the problem lies not so much in the language of the past—although that too can be a serious problem—as in the thought-forms of the present: a world without choices, where we keep all options open.

(b) *God and the All.* The conflict between the religion of ancient Israel and the paganism of its neighbors usually presented itself in terms of an opposition between biblical *monotheism* and pagan *poly-theism.* However, by the time of the early church, pagan polytheism was often taken by the more educated as merely an allegorical frame-work for the real content—philosophical monotheism, and often philo-sophical panthesim—God is the universe, the All. The conflict was thus no longer between the one God of monotheism and the many divinities of naive polytheism, but between the *One* personal God of biblical revelation and the impersonal *All* of philosophical speculation and mystical experience.

Just as philosophy in ancient times could continue to use the stories of the Homeric gods to clothe its own speculative monotheism or pantheism, *theology* in mid-twentieth century is perfectly capable of *presenting pantheism in Christian language.* Thus we satisfy the ideals of the modern mind, to avoid conflict, and to have everything. We have everything: the language of the Bible, the philosophical speculation of ultimate concern, the Ground of Being, the reconciliation of opposites, the devil-god of Blake, the myriad deities of Hinduism, the experience of L.S.D. But this is not possible. The God of the Bible demands that we choose between him and the All: "Hear, O Israel: the Lord our God is one LORD" (Deuteronomy 6:4). "There is one God, and one mediator also between God and men, the man Christ Jesus" (I Timothy 2:5). "He who rejects me, and does not receive my sayings, has one who judges him; the word I spoke . . . will judge him at the last day" (Jesus in John 12:48).

The choice is a choice between mutually exclusive possibilities. If we choose the God of the Bible, we reject the other, "everything," the All. We reject much of the world, and much of its self-styled wisdom. We certainly reject the twentieth-century mind. If we try for the All, in a certain sense we can have it: new theology, new morality, new politics, the world of sensation, of undifferentiated impressions of synthesis and absorption of opposites. We shall indeed be in step with the times, during the time of our lives. But we shall be out of step with Eternity. We shall be out of step with God. We shall escape responsibility here, perhaps, but—if the God of the Bible is really there, we shall not escape it forever. To fail to choose is to make the false choice, one for which, if we persist in it, there is ultimately no cure: "This is the judgment, that the light is come into the world, and men loved darkness rather than the light, for their deeds were evil" (John 3:19).

It is, then, a question of understanding the content. We cannot understand the God of the Bible unless we are willing to accept that words can be spoken in truth, unless we can choose between alternatives, unless we are willing to give up the desire to embrace the *All,* so that we can know the *One who is God.* To do this we must protest, we must rebel, against the mind of the twentieth century. For twentieth-century people, that is hard and costly. But it is better to have the mind of Christ (Philippians 2:5).

2. *The Differentiated Protest*

The 1960's are years of protest, of the protest song, of the protest march. Protest as such is not new, of course. Luther protested against some*thing,* four hundred and fifty years ago: the arrogance and errors of Rome; but we must realize that he also protested in favor of something: the authority and sufficiency of the Word of God. For us, protest first lost its positive aspect, then its specificity, and now, in the last third of the twentieth century, we have undifferentiated *total protest*. In America, you "drop out" of society. You repudiate civilization. Something is wrong: smash everything! Herbert Marcuse, whom we have already met as the patron saint of the extreme, anarchistic New Left in Germany, the "extra-parliamentary opposition," has sounded the call for a battle for the legalization of marijuana, "a means of total opposition."[10] It could not be stated better than by a representative of the *Living Theater,* an exiled American dramatic group working in Europe: "We want to smash the steel structure of laws which civilization has erected to protect itself from barbarism."[11]

Faced with this undifferentiated *total protest,* we must not fail to see that in practice, it will promote tyranny. If Marcuse's disciples succeed in destroying the "bourgeois tyranny" of West Berlin, what will succeed it is the quite different tyranny of East Berlin, which has much more effective ways of dealing with total opposition. The fact that a real tyranny would be the probable result of the success of these protesters, makes us wonder whether the New Left is as emancipated from the Old Left as it claims. But it may well be, for the twentieth century is the century of totalitarianism, and the total protesters would only be its obedient children if in fact they sincerely wished to destroy the present order and were altogether quite oblivious to the reality of the barbarism or tyranny, or both, which would follow upon it.

In the twentieth century, the Christian must rebel against the total culture *in its claim to totality*. He must protest without being a total protester. The differentiated protest is more difficult than the total one; to build is always more difficult than to destroy; surgery requires more skill than an axe murder. He must be a rebel in the sense of the American Revolution, with particular, limited goals—not in the sense of the French or Bolshevik ones, each of which rejected an *ancien régime* in it totality and spawned a new one which was even worse. In the twentieth century then, the Christian must differentiate in theology and in philosophy as well as in politics. He must be willing to see alternatives, and to choose between them. He cannot accept the twentieth century *en bloc* letting himself be swept along by it. But precisely by refusing to accept it—or reject it— *en bloc*, he will become the real rebel in the modern world—much more than the protesters of "total opposition." If anyone doubts this, let him simply try to differentiate, in his own circle of friends, between various twentieth-century fashions, accepting some and rejecting others. He will soon taste the hostility of twentieth-century man to discrimination in any form. The total protesters, by contrast, play the game—only on the other side. But—like gladiatorial combats— the whole game is wrong.

To be a Christian in the twentieth century, a man must allow his thinking to be reformed by the mind of God—his mind as it reveals itself in his revelation. This revelation may only be taken as it presents itself: therefore, in many parts, as objective truth, as communication of facts with significance. To do this, a man of today must work to shake off the mentality of his age and to free himself from the grip of the total culture. He will have to submit himself to a different, a higher authority, to that of the Word of God. Is this blind submission? Or is it rather absorption into our undifferentiating total culture, whether it be politically, philosophically, or theologically, which represents the real *sacrificium intellectus* for modern man? To put it differently, God demands obedience—but it is precisely the God of the Bible who is great enough to tolerate human freedom and loving enough to want us as children, not robots. He is the one whom, as the Episcopal prayer-book puts it, "to serve is perfect freedom." The twentieth century proffers total freedom, but on examination it is the freedom of the tribe, the freedom of the drug addict, and ultimately, the freedom of hell. Why else has hell been called the most enduring monument to the freedom of the human will?

3. *Protest in the Monolithic Culture*

Theology in particular has always presented itself as unique among the sciences studied by man. But actually, it was always carried along by the stream of the total culture. It can only free itself from it if it constantly resubmits itself, in Herman Dooyeweerd's words, "to the reforming power of the Word of God, even for science." Theology has always been torn by the alternative between fleeing from the claims contemporary culture makes on it, in order to remain safely in an orthodox citadel (a thing which is never possible), and succumbing to it. If it abandons contact with the total culture, it becomes irrelevant. If it succumbs to it, it becomes false. Today the task of theology is especially great, because never have the claims of the total culture been so massive. Never has its influence been so pervasive, so difficult to escape. Never has the number of outsiders with a different intellectual formation—for example, of old-fashioned, middle-class Christians—been so small. (This is neither an attack on nor praise of the middle-class Christian. If by virtue of the conservatism of his class, he has managed to keep what is of inestimable value, the historic Christian faith, he is fortunate, but even so he may experience the tragedy of not being able to communicate it to his children. Unfortunately, more often than not his habitual intellectual and religious conservatism does not even suffice to preserve a living faith for himself, but only a shell of one.)

Francis A. Schaeffer constantly refers to twentieth-century culture as *monolithic*. This is a very appropriate characterization. In spite of tremendous apparent variety, the twentieth century consists of a million different voices, all crying the same thing: nothing is real! The conviction that reality is an illusion was reached in India long before the Christian era; classical Greek thinkers were tempted by it, but it was banished from the Christian world by the biblical doctrine of a real creation. Now, as the Christianized portions of the world rapidly lose their biblical framework, the denial of reality sweeps back over us like a flood. This is the real apostasy of the twentieth century, not the denial of God, but the denial of any reality whatsoever.

In theology this loss of reality manifests itself in a preoccupation with formulas, with words. For German theologian Gerhard Ebeling, the reality of the Christian proclamation lies in the proclamation itself: the word is an event. The late Paul Tillich took comfort from his concepts of the Christ-event, the New Being, and the idea of Christ. He often said in lectures that it would not disturb his faith if it could be proved that no Jesus of Nazareth had ever lived. By a curious kind of irony, this banishing of the reality of the events and the people of biblical history, done in the name of science, has resulted in a new kind of *magic*. Mere words and formulas, completely cut off from tangible reality, are supposed to have the power to transform and completely to redirect our lives. The difference between the *kerygma* as conceived and proclaimed by a modern theologian and the curse or beneficent charm of a witch-doctor is not so very great.

This rejection of reality is a pervasive characteristic of our monolithic total culture. Theologians put it one way, and only a small number of people listen to them and really understand them. But it is not necessary to listen to academic theologians, for the omnipresent mass-media give us the same message. Nothing could show this more clearly than the new fascination of avant-garde theologians with the products of the entertainment industry. Church members often take offense at the fact that many ministers and theologians seem to feel it highly desirable to read, see, and quote all the sub-pornographic, pornographic, and super-pornographic productions of our publishing and motion-picture industries. In general, however, it is not the obscenities which attract them, but the philosophical message, *which is the same as that of modern theology*, namely, that nothing is real.

Examples are too numerous to begin to list, but perhaps three may be helpful. The first is the Beatles' song, "A Day in the Life." Rock music is making its way into the churches as a means of interesting the young, and even as an aid to worship. Before flying into a traditional, conservative fit of indignation at this because it is *new*, we must be careful to understand it. Many people have objected to the use of certain kinds of popular music in worship on the grounds that something in it contradicts the purpose of Christian worship. This charge has usually been brushed aside as evidence of cultural Philistinism. But now we can be grateful to the Beatles for making the message more precise in "A Day in the Life," where they tell us that nothing is real. The association of this song and of the rest of the album with drug-taking, which has prompted the B.B.C. to ban it, is not accidental: the world of drugs is the world where only fantasy is important and reality does not exist.

The second example is taken from the movie world: Michelangelo Antonioni's *Blow-Up*. With some of the most superb color photography ever produced, and with his "daring" display of two naked teen-age girls, and by giving his hero almost unquestioned dominance of everybody and everything with which he comes into contact, Antonioni has succeeded in fascinating most of the film's viewers. The more discriminating critics talk about the film's analysis of perception and reality, but its younger viewers seldom get that far into it. For them it is hardly a "serious" film, or if it is, its seriousness consists in its portrayal of the hero's freedom. Few of them recognize that they are being exposed to what a Lausanne critic called "the structures of Hell," but the fact that they do not recognize them does not prevent those structures from impressing themselves upon them.

The third example is the vogue enjoyed by the ostentatiously homosexual Allen Ginsberg among certain intellectuals and also in some of the mass-media. Ginsberg and his male paramour appeared at Harvard University, dining at Lowell House on Ford Foundation money under the portraits of Harvard's great Puritans of the past. It is not so surprising that this should happen at Harvard, where academic freedom is taken so seriously that it sometimes impairs normal judgment and taste. But it also happened all across the country, even in the Middle West and the Far West. Finally *Life* magazine gave Ginsberg an awestruck kind of write-up, expressing wonder and respect at the way he could disperse hostile city policemen with Hindu prayers.

Ginsberg's conquest of *Life* seals the case for the totality of the twentieth-century anti-realistic mentality. Nothing is more representative of the American establishment, of the good life as the best people in America see it, than the magazines of Time, Incorporated, especially *Time* and *Life*. (*Fortune* and *Sports Illustrated*, devoted to more specialized subjects, reflect it less.) When a small, artsy magazine eulogizes Ginsberg, it is nothing unusual, but when *Life* buys the Ginsberg package—or at least gives it the world's best advertising —it is a different story. *Time*'s movie critic, writing on *Blow-Up*, is unable to distinguish the message of Antonioni from that of St. Paul; its music writers can see no significance in the connection between the Beatles, drugs, and custom-tailored Hinduism. It is not that the brain children of the late Henry Luce are especially perverse, or especially dull-witted. On the contrary, they represent some of the best writing and reporting in America, and undoubtedly many men on their staffs still share something of Luce's ethical sensitivity. The point is that when *even they* cannot identify the message coming from such diverse quarters, when even they willy-nilly rebroadcast it, we see that the totalitarian grip of the total culture is virtually complete.

The monolithic culture is here, and we can accept it. That is the easiest course. But it is the course which ultimately leads to man's being alone in the universe, to his losing himself in an endless maze of blind corridors, and looking into an empty heaven with empty eyes. Or we can, if we choose, adopt the "total protest" exemplified by Marcuse's disciples, the hyperradical students of West Berlin, and in another way by America's hippies. But that total protest does not escape from totalitarian tyranny, either in the realm of the mind or in the realm of the realities of everyday life. We cannot totally reject our culture, because, like God's creation, everything that we have is wrapped up in it, both our goods and our liabilities. We can totally reject it only by annihilating ourselves. That is possible for the Buddhist, or for the Hindu (and thus the popularity of these religions, or of western variations on them, in our culture today), but not for the Christian, whose destiny is not personal annihilation but eternal life in fellowship with God.

Although we must be strangers in the modern world, we cannot be self-isolated hermits. The people of God have always been strangers and exiles, seeking a city built by him (Hebrews 11:13-16), even the Jews in the Promised Land and the Christians in the "Christian" Roman Empire. But it is *in* this world that we are exiles, and through it that we must make our intellectual as well as our physical pilgrimage. We cannot reject it *in toto,* and we must not accept it or succumb to it. In short, we must heed the words of St. Paul, "Do not be conformed to this world, but be transformed by the renewing of your mind" (Romans 12:2). He lived in the world of imperial, pagan Rome. He could not flee it, and remain obedient to his Lord, who had commissioned him Apostle to the Gentiles. It eventually killed him—and in the mid-twentieth century, if we wish to follow his advice, our world may eventually kill us. Is that so bad? In any event, something will kill us. We all have to answer the important question: on whose side will you live? But we must also be prepared to answer the other one: on whose side will you die? On Nero's? Or Paul's?

Notes

[1]There are excellent works with these titles, which serve as a good introduction to the fundamentals of Christianity: John R. W. Stott, *Basic Christianity* (London: Inter-Varsity and Grand Rapids: Eerdmans, 1958), and C. S. Lewis, *Mere Christianity* (London: Geoffrey Bless, 1952, and New York: Macmillan).

[2]Of course the Apostles' Creed was not actually written by the twelve Apostles, as the fifteenth-century scholar Lorenzo Valla already demonstrated. But it is quite clear that it represents the faith of the church of the Apostles, as Oscar Cullman states. (*Les premières confessions de foi chrétiennes.* Paris: Presses Universitaires, 1948). An excellent English work on the creeds is J. N. D. Kelly, *Early Christian Creeds* (London: Longmans, 1950).

[3]Worshippers should be alert to pious-sounding formulations like this: "Let us confess the *faith of our fathers* in the words of the Apostles' Creed. . . ." Such formulations often hide the fact that it is not the faith of the minister leading the recitation.

[4]To say that Hiroshima is an example of the triumph of evil in our century means neither more nor less than that just ends do not justify wrong means.

[5]Leighton Ford, *The Christian Persuader* (New York: Harper, 1966), pp. 81ff.

[6]Dietrich Bonhoeffer, *Letters and Papers from Prison,* ed. E. Bethge (London: S.C.M., 2nd ed. 1956), pp. 145-147. See Robinson, *Honest to God,* pp. 29ff. Harvey A. Cox, in *The Secular City,* also pictures modern man as confident, detached, competent—like a Marlboro man. But the works of major psychologists and psychiatrists, such as O. Hobart Mowrer, Paul Tournier, and Carl Gustav Jung, repudiate this theologians' image of modern man. Because modern man does not run to modern theologians for the answers does not prove that he is not aware of having any problems.

[7]Kurt E. Koch, *Christian Counseling and Occultism* (Grand Rapids: Kregel, 1965), thoroughly documents this assertation. In Germany, the Protestant Center for Philosophical Issues, Stuttgart, has collected evidence and statistics on the incredible prevalence of superstitious practices and beliefs among modern Germans—and surely no one represents "technical man" better than the Germans. For that matter, as we have noted, Bonhoeffer wrote about "man come of age" when most of his fellow-Germans were still enthusiastic Nazis.

The author himself, during his term as a tutor and member of the United Ministry at Harvard, witnessed the flowering of the spiritualist circle—to the concern of the deans and dismay of the university psychiatrists. What has happened to it since 1965 he cannot say.

[8]That the spirit of the age is against the ideas (a) that truth can be stated in words, and (b) that truth has intrinsic value is shown by the spectacular popularity enjoyed by the ideas of Marshall McLuhan, which may be epitomized by one of his chapter titles, "The Medium Is the Message" (*Understanding Media*. New York: McGraw-Hill, 1964. Chapter 1). Impression replaces rational content. Whether McLuhan has correctly analysed the twentieth century or not, it is remarkable how many twentieth-century opinion-makers hail him as he proclaims the abolition of intellectual, verbal, analytical content from human life.

[9]An essay which every thinking observer should read is Kingsley Amis, "Why Lucky Jim Turned Right," *National Review*, Vol. XIX, No. 41 (October 17, 1967), pp. 1211ff.

[10]*Pardon*, "the German satirical monthly," Vol. VI, No. 9 (September, 1967), p. 53. *Pardon* is published by the firm of Bärmeier & Nikel, a group interested in the promotion of drugs and the legalization and spread of homosexuality, at least to the extent of publishing works supporting them.

[11]Interview on French television, reported in the *Tribune de Lausanne*, Friday, October 13, 1967.

CHAPTER 12

· THE CHRISTIAN IN THE TOTAL CULTURE ·

For whenever I speak, I cry out,
  I shout, "Violence and destruction!"
For the word of the Lord has become for me
  A reproach and a derision all day long.

JEREMIAH 20:8 (R.S.V.).

However dubious the claims of theology to be a science may be, one thing is sure: it is definitely part of human culture. Whether it be orthodox or radical, the theology of a particular age will be deeply affected and either challenged or channeled by the total culture within which it arises. Both the Reformers and their Roman Catholic opponents in the sixteenth century were heavily indebted to Renaissance culture: one more in the sense of a reaction against it, one more in a kind of infatuation with it—but both were marked by it. Even when theology makes a conscious and successful effort to preserve its moorings in biblical tradition, its attachments to the great events of revelation, and its continuity with the heritage of the New Testament people, it will always bear the stamp of the age in which it arises. Once the moorings have been cast off, as is being done by more and more of contemporary theology, there is nothing to prevent the discipline called theology from becoming just another manifestation of contemporary culture. The fact that twentieth-century culture is oppressively monolithic means that in our century formal theology can hardly be anything other than a kind of cultural manifestation, in a different area, of the twentieth-century mentality unless it is deliberately subject to the Word of God and constantly being reformed by it. Since this is precisely what most contemporary theology is not, it cannot surprise us that by and large theology and the church today express the mind of the *Zeitgeist* but not of the Holy Spirit.

1. *Twentieth-Century Theological Man*

A year after Bishop Robinson burst on the theological scene, Marshall McLuhan published *Understanding Media: The Extensions of Man* (1964). It took a bit longer to make an impact than Robinson's little book, but now it is hailed by hundreds of voices, and not least by theologians, as being *the* work to give us insight into the twentieth century and its transformation of man. *Understanding Media* and *Honest to God* have this in common: examined in detail, each reveals many internal contradictions, making it unclear just what its author really meant to say. Further, like Robinson for modern theology, McLuhan seems to have a kind of patent to speak for as well as to the total modern culture. It is possible that just as the one is a very bad guide to what Christian theology really is, so the other may be a highly inaccurate and misleading interpreter of what twentieth-century man really is,[1] but the acclaim with which they have been greeted shows that they represent what a good portion of the twentieth-century church, in Robinson's case, and of the total culture, in McLuhan's case, thinks that it is or should be. As a result, works like these ought to be required reading precisely for those who disagree most with them. They are not only symptoms of what is happening to us, but they are very effective tracts to push the process along.

From one point of view, it is hard to see how McLuhan and Bishop Robinson can really both be spokesmen for the twentieth-century mind, i.e. for what we have called the monolithic total culture. On the one hand, Robinson, like a number of other popular theological figures of our day, follows Rudolf Bultmann and Dietrich Bonhoeffer in their vision of confident, competent modern man. Bultmann, despite the fact that the *Sitz im Leben* of much of his important writing was the myth-mad Germany of Adolf Hitler, has remade theology to suit modern man as Bultmann sees him—objective, rational, logical, unable to believe anything but the evidence of his own senses or the statements of prominent scientific theologians. Bonhoeffer too, although he himself was destroyed by the madness to which Germany fell victim, held a similar illusion that man was mature, sure of himself, living only in the realm of fact, technology, and this-worldly sufficiency. McLuhan, by contrast, thinks that precisely technology is turning "modern" man back into a primitive creature, a kind of emotional sponge, bathed in multicolored fluids representing the different sensory impressions he absorbs, soaking them up greedily and indiscriminately, to extrude them equally uncritically when squeezed.

It is easy to see that if McLuhan's concept of man is right, Bultmann's theology is built upon the sand of a vision of man which is simply false. From this point of view, Bultmann and his disciples should fight McLuhan tooth and nail, precisely as Bultmann fights all those who oppose modern theology by pointing to the susceptibility of modern man to superstition and the occult and to the evidence for the reality of demonic powers. However, in practice they do not fight him, but greet him as one of their own. This is possible because for both parties, as McLuhan says, "the medium is the message." Both are opposed to meaningful content, and thus are representatives of the twentieth-century mind.

Bishop Robinson, his mentors, and his colleagues would protest that they are very much in favor of meaningful expression, and that they criticize the content of the Bible precisely because they believe its message to be wrong on factual grounds. This is largely a posture, unconsciously or consciously assumed to further their argument, as we see by the glaring fact that they do not protest against false messages elsewhere, even those diametrically opposed to their principles, other than in orthodox theology. That Robinson, for example, does not attack McLuhan in his zeal for enlightening the church may be understandable—after all, McLuhan is not a theologian and one man can do only so much. But that none of the modern theologians comment on the promotion of gross error and superstition from within their own ranks is something else again. Perhaps tact prevents people like Robinson from commenting on another man's venture into spiritualism. Yet surely the office of a bishop must be to protect the people from dangerous error. Modern theologians are not waging war on spiritism, nor on drugs, nor on sexual promiscuity and perversion, each of which can imprison man far more effectively and cruelly than "fundamentalist" theology, even from a purely medical and not specifically Christian point of view. Modern theology directs its enlightening zeal chiefly against historic orthodoxy, and—except in the social sphere, where it can be quite vigorous—is content to let all other errors, as well as almost every vice, flourish unrebuked.

Speaking of modern theologians, the Jewish philosopher Jonas says, "The very idea of a true doctrine vanishes, and with it that of heresy."[2] Not only the theologians but also the church administrations have virtually abandoned the concept of heresy—although it should be clear to any child that *if the church has no right to say that any doctrine is false, it also cannot say that any is true.* Faced with the choice between holding a heresy trial to defend its objective doctrines against Bishop Pike's attacks, which would have exposed it to much unfavorable publicity, and abandoning its procedures against heresy, the Episcopal Church by 1967 had given up every practical possibility of defending itself against heresy.[3] Thus too— although Tillich was disturbed by Altizer—no major avant-garde "scientific" theologian has taken pen in hand to reject the teachings of the death-of-God school, which whatever they are, are not scientific theology.[4] There is only one exception—those who defend the traditional, still formally official faith of the church may expect the solitary distinction of being accused of dangerous error and of leading the people astray.

In the area of ethics, as well, supposedly scientific modern theologians are united in a puzzling tolerance of the public advocacy of conduct which in general they would reject for themselves. Today only the "arch-conservatives" (i.e. the orthodox Christians), and enthusiasts like the Pentecostals will speak out against promiscuity, pornography and homosexuality,[5] or commit themselves to the fight against drugs.[6] A curious blindness exists towards real moral evil on an individual level. Without denying that conservative Christians are often guilty of inconsistency and hypocrisy, we cannot help contrasting the venom with which some modern theologians attack Christians who simply restate traditional Christian moral teachings, with the benevolence with which they regard individual moral corruption, for instance, or government terror and oppression—in the people's democracies—for another. There is a terrible inconsistency here which would almost seem to cry out for the explanation of deliberate deception on the part of many of these men. But while there undoubtedly *are* cases of Western theological leaders who are consciously in the service of Communism, to accept the conspiracy solution is to fail to see the depth of the problem which confronts us, namely, the loss of meaningful content in theology and doctrine.

Twentieth-century theological man, unless he consciously submits himself to the authority of God and his Word, is bound to represent the mind of our century in the theology he writes. This much is vigorously opposed to the very concept of reliable, authoritative, binding communication. By reliable communication is meant that the factual, literal content corresponds to objective reality. By authoritative is meant that it comes directly from one who has authority, and by binding, that we are responsible to act on what is communicated or suffer the consequences for our failure to do so. Despite apparently basic differences of conviction between them, we see that people like the New Testament scholar Bultmann, the religious sociologist Harvey Cox, and the secular "media scholar" McLuhan all reflect this basic prejudice of the twentieth-century mind against reliable communication of objective content.

Bultmann attacks the communication of truth in the Bible as unreliable (not factual) and often as unauthoritative (not coming from the sources it claims for itself). He would like to keep it, or at least his proclamation of it, *binding*. The folly of this hope is shown by the fact that never have so many German scholars made such strenuous and often fantastic efforts to make the Bible speak to modern man, and never has the Bible enjoyed less respect and interest in Germany than it does today. Cox disregards the critical questions which preoccupy Bultmann and cuts a new Jesus out of whole cloth, who turns out to be saying much the same things as Harvey Cox. *The Secular City* enjoys a considerable vogue in its German translation, but no modern German theologian has warned the church against Cox as many have done against the orthodox Bergmann. Aside from his theology, many people have been impressed by Cox's genial sociological analysis of modern, technicopolitan man. Now a professional sociologist has seriously challenged the competence of his performance in the area.[7] Unfortunately, detailed refutations, either of individual points or of a writer's basic position make very little impact—for here the twentieth-century mind reacts as McLuhan apparently thinks it should, and rejoices in the impressions, neglecting the content. Finally, McLuhan himself says that modern man is dispensing—and apparently properly so—with contentful communication, to respond only to the medium, and to whether it is "hot" or "cool." Naturally McLuhan realizes that somewhere in modern technical society someone has to know and understand facts, or otherwise the reversion of the world to a tribal village culture will be only too real. But he seems to be willing to leave this knowledge to a few archaic specialists and—for the most part, to computers.

2. Biblical Theological Man

To the vision of man as floating free in a world of impressions, with real knowledge left to a few specialists and otherwise to machines, the Judaeo-Christian religious tradition opposes its vision of a different kind of theological man. It envisions each individual man knowing God because His statutes are written in his heart (Jeremiah 31:33). Jesus Christ speaks of knowing God and his son, which he equates with life eternal (John 17:3). That this is not to be merely a kind of undefined mystic vision was shown clearly enough by Jesus himself when he told the disciples that they were his friends, not his servants, because he had thoroughly informed them of what he had heard from his Father (John 15:14-15). Because the biblical knowledge of God can be communicated, when Paul met Christ on the road to Damascus, it was not an ineffable, mystical encounter but Christ spoke to him "in the Hebrew tongue," that is, in a distinct, definite language, saying words that could be repeated (Acts 26:14). There is, of course, a transcendent, ineffable vision of God which cannot be communicated in human words. The Bible does not exclude all genuine mysticism, nor does it claim to be total revelation, but it gives us something which we can understand without being or becoming mystics, and which we can communicate. St. Paul stresses holding fast to sound doctrine (II Timothy 1:13); by doctrine he understands precisely the kind of reliable, authoritative, binding communication which is so obnoxious to the modern mind. To the modern mind, the problem with historic Christianity is not that it is hard to believe, but that there is something definite to believe.

The individual Christian in New Testament times was expected to have a personal knowledge of his faith. In the days of the early church, the greatest of care was given to the instruction of converts, and later of believers' children. Even in the late fourth century, after Christianity had received the imperial blessing, the amount which a catechumen had to learn before being admitted to communion was impressive. This later declined, so that in medieval England examining bishops often thought that a priest was doing well if everyone in his congregation knew the Ten Commandments, the Lord's Prayer, and the Apostles' Creed. During the Reformation, the major Reformers revived the early church's interest in the instruction of all their people. The seventeenth-century Presbyterian Richard Baxter prescribed that a minister examine everyone in his congregation yearly on his knowledge of doctrine. In our century in the United States, thanks to parochial schools and to the competitive spirit fostered by minority status, Roman Catholics often show a greater knowledge of Christian fundamentals than Protestants. But today a genuine religious knowledge is in decline almost everywhere. Despite some ambitious and praiseworthy efforts to restate the orthodox doctrines of Roman Catholicism in easily-understood terms, such as the Paulist Press's *Come to the Father* set of catechetical materials, the Roman Catholic performance in this area is declining. Most new Protestant teaching materials are moving in the direction of the replacement of revealed truths with current nostrums. As a result, attendance at catechism classes, discussion and study groups and the like is no guarantee whatsoever that one will receive any help toward becoming a *theological* man in the sense of John 15:14-15 and 17:3, of knowing something tangible of God the Father and the Son.

Therefore the individual Christian, even in his own church, must be prepared to swim against the tide. Of course there are many individual pastors, teachers, churches and even perhaps smaller denominations where the tide is still running in the right direction. The Christian who is fortunate enough to find such a fellowship should support it if he already belongs to it or join it if he does not. But even as a member of a thoroughly sound fellowship, he himself, his children and his associates cannot help but feel the impact of the total cultural climate in theology. The church no longer has soundproof walls. Therefore no Christian has the right to neglect his own theological formation—not even in the best of church fellowships.

In Germany, more so than in the United States, the modern theologians claim to be concerned about the layman's theological knowledge. There is much altruistic talk of making each individual church member acquainted with the results of modern theological science. They present their program as one intended to educate and enlighten those held in mental bondage by fundamentalistic oversimplifications. Whatever the sincerity of the modern theologians, it does not lead them to try to defend the ordinary individual from being completely disoriented by the ravings of the death of God theologians. No modern German theologian protested that Dorothee Soelle was given a chance to publicize her eccentric ideas at the *Kirchentag* of 1965, but what an outcry there would have been had Gerhard Bergmann been given a major address! The willingness to tolerate the most eccentric babble from one wing and the complete unwillingness to allow even a presentation of orthodox views from the other certainly discredits the modernists' claim to be interested in spreading knowledge. In any event the Christian cannot go to the church's popular pundits for guidance towards theological knowledge in the New Testament sense. Nor—sad to say—can he find it among the church and denominational leaders. The present Archbishop of Canterbury is much readier to warn people against trusting Billy Graham than to do anything about Bishop Robinson. German church officials, for the most part, tremble at the bark of their own radical theologians and at the prospect of ridicule in the German press if they challenge them. And so it goes. In the United States the situation is equally ridiculous. Perhaps its brightest aspect is that few spiritually sensitive Christians expect much of the typical academic theologian or church official.

For twentieth-century man, then, if he wants to be theological in the biblical sense—and to be a true *theologian,* knowing the Father and the Son, is, in Jesus' words, eternal life—he must go back to the sources. There is no alternative to a personal knowledge of the promises and commandments of God. Faith involves trust, trust in the promises and in the one who has promised. This means a personal knowledge of the Bible itself. Knowledge of the catechism, even a *good* catechism, is no substitute. Of course it is true that many passages permit a variety of interpretations. But there are quite enough which are abundantly clear to give the one who believes their message a great head start over the sophisticated theologians.

Commentaries, introductions, and works of theology may be helpful. On the whole, however, the Christian or interested non-Christian will do better to learn to know the text of Scripture, especially the New Testament, in a good, readable translation. Here he should note that while a free translation or a paraphrase, such as the *New English Bible* or the translation of J. B. Phillips, is valuable, it should be read in connection with a straightforward translation, such as the *New American Standard Bible,* the *Revised Standard Version,* the *Berkeley Version,* or the older *Authorized* ("King James") *Version* of 1611. Introductions to doctrine, such as John R. W. Stott's *Basic Christianity,* or the works of C. S. Lewis, J. B. Phillips, O. Hallesby, and others are useful, but it is the Bible itself which has, in Phillips' words, "The Ring of Truth."[8]

The English-speaking world is fortunate in that there is more than enough biblically sound literature available to supply the Christian with ammunition against destructive theology.[9] This situation does not exist in Germany. But to some extent it is not altogether satisfactory in the United States and Britain either, for the modish modernists compliment and acclaim one another and ignore their opponents, thus giving the impression of a much more monolithic theological liberalism than the facts warrant. Consequently one must know where to look. It would be possible to recommend many recent works,[10] but to do so involves one in the problems of conflicting evaluations. A better policy is to read the classics of Christian history, many of them printed in excellent modern editions by Westminster Press of Philadelphia in *The Library of Christian Classics.* The older *Library of Nicene and Ante-Nicene Theology* has been reprinted by Eerdmans of Grand Rapids and there are several good Roman Catholic editions. The great books of the Reformation era are available in good English editions. Noteworthy is the joint Concordia Publishing House-Fortress Press edition of Luther's works now in progress, and the fine Westminster Press version of Calvin's *Institutes of the Christian Religion.* Even these classics of faith and theology, which have moulded generations of Christians, are no substitute for personal acquaintance with the Bible itself, but they are far more valuable than the typical product of a modern theologian's pen. Commentaries and sermons on the whole Bible can be found, in good English editions, by Luther and Calvin, not to mention the lesser Reformers. There are many commentaries by early Christian fathers, such as Augustine and John Chrysostom. American Presbyterianism made a great contribution in the works of the Princeton theologians Charles Hodges, A. A. Hodge, and Benjamin B. Warfield. Some excellent English Reformation and post-Reformation writing is contained in the old collection, *The Library of Anglo-Catholic Theology*, which can be found gathering dust on many a public and university library's shelves.

The list could be prolonged almost indefinitely. We in the English-speaking world have no lack of access to the great works of Christian faith and life, ancient, medieval, Reformation, or modern.[11] The interested reader can only be encouraged to pay special attention to the works of the really great men of the past. They are often easier to read than those of their disciples or of their modern interpreters.

3. The Task

The task facing every Christian in today's theological culture must be to heed the old Christian humanists' war-cry: *Ad fontes!* To the sources! The challenge is not only to the intellectually-inclined Christian. He may have the incentive to study in greater depth and variety than others, but the task is the same for every Christian: to know God's Word and his promises, so that they can trust them and him, and say with St. Paul, "I know whom I have believed" (II Timothy 2:12). First we must know the Book itself. Then we have all the resources of Christian literature to aid us.

Three things will be enough for the necessary minimum. But something more is needed. We cannot accept the message of Eugene Carson Blake to the 1967 German *Kirchentag*, to the effect that we can only understand the Bible if we are all together in one unified church. If total fellowship among all real and nominal Christians were a necessary condition, it would also be an impossible one. But for the individual a fellowship of like-minded believers is a psychological and a spiritual necessity, as well as a New Testament imperative. However, in order to identify such a fellowship, and to trust it, he must be able to recognize its conformity to what the Bible teaches. And that again brings him back to the necessity of personal knowledge and comprehension. Implicit faith is impossible in our century: either one knows for himself, or one does not know at all.

This personal knowledge of and commitment to the content of historic Christian faith repudiates McLuhan's dictum that the medium is the message. It repudiates the conviction of modern theologians that they, not the martyrs of the past or the present, understand what the Bible means, and find it wanting. It accepts the word of the Psalmist to God,

> "Thy righteousness is righteous for ever,
> and thy law is true.
> . . . and all thy commandments are true."
>
> Psalm 119:142, 152 (R.S.V.)

Notes

[1]For a critique of McLuhan's coherence, see Geoffrey Wagner, "Misunderstanding Media: Obscurity as Authority," *The Kenyon Review*, Vol. XXIX (March, 1967), pp. 246-255.

[2]Hans Jonas, "Heidegger und die Theologie," *Evangelische Theologie*, Vol. XXIV, No. 12 (December, 1964), p. 636. The English version is in the December, 1964 *Review of Metaphysics*, unavailable to me.

[3]For reports, see *Christianity Today*, Vol. XI, No. 23 (September 1, 1967), pp. 1156-57, and Vol. XII, No. 1 (October 13, 1967), pp. 44-45.

[4]It is always dangerous to say "no one," and perhaps there is an exception which has not come to the author's attention. Even if such criticism on the part of modern theologians existed, it would certainly be insignificant in comparison with the regular broadsides they fire at conservatives for holding onto historic doctrines.

[5]Klaus Bockmühl, chaplain at Heidelberg University, gives a withering account of theologians' repudiation of the biblical teaching on homosexuality in "Die Diskussion über Homosexualität in theologischer Sicht," *Evangelische Theologie* Vol. XXIV, No. 5 (May, 1964), pp. 242-266. Needless to say Dr. Bockmühl is now *persona non grata* in liberal theological circles.

[6]It is a Pentecostal minister, the Rev. David F. Wilkerson, who has undertaken to free teen-agers from the curse of the drugs to which other theologians recommend easier access. See his remarkable *The Cross and the Switchblade* (New York: Bernard Geis, 1963).

[7]Samuel A. Mueller, "Relevance, Community Organization and Sociology," *Christian Century*, Vol. LXXXIX, No. 41 (October 11, 1967), pp. 1282-1284.

[8]Phillip's valuable book, *The Ring of Truth* (New York: Macmillan, 1967), was written because, the author says, "I do not care a rap what the 'avant-garde' scholars say; I very much care what God says and does."

[9]For an up-to-date reading list, see Robert L. Cleath, "Read Your Way to Theological Literacy," *Christianity Today*, Vol. XI, No. 24 (September 15, 1967), pp. 1200-1202.

[10]For a good introduction to the New Testament, I can highly recommend Donald F. Guthrie, *Introduction to the New Testament*. 3 vol. (London: Tyndale, 1961ff). Edward J. Young has written the most reliable conservative *Introduction to the Old Testament* (Grand Rapids: Eerdmans, 3rd ed. 1960). There is no better interpreter of Scripture in English than G. Campell Morgan, many of whose books have been reprinted by Revell.

[11]The Roman Catholic can profitably read the great fathers and doctors honored by the whole of Christendom. Lack of space and knowledge prevent me from recommending more recent Roman Catholic works, but I can say, despite my doctrinal objections to Roman Catholicism, that some excellent works of biblical scholarship are being produced by Catholics. Unfortunately there are also some which are completely captive to the modern mind. It is hard to go wrong with Augustine.

CHAPTER 13

· THE ECUMENICAL
IMPERATIVE ·

Then said Samuel, Bring ye hither to me Agag the king of the Amalekites. And Agag came unto him delicately.* And Agag said, Surely the
bitterness of death is past.

I SAMUEL 15:32, A.V.

Saul, the first king of Israel, was a well-intentioned sort of fellow,
and inclined to talk things over reasonably—except when he was
overtaken by what Samuel calls an evil spirit. In such a mood he tried
to pin David to the wall with a javelin. But normally it was possible
to reason with him. After he had defeated the Amalekites, instead of
destroying them all, as the Lord had commanded, Saul spared Agag
and kept the best of the Amalekite booty, in order, as he explained to
Samuel, "to bring sacrifices to the Lord your God at Gilgal" (1
Samuel 15:21). Apparently when he saw Samuel, Saul had a pre-
monition that he had made the wrong decision in disobeying God's
command, even for a plausible reason. Hence he spoke to Samuel of
"your God" rather than of "my God." Agag, who was undoubtedly
expecting the worst when he was captured, was relieved by Saul's
treatment of him, and when he was brought in to Samuel, he greeted
him cheerfully. Samuel replied, "As your sword has made women
childless, so shall your mother be childless among women," and cut
him to pieces (15:33).

This severity was not exactly Samuel's own doing: he was acting
at the express command of the Lord. And since in those days the

*cheerfully

Lord could be quite prompt about dealing with anyone who dis-
obeyed a direct order, we must not blame Samuel for his promptness
to obey. It is less Samuel's obedience which poses the problem for
us, for twentieth-century Sunday school teachers as well as for
atheists like Bertrand Russell, than the character of the God who
gave him the command.

Our tender conscience on this issue is a bit hypocritical, of course.
In the century of extermination camps, atomic and nuclear weapons,
and intercontinental rockets, we are hardly in a position to reprove
the ancient Israelites for wiping out some of their enemies. Harry S.
Truman gave the orders to incinerate the populations of two large
Japanese cities, Hiroshima and Nagasaki, without any command
from God, and apparently without any compelling political or military necessity. We look on with only mild interest as Ibos are mas-
sacred in Nigeria. Better publicity permits more horror and dismay
at the use of napalm against mixed targets in Vietnam. But what the
United States is doing with technology is hardly more horrible than
what the Viet Cong is doing with old-fashioned knives and bamboo
stakes, and neither is much compared to what the United States, the
Soviet Union, and several smaller powers have carefully prepared for
anyone who becomes too much of a threat to them.

We boast of our ability to exterminate hundreds of millions of
people, perhaps the whole world, for reasons of our own. We actually
kill thousands annually in Vietnam. All this is without even a decla-
ration of war or clear instruction from Congress, much less a command from God. We surely have no right to be self-righteous in our
criticism of God for telling the Jews to wipe out certain of their
enemies. It is reasonable to expect him to show more reverence for
human life which he created than we who are humans do? This
kind of an argument against God is based on the traditional human
desire to have gods in "our own image"—not in the image of what
we actually *are*, because such gods would be too horrible, but in the
image of what in our more altruistic moments we would like to be.
It does not understand the character of the God who is. To understand what God is really like and what his purposes are is much
more useful than to reproach him for not thinking more highly of
human life than we ourselves do.

In actual fact, of course, God thinks much more highly of man than man himself does. The whole story of the Bible is in a way God's attempt to persuade man to revise the wrong opinion he has of himself. Sometimes God must work to rid man of arrogance and presumption, but more often, it seems—particularly in our century—he has to teach man a higher opinion of himself. Modern man thinks of himself as a desperate emptiness, but God knows better. He knows that man can be his child, with all the honor and joy that that entails. But man will not believe it. Therefore St. John says, "This is the condemnation." He might have said, "This is the tragedy," except for the fact that according to Christian teaching man's rebellion against God is precisely *not* tragic, not something to which he is driven by his destiny, but his own choice—hence, his condemnation: "that light has come into the world, and men loved the darkness more than the light, because their deeds were evil" (John 3:19). It is in the context both of man's privilege to be a child of God and of the condemnation which results from his disobedience that we must see this divine command to Israel to kill her enemies.

The possibility of being a child of God brings with it great honor and grave danger. A child must be responsible to his father: he must be able to answer to him, not only in the sense of having a dialogue with him, but also in the sense of being called to account for his conduct. The automaton is not called to account, because it does only what it is programmed to do. But it is not a child and cannot inherit. According to New Testament teaching, men are not by nature children of God, but they have the possibility of adoption as children (see John 1:18).[1] If men were God's children by nature, then much of his action with them would be pointless. One does not, under most circumstances, kill disobedient children. But if men are not his children because of being men, but have the potential of *becoming* such by obedience and faith, then their actions and decisions have a momentous significance—so momentous that killing no longer seems disproportionate.

It is in the light of man's potential fulfillment, as God envisions it, that the particular commands to Israel to destroy her enemies take on a clear and understandable meaning. An individual or a group has the right to rebel against God and to reject the offer of sonship. But he does not have the right, in God's sight, to infiltrate and destroy the community in which God is creating a renewed and redeemed humanity, a family of his children. Individual rebellion against God often appears to go unpunished in this world, even in the Old Testament. But what God was not willing to tolerate was the corruption of his people's heritage. It is to prevent this that we see him, in the Old Testament, unleashing his wrath.

Before going further in our consideration of the wrath of God, it is necessary to remind ourselves that it is not limited to the Old Testament. This is one of the suggestions at which the confused Sunday School teacher or the bland liberal theologian clutches in an effort to come to terms with this aspect of God's character: "He was like that long ago, in the *Old* Testament, but the God of the New is a God of love." It is worth emphasizing again that both the Old and the New Testaments disclose the same God: the Old Testament proclaims his patient, fervent, covenant love. The New speaks of the Lamb of God, but it also tells us of *the wrath of the Lamb* (Revelation 6:16). The familiar lines of Jesus, "For God so loved the world . . ." (John 3:16) go on to warn of the danger of being eternally lost, and two verses earlier he had made a veiled reference to the fact that he would be crucified. No one speaks of hell more often than Jesus did, and well he might, for he had to suffer and die to free men from its power.

We cannot, therefore, speak as though there were "progress" from wrath to love between the Old and the New Testament. Both wrath and love, both justice and mercy are present in the whole Bible, for both are aspects of God's character. When Jesus talks of God's anger and warns of his exacting judgment, it is not in spite of being the Suffering Servant and the Lamb. He had to be the Suffering Servant to satisfy his Father's justice. As the Son of God who is faithful and true, he cannot conceal from us this essential aspect of God's character, which it is so important for us to know. It is more than a trifle facetious for us to discuss what God ought to be like to please us when we have authoritative sources to tell us what he *is* like. There is no sense in objecting to the wrath of God; all that we can reasonably do is to inquire about its purpose, and to ask how we can avoid it.

1. *The Wrath of God and the Purity of His People*

God's anger reveals itself in the Old Testament when the integrity and purity of his people is at stake. This characteristic of his wrath is so pronounced that we can call it a principle of his conduct. Those who wanted to destroy the Hebrews physically, like the Pharaoh of Moses' day, felt it, and so did those who would have corrupted them religiously, such as Korah (Numbers 16:1-50) and the prophets of Baal (I Kings 18:25-41). Although, as has been noted earlier, physical Israel no longer occupies the same position under the New Covenant as it did under the Old, even in our own day we have seen terrible punishments exacted on nations which have taken it upon themselves to destroy the Jews: in 1945 upon Nazi Germany, and in 1967 against the Arabs.

This divine anger testifies to the preciousness of God's chosen people in his sight. In a similar way, early Christians recorded the dismal fates which befell the Emperors who distinguished themselves by their persecution of the church. Naturally any attempt to view a particular historical event as a divine judgment must be speculative, except for events specifically described in these terms by the Bible itself (e.g. the destruction of Pharaoh's army during the Exodus, the fall of Jerusalem to Babylonia, and Babylonia's subsequent defeat by the Medes and the Persians). And of course there are many examples of the persecution of Israel or of the church which do not yet appear to have fallen under such judgment. Nevertheless, the principle remains: the wrath of God is most strikingly and signally revealed when the integrity of his people is being threatened.

The whole of the Old Testament is a preparation for the coming of the Redeemer, whom God promised in the so-called proto-evangel given immediately after the Fall (Genesis 3:15). The history of Israel was intended to prepare it to receive the Messiah who would come in the fulness of time. Since the promised Saviour was rejected by the greater part of the physical nation of Israel, Israel's prerogatives have passed over to the spiritual Israel, the church. Racial purity is no longer a kind of condition for religious faithfulness, as it was in the days when Israel was moving into Canaan. In fact, the tragedy of modern Judaism may be that it has preserved or recreated its racial sense and lost its religious sense. The tension between the religious and the secular elements in the present-day State of Israel has not yet been resolved, and its eventual outcome is still uncertain. Religious feeling in Israel has received a strong stimulus by the conquest of the Old City of Jerusalem from the Kingdom of Jordan. Despite it the State of Israel seems to be headed in the same secularist directions as are large segments of the Christian church. We may some day see the curious paradox of a nation fighting against overwhelming odds to preserve its claim to a "promised land" promised by a God in whom most of its citizens do not really believe. If this becomes true, it will not represent a particular apostasy on the part of modern Israel: it will only mean that the omnipresent mentality of the twentieth century is triumphant in the former Roman province of Palestine as it is in what was formerly Christian Europe.

Because of the unholy alliance which has sometimes been made between biblical teaching and racist ideology, it is necessary to point out that racial purity in the strict sense of race was not crucial even for ancient Israel. Moses had an Ethiopian wife (Numbers 12:1) and the only women named in Christ's genealogy, except for Mary, were non-Jews: Rahab of Jericho and Ruth of Moab (Matthew 1:5). They decided whole-heartedly to share the fate of the Jews, saying as Ruth did to her mother-in-law, "Thy people shall be my people, and thy God my God" (Ruth 1:16). This was what was required of them. The contemporary analogy to racial purity and to loyalty to one's adopted people has to do with the church. For the church, doctrinal and disciplinary purity are necessities. For the individual, it is necessary to identify oneself wholeheartedly with a sound church. To do as some intellectually-inclined, would-be Christians do, who claim to be disciples of Christ while completely keeping their distance from every visible form of the church, is not sufficient.

Without purity, the church loses its integrity, its wholeness, and thereby its possibility of being a community in which God's plan of salvation is worked out in practice among men. On the one hand, we have spoken of the true church as invisible. It is invisible, in the sense that all who truly believe in Jesus Christ as Lord and Saviour according to the Scripture in fact belong to it and constitute it, and also in the sense that its full extent is visible to no man. Those who appear now to be in it because of their professions of faith and the conduct of their lives may yet reveal their professions to have been shams and their conduct hypocrisy; those who appear deliberately and permanently to have excluded themselves from it may still, in the mercy of God, experience a genuine change of heart before their deaths. Therefore we must speak of the church as *invisible*. Yet there is also on the other hand a doctrine of the *visible* church.

The doctrine of the visible church is the subject of tremendous contention among various Christian denominations. Its various forms cannot be discussed here. Traditional Reformed teaching holds that a visible local church or larger body is a true church if in the Word of God is rightly preached and the sacraments and discipline are administered according to the Word. This definition has the great advantage of conformity to biblical teaching; it has the disadvantage that according to it virtually all of the confessions and denominations and most of the individual churches as we know them today would have to be denied the name church, for the simple and sufficient reason that they do not exercise any discipline among either members or officers in either doctrine or morals. The difficulty of finding a suitable form of the visible church must not be minimized, but it may not serve us as an excuse for indifference.

The doctrine of the visible church has been hotly argued during all the Christian centuries, and this is not the place to recapitulate its history. Roman Catholic thought has traditionally identified the visible church with the Roman pope at its head with the invisible church. The famous bull of Pope Boniface VIII, *Unam sanctam* (1302), declared that it was absolutely necessary to be subject to the Roman pontiff in order to be saved. Unfortunately for him, Boniface VIII immediately ran afoul of King Philip the Fair of France, who had him kidnapped. Though rescued, the pope never recovered from the shock, and died a few weeks later. This event was followed by the "Babylonian captivity" of the papacy (1309-1377), when the popes lived at Avignon in France and were virtually the pawns of the French kings. The return of the papacy to Rome under Pope Urban VI in 1378 was followed by the Great Western Schism, during which there were two and even three rival popes at one time (1378-1415).

This kind of development obviously plays havoc with faith in the visible organization as the equivalent of the invisible church. Today we are plunged into even greater confusion on the subject of the visible church than devout Catholics were when faced with three rival popes in 1409. Apparently no major church possesses the third mark of the true church, which is the appropriate exercise of discipline for doctrinal and moral error. In some churches it is still theoretically possible to discipline a person for teaching false doctrine; in others, such as the Protestant Episcopal Church, recent developments seem to have made it virtually impossible. But even where it is *theoretically* possible, as in the Evangelical Church in Germany, or theoretically *obligatory*, as in the Roman Catholic Church, it seems to be a thing of the past in practice. Whatever the official position of any major church may be on preserving doctrinal integrity, we must concede that the formal structures of church organization are evidently unable to accomplish it.

In today's intellectual climate, the ordinary safeguards of church membership qualifications, ordination, theological degrees, and the like, mean virtually nothing. Today's bishops and clergy put on theological and priestly robes to mock Christian truth just as Nazi and Communist judges donned legal robes to pervert justice. But this does not mean that the question of the *purity of the church* is unnecessary or irrelevant. It means instead that the responsibility for preserving it is no longer adequately exercised by church officials, and now devolves upon the individual believer. It is just as important in the sight of God today as it ever was—and however difficult it may be for us to fight for it today, it was often equally difficult in the past.

Was it easy for the nomadic Hebrews, as they entered Canaan after forty years of desert wandering, to preserve their moral law and their severe religion in the face of the profligate temple cults of the richer and more sophisticated Canaanites? Was it easy for the unlettered Christians of the second century to preserve a biblical faith and discipline in the face of Roman persecution and amidst the competition of pagan syncretism and Gnostic speculation? The task which faces the twentieth-century Christian is probably no easier, but it is no less essential than theirs was—nor, with God's help, is it any less possible to accomplish.

Except in the chemical and drug industry, the word "pure," like so many other words associated with traditional virtues, has taken on a more or less pejorative connotation. Is it not terribly stiff and conceited to be concerned about the "purity" of any human organization, even the church? Can we not live and preserve our own biblical faith in a morally and doctrinally mixed church? Obviously the answer to the second question must be affirmative. There are numerous examples of thoroughly orthodox Christians who survive within, or are even produced from highly mixed churches. But the fact that this is possible does not mean that it is desirable. The convinced Christian, who knows what he believes and why he believes it, is often capable of surviving in a theologically or morally corrupt congregation or denomination. But difficulty arises for those who depend on his testimony and example. All too often they will take his membership in a congregation or denomination as a sign that all that is taught in that denomination is acceptable to him. Thus the conservative, evangelical Episcopalian who merely leads an exemplary and pious life within the Episcopal church, for example, may be cited in support of Messrs. Pike and Robinson. "Mr. So-and-So is a fine, devout Christian man—you couldn't ask for a more genuine Christian—and *he* is an Episcopalian. So why do you find fault with Robinson?" This type of argument wins no prizes for logic, but it often carries a lot of weight in practice. It shows that to preserve one's own doctrinal convictions within a theologically mixed or errant church is not enough. Individual orthodoxy or moral rectitude is no answer to the problem of the purity of the visible church, which must be dealt with before it makes any sense to speak of church unity.

(a) *Moral Purity.* Traditionally there have been two major reasons for excommunication from a Christian church: serious moral failing and serious doctrinal error. In both cases, these offenses were punished with excommunication for the sake of the offender *and* for the sake of the congregation. The offender as a last resort had to feel the sharpness of exclusion from the visible Christian community, in order that he might recognize that his moral or doctrinal error could cut him off from the invisible church as well. The visible church itself had to be protected, as a last resort, from the presence of unpunished gross sinners or flagrant heretics, whose teaching and example would lead others astray.

Whatever inexcusable excesses have taken place in the administration of these principles during the course of the church's history, the principles remain valid. The problems have come in the past when (1) entirely wrong means have been chosen to enforce them, as when heretics were persecuted and killed; (2) the enforcing body was itself unfaithful to the whole body of biblical principles, and contented itself with enforcing only a portion of them.

During the Middle Ages, moral corruption was widespread among the clergy. When the Reformation came, many abuses were resolved by Protestant teachings. On the Catholic side the necessity to compete with Protestantism greatly reduced gross moral problems within the Roman church. Of course, the Reformation did not change the heart of man, nor make him stronger to resist temptation. Perhaps its greatest contribution to raising the standards of clerical morality was that it abolished the special status previously enjoyed by the clergy. The elimination of clerical celibacy and the establishment of a married ministry solved one major problem. The doctrine of the priesthood of all believers removed the layman's fear of criticizing a minister, and kept the minister from hiding ordinary human faults behind some kind of a priestly cloak. The resulting moral competition certainly resulted in greater consistency among Roman Catholics, particularly in those regions where their influence was actively challenged by the Protestants.

Until relatively recently, the clergy of almost all denominations usually shared a relatively high standard of personal morality. This fact is amply attested by the reputation which the clergy have enjoyed—or suffered from—of being otherworldly and unfamiliar with the facts of life. Naturally no group of human beings is ever free of moral failings, but whenever failure occurred, discipline was expected and usually received. It is only in recent times, with the advent of situation ethics, that one must ask how much moral standing the present-day clergy still has. Whatever Roman Catholics may feel about those priests who renounce their vows and leave the church in order to marry, they pose less of a problem than those clergy of various denominations who encourage and perhaps take part in sexual profligacy, financial misdoings, and political insurrection in the name of situation ethics and social relevance.

Passing moral judgments on other individuals is a difficult and dangerous thing to do. It is God whose standards they must satisfy, and not ours (Romans 14:4). The fact that a Christian, be he clergyman, church official, or ordinary layman, has involved himself in serious sin does not necessarily disqualify him for future service. St. Paul was a persecutor of Christians, and the Swiss Reformer Ulrich Zwingli committed adultery with a woman from his congregation. But in both cases the sin was followed by public confession and repentance, and by an amended life. Today the situation is different, for we find "Christian" leaders apparently associating themselves with everything from witchcraft to sexual orgies. Instead of remorse and public penance, they have newspaper interviews and receive honoraria. Under such circumstances, we can say that the moral purity of the visible church is threatened. Such people will pay a heavy penalty unless they repent; but in the meantime, before the Last Judgment, the Christian must point out again and again that the Law of God does not change. Pretended Christian leaders who flout the moral law, in the name of whatever set of values, will have to answer not only for violating the law, but also for all those who have been corrupted by their example.

Since even the evil which takes place in this world, although not willed by God, can fill a positive role in his plan, it is likely that the present swarm of morally renegade clergymen who infect various denominations has something positive to teach us: firstly, the necessity for each individual to conform his own life to the Word of God, and not to the example or doctrine of popular ecclesiastical figures, and secondly the inevitability of the final judgment. In our generation clergymen who are moral hypocrites are praised by the secular world, not condemned as they would have been a few decades ago. This should remind us all the more distinctly that God has reserved a final settling of accounts for himself, and that on that day no one will fare worse than those who have eaten the bread and enjoyed the revenues of his people while devoting themselves to the service of the Adversary. To speak of the Last Judgment is theologically highly unpopular, but in the present theological confusion it more than ever appears a kind of inevitable necessity, if the sovereignty and justice of God are not to be stripped of every significance.

Faced with severe moral disorders within his own church, the individual Christian must be careful not to condemn their authors as persons; ultimately such condemnation rests with God. But he must be willing to stress the principle of the moral purity of the visible church. Sin, even the most serious sin, cannot be kept out of the church, as long as the church is human, but where there is sin, there must also be repentance and amendment, if the church is to be the church. Failure on the part of individual Christian officials to recognize this does not change the Law of God. We are not speaking of doubtful matters, but of clear commands.

When a church fails to discipline its responsible officials for advocating or participating in things which transgress God's commandments, such failure may properly be tolerated for a time on the grounds that we do not know all the circumstances. In certain Communist countries, for example, churchmen have been jailed by the state for attempting to exercise discipline within their churches. (The reason why a Communist state does not want the church to defend itself against moral decay is obvious.) In certain Scandinavian countries pastors attempting to exercise biblical principles of church discipline have been punished by the civil authorities, on the ground that every Swedish or Danish subject is entitled to the full benefits of the ministry of the Swedish or Danish church, quite irrespective of what the Bible may have to say on the subject. When a church finds itself in such a situation, we cannot judge it too harshly. But when—as is happening with increasing frequency in the United States and Great Britain—church leaders condone sexual promiscuity and perversion as "love," racial hatred in the guise of Black Power, slavery to drugs as "religious experience" and do so without being disavowed and disciplined by their churches, a time is not distant when we will have to concede, in St. John's words, that we have before us no church, but a synagogue of Satan (Revelation 3:9).

(b) *Doctrinal Purity*. If the churches of today are remiss in exercising moral discipline—except, of course, where church funds have been misused—doctrinal discipline has virtually reached the vanishing-point. A concern for doctrinal integrity is a prominent feature of the teachings of Christ and his Apostles. Jesus warned his disciples to teach men *everything* that he commanded (Matthew 28:20), and St. Paul frequently stressed the same necessity. In his farewell speech to the elders of Ephesus, Paul reminded them that he had taught them "the whole counsel of God," keeping nothing back (Acts 20:27). In today's churches, from the greatest to the smallest, with all too few exceptions, the trend is to keep back what God has said, and to display the greatest ingenuity in making plausible things which he has not said, or which he has expressly forbidden.

Nevertheless, the question of doctrinal purity cannot be dismissed with a wave at this almost hopeless muddle into which the teaching and disciplinary authorities of most churches have gotten themselves. The presence of false doctrine within a church fellowship does not necessarily require the immediate withdrawal of all those who disagree. Some of the great men of church history, for example Savonarola, never actually withdrew from the church they criticized; others left only when they were forced to do so, as was the case with Luther in the Roman Catholic Church, or with John Wesley in the Anglican. It is essential that we clearly see the principle which is involved: are we dealing with a situation in which the concept of true doctrine is recognized and respected, but inconsistently practiced, or with one in which the very concept of true doctrine has been abandoned?

In the German Protestant churches at the present time ministers are still required to profess their faith in the terms of the historic creeds and the Lutheran confessions. Despite this, virtual chaos reigns in Christian doctrine among Protestant clergy in Germany. However, a minister in a German evangelical church who in fact does believe what he publicly professes at the time of his ordination may plausibly claim that *he* represents the church, and that the modernists, who are more numerous, are illegitimate. Why should he resign and leave it to them? Likewise, a conservative Episcopalian can claim that, believing the faith as expressed in the Thirty-Nine Articles, he is a legitimate member of the church, while people like Pike and Robinson are impostors. As long as the major churches profess their allegiance to creeds which embody the essential, true doctrines, a strong case can be made for staying within them.

Whether a believing Christian can remain within a church which professes a false or seriously inadequate creed is a different problem. (The problem is complicated by the fact that some churches, including some of the more conservative ones, profess to have *no* creed. Of course, in practice they do have some kind of minimum standard of faith, but that has no bearing on the present argument, which is concerned with what the church formally and officially professes and requires of its members and clergy.) The United Presbyterian Church in the United States of America, by adopting the so-called Confession of 1967, has confronted its conservative members and ministers with a difficult situation. The new confession is not *per se* wrong or false; it does not deny historic Christian convictions. But it expresses some of them in an ambiguous or guarded way, which is precisely what a confession is not supposed to do. If a new denomination were being formed, and it produced the Presbyterian Confession of 1967, we could not well accuse it of *false* doctrine because its confession is vague. But when the Presbyterian church, which formerly subscribed to a much clearer set of articles, namely the Westminster Confession, adopts a watered-down version, it inevitably suggests to us that it intends to dissociate itself from some of its historic convictions. This puts a conservative Presbyterian minister in a more difficult situation than that of a minister in the Evangelical Church in Germany. On the one hand, there is doubtless a larger percentage of conservative evangelicals in the United Presbyterian Church than in the German one, but the American Presbyterian minister is tied to a denomination which officially seems to be veering away from the historic faith, whereas his German fellow-minister is in a church which is still formally orthodox, however bad the actual situation may be. The Roman Catholic Church, long regarded as doctrinally monolithic, now too confronts its priests and members with a similar problem. If a church in which doctrinal purity has been stressed to the point of the Inquisition suddenly begins to tolerate views which clearly contradict the historic faith, is it not necessary for someone who really believes it, for the sake of his own consistency, to separate from a church which is falsifying its faith?

The question of doctrinal purity within a church in flux is a difficult one. The counsel of immediate and total separation is evidently no answer. Many if not all the present church divisions came from a concern for doctrinal purity, and yet many if not all of the confessions and denominations which separated for doctrinal reasons are now themselves hopelessly muddled. On the other hand, unity at all costs certainly is wrong. For each believing Christian, the problem of church loyalty versus separation from his church is divided into a question of principle and a question of prudence.

The principle must be that doctrinal integrity is a *requirement* for the individual and the church. Both must be willing to confess an integral, fundamental Christian faith. Where there is formal repudiation either of specific doctrines or of the concept of true doctrine there can be no fellowship. Thus, to take a glaring example, a Christian can hardly be a member of a Unitarian church or have *Christian* fellowship with Unitarians. Even as vague an organization as the World Council of Churches sees quite clearly at this point. (Of course, a certain practical fellowship and cooperation with Unitarians and other non-Christians is possible and even desirable, for Christians, but it is not *Christian* fellowship or cooperation. It should in fact be easier for a believing Christian to cooperate in certain projects with an out-and-out Unitarian than to remain within groups which retain the name Christian but repudiate essential ingredients of the historic faith.) In a sense it seems inconsistent for the World Council to deny membership to Unitarians who openly confess to be such, and yet to admit others who in practice are no more orthodox, simply because they still have an orthodox confession on their books. Surely the point must come where what an individual or denomination actually believes is seen to be more important than what he formally professes. This is true, yet for formal, structural purposes a formally orthodox confession can suffice. Where such a confession is repudiated, it is clear that there must be formal separation, but where it is still honored, separation may be premature.

Neither an individual nor a church has the right to accept a false confession of faith. This is a matter of principle. The problem of accepting a confession which is true but inadequate becomes a matter of prudence. Probably *no* confession of faith which exists or can be imagined can include *everything* which is essential and *nothing* which is non-essential. In asking whether he can associate himself with a certain church, or remain within it, the individual must not only ask himself what its formal statements say, but he must also try to understand what they mean and where they are headed. Thus we could say that a Missouri Synod Lutheran ought to fight tooth and nail against accepting a doctrinal statement with which an evangelical Episcopalian could easily live. The reason is that the Missouri Synod has a long tradition of doctrinal fidelity, and even a slightly vague statement might well be symptomatic of a dangerously destructive trend within that denomination. Episcopalianism on the other hand, like the Church of England, has a long tradition of doctrinal vagueness, and it is not likely that it will suddenly rouse itself to make a perfectly unambiguous statement in our generation. Thus there is less reason for an Episcopalian to be alarmed over a new vague statement.

The example of the fate of many groups which have separated from their parent bodies in the interest of orthodoxy only later to lose it themselves should teach us that the battle for purity of doctrine can never be definitely and finally won by any group, no matter how clear its stand may be at certain times. It can, however, be definitely lost, and when this happens an individual must either withdraw or hopelessly compromise himself and his theological trustworthiness. The decision about exactly *when* the battle has been irrevocably lost within one's own group is a decision of prudence, and each man must decide it according to the insight which God gives him. But if a man is unwilling to admit that it *can* be lost, and that there could be circumstances under which he would separate from the church to which he belongs, then he has already violated the principle of the purity of doctrine.

Purity of the church, then, in doctrinal and in moral matters, is something which must be recognized without reservation as a principle. To fail to do so is foolishly to court the severity of God's judgment upon the institution and upon the individual, for never is his anger more dramatically revealed than when the integrity of his people is at stake. To put the principle into practice, each man must make his own decision carefully, and must avoid hastily counseling or condemning others—except to say, again, that where the possibility of actual withdrawal is considered "out of the question," then the principle has already been lost and all the prudence in the world is useless. Thus to talk of the "sin of separation" is dangerously misleading. There can be a duty of separation. The sin is in separation for the wrong reasons, not in separation itself.

How this principle is to work in practice cannot be predicted, for it will depend on the circumstances in which an individual finds himself. It may mean leaving a well-known, socially respected church to associate oneself with a little band of really committed Christians. It may mean taking such a clear stand for the essentials of historic Christianity that one will be expelled from one's wavering church. Or it may mean staying within a creaky, groaning old church structure, as long as one can still testify to the totality of Christian truth. In the last case, the obligation to be perfectly clear and unambiguous in one's own commitment and in making it known to others is doubly important. For the trained theologian this may take the form of speaking out in simple, unambiguous language, to the scorn of his sophisticated colleagues—rather than in sparring with them according to their rules, in terminology the troubled layman cannot understand. For the trained layman, it means to make a clear, humble confession; for the untrained layman, it means to make the same confession—but it also means to get some good training so that he can understand what he believes. There is no excuse for the twentieth-century Christian, if he is not mentally handicapped, not knowing enough basic Christian theology to tell theological truth from falsehood.

The true church is an *invisible* fellowship, but it is not an *imaginary* one. To be in it, you do not step inside four walls, but you accept a whole framework and orientation towards truth by entering into it with your whole understanding as well as your will. From the simple, unsophisticated, straightforward man—the subsistence farmer, perhaps—God expects an understanding and a loyalty on his level— on the same level on which he operates in his daily life. From him, a simply phrased, naïve understanding is honest. For the most complicated man—an I.B.M. executive, perhaps—He expects exactly the same thing, namely honesty, but this means something different in practice. It means loyalty and understanding on the level on which *he* operates in *his* daily life, which probably is different from that of the farmer. In the final analysis, the purity of the church cannot be guaranteed by decrees—it can only be guaranteed by church members who know their faith, both its vital elements and its secondary ones, and the difference between them.

2. *The Ecumenical Imperative*

In the preceding chapters, much has been said against some of the current efforts to create an organizational ecumenical unity. Precisely because so many of these efforts, particularly as represented by the great, official ecumenical organizations, are surrendering the essentials and distinctives of the Christian faith, it is necessary first and always to be on our guard against all *such* effort at unity. But when this is said, we must recognize that just as no Catholic (or Protestant) can be a Christian unless he is *evangelical,* no Christian can be obedient unless he is willing to be *catholic.* This does not mean that he must go along with one or another official ecumenical institution: No. But if the Christian is attentive to God's voice in Scripture he

cannot fail to see that there is an *ecumenical imperative,* which he
must heed.

The standard proof-text of the ecumenical movement is John 17:21,
"that they may all be one . . ." This line is taken from the prayer
spoken by Jesus the night before his crucifixion, called the High-
Priestly Prayer. Organization-minded ecumenists who use this text to
coerce people into structural unification evidently abuse it, for Jesus
continued, "even as Thou, father, art in me and I in Thee . . ." That
is obviously *not* organizational unity. The antiecumenists do well to
protest the misuse of the text. But it does express Jesus' fervent wish
—which must be seen as a command by those who love him—that
there be unity among his followers. It is necessary to understand that
this fervent desire was expressed by our Lord and that it is our duty
to respect and to fulfil it.

(a) *The Nature of This Unity.* If the unity Jesus had in mind is
not organizational, what is it? It is like the union between him and
God the Father. Naturally, there are elements in the unity of the
Holy Trinity which the unity among Jesus' disciples cannot remotely
resemble. But it can be like it in some ways. First, it too is a unity of
will and purpose. What the Father willed, Jesus also willed. Among
Christians, this means agreement with each other in doing Jesus' will
—which is also the will of the Father. Thus there is unity *among*
Christians and *with* Christ and the Father.

Where Jesus' will is not obeyed, there can be no true unity. All too
often official ecumenism disqualifies itself by its implicit universalism
—the idea, becoming more and more explicit, that all men are saved,
and that the church's task is only to make them aware of it. This is
plainly contrary to Jesus' "Great Commission." The Christian task is
to do Jesus' will in this respect as well as in others; to proclaim the
Gospel to every creature. To take refuge in speculation about universalism is disobedience, and certainly is not ecumenical, simply because it is not Christian. Jesus was not explicit about church allegiance. Partisans have looked hard to find in the Bible the authority
for one particular form of church government, and the learned discussions continue. But there is no room for discussion about whether
it is the will of God that people repent, and come to personal faith in
Christ. It most certainly is.

The encounter between evangelist Billy Graham and Roman Catholic Cardinal Richard Cushing of Boston before Graham's Boston Crusade in 1964 was an example of practical ecumenism in the sense of John 17:21. The cardinal, without accepting Billy Graham's whole position, was forced to recognize that the evangelist does in fact preach basic Christian truth. Dr. Graham, who by no means accepts the cardinal's authority and would not hesitate to lead Roman Catholics into a Protestant church, had nevertheless to be grateful to the cardinal for this fraternal endorsement. Many more rigid Catholics and Protestants were irritated by this "compromise." But seen clearly, it was no compromise at all—both these men were obeying the plainly-stated will of God. If they had been discussing other matters, there would have been serious differences. If the cardinal had accepted Dr. Graham's view of baptism, he would have been compromising. If Graham had accepted Cushing's view of papal authority, he would have been surrendering. But that was not the question. The question was whether the cardinal wanted the people of Boston to hear what the New Testament says about sin and grace, about God and man and about Jesus Christ, the Son of Man who is also the Son of God. The cardinal *had* to approve that—or be disobedient to his Lord. Billy Graham had to appreciate the cardinal's approval— or likewise be disobedient. This encounter, brief and incomplete though it was, was an example of a more Christian ecumenicism than what is being officially organized in Geneva or Rome, because it was unity in obedience to the instructions of Christ. Anything less would have been disobedience.

Whenever professing Christians unite in obedience to a clear command of Christ, whether it be to proclaim the Gospel, to feed the hungry, to clothe the naked, to heal the sick, or any other work of love, there is no doubt that they *have* a certain ecumenical unity. This is far short of the ideal of doctrinal and structural unity, but it is *not nothing*. Certainly for Catholics and Protestants, doctrinal unity, sacramental unity, and structural unity are impossible without one group or both giving up major elements in its faith. Such a thing may happen with individuals or even with groups; it is certainly possible for the Holy Spirit to bring it about. But it cannot and should not be counterfeited. Among the marks Jesus gave by which his disciples could be recognized were obedience and love (John 14:15, 13:35). When we fulfil the tasks of love in obedience to Christ and in cooperation with Christians of other affiliations, we have a certain unity. It is far from perfect, but it is real, and it is obedient. The unity which is counterfeited by disregarding unresolved differences on important questions of faith is neither pleasing to God nor impressive to men.

One of the chief reasons behind the present ecumenical movement was to make Christianity more plausible and attractive to non-Christians who, it was felt, were put off by the divisions of Christendom. Certainly organizational, structural ecumenical unity has made great strides in the past half-century, particularly in the last ten years. That this "progress" has been accompanied by, even if it has not itself caused, a progressive loss in doctrinal clarity in all the denominations associated with the ecumenical movement is something no one can deny. That it has brought any increase in new Christians is something no one can claim. In fact, the reverse is true: to the extent that Christians have forgotten their rival distinctions in ecumenical dialogue, they have been deprived of the time, energy, and interest in talking about Christ to non-Christians. The outcome of the ecumenical movement could well be a fully unified, thoroughly impotent church. This is not the *only* possibility; with God all things are possible. It would be unfair to deny the genuineness of many ecumenists' desire to spread the historic Christian faith. But it must be said that up till now the ecumenical movement certainly has not succeeded in making Christianity more effective in its efforts to convert the world.

It requires no theological training to recognize why this is so. There have been two major reasons why people have been won to Christ throughout church history. (We exclude a major reason why people have joined churches, i.e. following the example or wish of the ruler, because joining a church is not synonymous with conversion, and even the most fervent ecumenists aim higher than just increasing the numbers on the roll-books.) The first reason is persuasion. They have heard the Gospel presented in an understandable, attractive, distinct, and compelling way, and have been persuaded that it is worthy of their acceptance. The second is example: many people have been won to Christ by the silent but eloquent witness of a faithful Christian's self-forgetful love, or of his courageous martyrdom. But how many people have been converted to Christ, in any real sense of the word, because they were impressed by the majesty, power, organization, and unity of the institutional church? There have been times and places where the organized church was to all extents and purposes united and unchallenged: the Catholic church in Western Europe during the Middle Ages, or the Lutheran in Scandinavia and Anglican in England after the Reformation. But no one will claim that those were ideal situations as far as meaningful Christian faith among the broad masses of the people is concerned. (This is not the place to go once again into the Romantic illusion that medieval Europe was deeply Christian. A form of Christianity was dominant and influential and there were many great saints, but the mass of the people and even a large percentage of the clergy had only the most distorted ideas concerning either Catholic doctrines or the simplest elements of the Gospel. G. G. Coulton, in his extensive writings, has shown this beyond all question.)[2]

(b) *What the Unity is Not.* There is a great deal too much talk about "the unity we seek." It would make far more sense to talk of "the unity we have." We can only do this if we *have* it, and we can have it not through discussion but through faith and obedience. Realization of unity in Christ depends, then, on *obedient listening* to God. This means first an individual knowledge and understanding of God's Word. That is essential. A formulation of the meaning of God's Word in a valid system of doctrine is also important. Then, on the basis of our own willingness to obey, we can accept without reservation the Christian obedience of those with whom we cannot avoid all theological conflict. Out of practical obedience we can receive and give sharp mutual criticism, and still have a basic unity.

There are things which this real unity does not mean and will not do. For example, it will never accept organizational unity at the cost of Christian truth, for without truth unity is a mere façade. It will prohibit all experiments in so-called ecumenical worship which transgress the convictions of the participants. It will not substitute vague, contentless, least-common-denominator functions for the reasonable service God expects of every believer, namely, worship in a form and with a content to which the worshipper can give assent. An ecumenical assembly cannot replace the church or private prayer. Above all, a true ecumenism will not mock the sacraments, such as the communion, by cutting them adrift from their basis in New Testament teaching or from their historic development in the life of the church. (Reformation of the observance of the sacraments, where it is necessary, should be decided upon for good and sufficient reason, not produced by experimental tinkerings.) If we *have* unity in obedience, we will not need to pretend to have it by staging an imitation communion service. If a Catholic and I together help disaster victims, we are one in our obedience to Christ. But if we have a communion ceremony together which violates the principles of both our churches, we are engaged in a dishonest farce. The fact that Christians of different denominations cannot all attend the same communion is sad, even tragic. But to remake the communion without agreeing beforehand on what it means is a blasphemous mockery. It is to make the sacrament which shows forth Christ's death, something real, into a token of something false, a unity we do not have. This is to make it the sacrament of the unclarity of our thinking and to be united only in rebellion.

Finally, we must say a word about cooperation with non-Christians. Of course many non-Christians, for different reasons, fulfill requirements of the Christian moral code. We can be happy at every such fulfillment, firstly because moral sensitivity, if it does not lead to hypocritical smugness, can be a valid preparation for the Gospel, and secondly because God's moral laws are good and beneficial even if one is not aware of the fact that they are *His* laws. The Christian can rejoice in the cooperation he receives from morally and ethically sensitive non-Christians. But, here, perhaps most of all, he must have a clear understanding of the framework of Christian truth. Without it he might lose his own perspective, and be blinded by the comparative moral uprightness of a good non-Christian vis-à-vis an inconsistent Christian. Without it he cannot bear witness to the non-Christian of the only One who is able to make a sacrifice on behalf of virtue ultimately meaningful and worthwhile.

(c) *Co-belligerency.* The situation of the church in the spiritual and intellectual warfare of the mid-twentieth century is not unlike that which confronts the United States in Vietnam. It is faced with several different kinds of internal and external enemies. The outspoken atheists who openly seek to destroy Christianity are like North Vietnam. We know clearly who they are and what they want to achieve. The secularists who claim to be neutral or objective towards religion while actually throttling it, such as several Supreme Court justices have shown themselves to be in recent decisions, are like the Viet Cong. They claim to want only what is good for the people, but really are pursuing their own quest for power, ruthlessly trampling those who trusted their objectivity and did not recognize their deadly seriousness. Within the structure of the church itself, the radical theologians and social activists are like the rioters, draft-card burners, and anarchist pacifists in the United States. For a variety of motives, some genuinely honorable, some very mixed, some downright treacherous, they effectively serve the enemy from within the church's own camp.

Under such circumstances, the concerned conservative Christian must try to see the battle-lines clearly and to make his friends and allies where he can find them. Today no single church body is strong enough to stand alone. In addition, no church is pure enough to be able to trust all its own members or even all its own officers. The boundaries between people of different convictions within denominations are greater than the lines between the denominations themselves. An evangelical Protestant has some very important things in common with conservative Roman Catholics, both with the more evangelical ones and with the traditionalists. On the other hand, among reform-minded Catholics he must be careful to distinguish between those who seek to conform their institutions more closely to biblical norms, and those whose motive is accommodation to the secularistic spirit of our age. An *evangelical* Catholic may slight his own traditionalists, but he will fight the modernists and stress the great truths of biblical revelation. His hostility to traditionalism is for the sake of the simplicity of the same Gospel the truth and importance of which the Catholic traditionalist also defends. With the traditionalist Catholic and with the Catholic who is reform-minded for biblical reasons, the conservative Protestant can make common cause, but not with the Catholic modernist or secularizer. This distinction is not too difficult to make in practice. An evangelical Catholic may sound radical as he casts doubt on the authority of the pope, but he will uphold the authority and divinity of Christ all the more strongly. The modernist who doubts the reality of the resurrection or whether God is alive has no more right to call himself a Catholic than to call himself a Christian.

We have seen that evangelical Protestantism has a heritage of opposition to the Roman Catholic Church, and that many of the reasons for this old antagonism are still quite valid today. Nevertheless, to the extent that a Catholic and a Protestant are orthodox, there is more by far that unites them than divides them, particularly over against the monolithic secular culture of today. Both are committed to absolutes, to real truth, and to abiding moral laws. This commitment to absolutes itself distinguishes them from the rest of the contemporary world more sharply than the monotheistic Jews of ancient Israel were distinguished from the polytheistic pagans who lived around them.

Without either in any way compromising his position, the conservative, evangelical Protestant and the conservative Roman Catholic can and should join forces as co-belligerents against their common enemy, the mentality of this age. The spirit of our age does not merely happen to be opposed to Christian truth: in the New Testament, "the present age" is influenced and dominated by the "god of this age," that is, by the ancient Enemy of God and man. Catholics and Protestants will not agree on every point of their confessions of faith—not even on every important point—but they can agree to fight together against the god of this world. This is all the more important precisely because the Enemy seeks to maximize the differences between rival confessions, in order to say that no one really knows what Christianity is. He suggests that because Catholics and Protestants cannot easily agree among themselves on the interpretation of the Holy Communion, the fact that they do agree on the divinity of Christ, on eternal life, or on a final judgment is unimportant. We must not pretend to a complete unity, for it does not exist in our present situation. But we can, indeed we *must* recognize that we have a common enemy in the god of this world and in the intellectual and moral relativism he advocates, and that we have a common Lord, the true God of Time *and* Eternity. We are not identical with each other; we still have rivalries and differences. But in this great warfare we can be vigorous *co-belligerents*. We must be, if we really believe in truth and in justice and if it really is our desire to be servants of the God of all truth.

(d) *Conclusion*. The evangelical Christian—or orthodox Catholic —can legitimately reject the present ecumenical machinery, and indeed *must* do so as far as much of it is concerned. But the grounds on which he should reject it, namely belief in historic Christian doctrine and the necessity to obey God, require him to affirm a true ecumenism at the same time. Merely to reject is sterile and disobedient. Much modern ecumenism is like the golden calf Aaron made. It is not a false goal—as the calf was not a false god, but a wrong way of worshipping the true God. It is a false way of achieving a right goal. After Moses destroyed the calf, he instructed the people—just abolishing calf-worship would not have been enough. We must oppose shallow or false ecumenism with a true, evangelical, biblical ecumenism. And we have a great advantage: we do not need to build the unity laboriously. We have it already, if we believe in Christ and actively obey him. The key to true ecumenism is not more talk, but more work. If we share obedience where our Lord's commands are clear, without sacrificing or compromising our commitments, we may learn how to reconcile them—or, where necessary, to amend them. But our goal must be obedience first, in the things we see clearly, not unity at all costs. Only then will His prayer be fulfilled, "that they may be one."

Notes

¹Alan Richardson, in his *Introduction to New Testament Theology* (London: S.C.M., 1956), pp. 153ff., restates this fact about the teaching of Jesus, which ought to be obvious but is not. Biblical Christianity does not teach that men, simply because they are men, are God's children.

²See, for example, his four-volume work, *Five Centuries of Religion* (London: Oxford, 1922ff.).

Chapter 14

· UPPSALA 1968 AND AFTER: UNITY OR UNIFICATION? ·

But some of the Jewish exorcists, who went from place to place, at-
tempted to name over those who had the evil spirits the name of the
Lord Jesus, saying, "I adjure you by Jesus whom Paul preaches."

Acts 19:13

Why has it been necessary to discuss ecumenism or the ecumenical imperative in general terms when a specific attempt to implement
this imperative is being made today in the World Council of
Churches? This vast body, embracing two hundred and thirty-five
member churches, was formed in the optimistic years after World
War II, not too long after the United Nations. It would like to be
considered—perhaps in tandem with the Roman Catholic Church—
as the legitimate expression of the universal church of Jesus Christ.
Yet obviously we reject this claim. For what reasons?

Formed in 1948 in Amsterdam as a fusion of the older "Faith and
Order" and "Life and Work" movements, the World Council of
Churches began with a certain Western, Protestant, and missionary
orientation. In 1961 the International Missionary Council became
part of the W.C.C.; that same year the Russian Orthodox Church
of the U.S.S.R., together with a number of other churches in Com-
munist-controlled lands, joined. Both the absorption of the I.M.C.
and the adhesion of Iron Curtain churches had a similar effect, if
for different reasons: the evangelistic, missionizing, converting thrust
of Christianity was further blunted, and more Christian energy was
diverted into inter-church and inter-religious dialogue.

At the present time—or perhaps it would be better to say, prior to the W.C.C.'s Fourth Assembly in Uppsala (July 4-19, 1968)—the World Council seems to be *the* expression of ecumenism. But precisely because it is a *bad* expression of church unity, it was necessary to consider what a valid ecumenism would be like before discussing the W.C.C. Since Uppsala, two things have become clear: one is the desire of the W.C.C. leadership to move world Christendom in a direction it does not want to go; the second is the extent to which the attempt of the W.C.C.'s planners and leaders to put the church "where the action is" has been sidetracked by the rush of events.[1]

What was the most important religious event of 1968? For traditionally-inclined Catholics, there was the proclamation by Pope Paul VI of his personal creed on June 30, followed only a few weeks later by the encyclical on birth control, *Humanae vitae*. Both papal declarations are firmly in line with Catholic tradition and show that as far as Catholic doctrine is concerned, the Pope has not been convinced that "the more it changes, the more it is the same." Perhaps future historians will find these two pronouncements deeply significant. In any event, they accidentally (or cleverly?) bracketed what was intended to be *the* religious event of 1968, the Fourth Assembly of the World Council of Churches at Uppsala.

During two weeks, July 4-19, over seven hundred delegates and double that number of advisers, observers, relatives, staff, press, and others met in the medieval Swedish archepiscopal town of Uppsala. They met under the motto, "Behold, I make all things new" (Revelation 21:5), and wrestled in working "sections" and in plenary sessions with topics as diverse as "The Holy Spirit and the Catholicity of the Church" and "Towards New Styles of Living." A new category of non-voting delegate, that of "youth participant," was created to permit the younger members of the Christian community to express themselves. According to one "y.p.," an Australian, the Assembly's organizers had chosen them to challenge and prod the voting delegates. This task they accomplished, although perhaps not always in the most constructive way.

The Fourth Assembly met during the "Prague Spring," while Czechs and Slovaks were enjoying a fresh breath of freedom and Soviet tanks massed on Czechoslovakia's borders. It debated the "unilateral intervention of a great power" in Vietnam to the echoes of ringing denunciations of the United States by Soviet and British delegates. The attempts of Norwegian, Philippine, and Japanese speakers to apply the criterion of historical accuracy in the debate were pigeonholed by the American General Secretary or drenched in the self-condemning tears of other Americans, such as Robert McAfee Brown and Harold Bolsey. The harsh, premature winter which followed upon the Prague spring, the blitzkrieg-like occupation of Czechoslovakia by half-a-million Soviets and obedient satellites, also blanketed the Assembly at Uppsala, making its attempts to be politically relevant appear either hopelessly naïve or hopelessly compromised.

The problem involves far more than mere timing, more than merely the fact that the W.C.C. Assembly was bracketed in theological matters by Pope Paul's double broadside and completely swamped by the tidal wave of Russian military determination which overwhelmed its political ventures. If we accept the symbolism of the boat which the W.C.C. has chosen for itself, the giant metallic sculpture behind the presidential platform in Uppsala's Fyris Hall may give us a clue as to what went so wrong. In the sculpture, made especially for the Fourth Assembly, the boat's rudder is firmly fixed to its mast. In normal sailing, the winds provide the power, but the rudder, controlled by the helmsman's intelligence, determines the direction. As the rudder of the W.C.C. boat is fixed to the mast, the direction as well as the power must come from the winds; the winds are the winds of change, and not the "rushing, mighty wind" of the Holy Spirit, speaking through an authoritative Bible. The W.C.C. made use of biblical texts, from its charter-text, John 17:21 ("That they may all be one . . .") to the Assembly motto, Revelation 21:5. Unfortunately, as Anglican observer John R. W. Stott remarked, the W.C.C. uses the Bible as a drunk does a lamppost—for support, not for illumination.[2]

The tragedy of the W.C.C. does not lie in the fact that it exercised bad timing at Uppsala. It is rather that it never could have reached a worthwhile mark, no matter how good its timing or how considerate the Pope and the Russians might have been about not stealing the stage. It never will be able to do so, either, until it can take its direction from the One it formally acknowledges as Lord and not from the world it wants to serve and to help.

In almost all the comments which have been published on the

Uppsala Assembly, attention has been drawn to its sociological, political, even "revolutionary" emphases. This is understandable enough. For the secular media which covered the conference, revolution makes better copy than tradition and—as the "youth participants" charged—the Assembly's theology was much more traditional than its sociology. The liberal religious press, on the one hand, has a vested interest in publicizing the W.C.C.'s political-social activism, which it has itself largely stimulated if not sponsored. The conservative religious press, on the other hand, is often on the look-out for something with which to shock or even frighten its readers, and that leads it, too, to chronicle the social-action lobby. As a result, most of those who were not actually present at Uppsala are completely unaware of the strongly theological bent of a large number, perhaps even the majority, of the delegates.

Of course the delegates have left Uppsala now, and the W.C.C. headquarters staff have gone into winter quarters—but not hibernation—by the shores of Lake Geneva. There they will make the important decisions during the seven or so long years which will precede the Fifth Assembly. Will they feel bound to respect, during their absence, the delegates' interests and convictions, which they tried to ignore when they were present at Uppsala? It is hardly likely. Thus we can conclude that while the unbalanced press coverage did not adequately portray the Assembly at Uppsala, the impression which it gave of the W.C.C. as a secularly-minded organization may well be accurate. One Eastern Orthodox priest—a veteran of the World Council since its birth in Amsterdam—told a reporter, "You must not think that this is a *Christian* organization." The same sentiment, voiced by other ecumenical veterans, speaks only too clearly of the disillusionment of faithful servants of Christ with the trend of the ecumenical organization. From uncertain but hopeful beginnings, it has developed badly.

1. Dichotomy and Ambiguity at Uppsala

The Assembly had many faces. Whereas the W.C.C. leaders, particularly since the 1966 Conference on Church and Society, seem to have taken pride in the W.C.C.'s increasingly aggressive involvement in social and economic concerns, the delegates, advisers, and observers by contrast, had more traditionally theological interests. The old dichotomy between those interested in clarifying and confirming common beliefs ("Faith and Order") and those with a zeal for action ("Life and Work") was intense. Whereas the delegates and their advisers often seemed preoccupied with Christian belief, the W.C.C. staff seemed far more concerned with political and social activism. At Uppsala there was an atmosphere of greater theological concern and seriousness, as well as of more piety, than reigns in the W.C.C. offices in Geneva. On the other hand, Uppsala is now over, and the Geneva administration will shape the destiny of the W.C.C. for the next several years. In trying to reach a balanced evaluation of the different emphases and interests represented at Uppsala, it is necessary to bear in mind the fact that they will not necessarily be given equal weight in the decisions Geneva will make in the future.

The dichotomy between belief and action was represented in the tasks assigned to the six "sections" or commissions into which the Assembly was divided, which presented reports ultimately approved by the Assembly and submitted to the member churches. Three were devoted to largely "theological"* topics: catholicity, mission, and worship; three to "social" concerns: development, peace and justice in international affairs, and "new styles of living." The largest number of delegates was interested in the section on mission, and the largest number within that section in the theological basis for mission. The W.C.C. officials and staff, on the other hand, were obviously far more partial to the issues of development, international affairs, and "new styles of living."

The sections on catholicity and on worship were influenced by the theological conservatism of Eastern Orthodox delegates and Roman Catholic observers; the section on "Renewal in Mission" was marked by a major effort of conservative, evangelical Protestants to see to it that the priority of proclaiming the *content* of Gospel not be lost. Listening to individual delegates, participating in worship, or reading some of the drafts on "theological" topics gave one kind of an impression. Watching the rapid railroading of measures

*Naturally the "theological" topics have social implications, and vice versa.

through plenary session, listening to the partisan political harrangues of various delegates—the impassioned self-defense of the Nigerians on the question of Biafra, the pathetic self-condemnation of Americans on Vietnam—or observing the films being shown in a corridor corner by a W.C.C. official gave another.

The dichotomy between faith and activism, between concern for theological truth and captivation by political slogans, was only one facet of the ambiguity of this W.C.C. Assembly. In another area— the area of Assembly mechanics—it took on almost grotesque features. There was a remarkable contrast between the well-planned application of American parliamentary and business procedures and the near chaos which ruled among the delegates who were trying to understand them and use them in a responsible and intelligent way.

In one very significant respect the whole Assembly was dominated by the nearly frenzied manner in which reports and resolutions had to be presented, discussed, and voted upon and in which officers were nominated and elected. Mimeographed reports, documents, and lists of candidates were constantly being distributed in three different languages. A delegate from the Waldensian Church of Italy described the Assembly as "bedlam," incapable of coming to any kind of a rational decision and serving only as "window-dressing" to conceal from the delegates and member churches the fact that everything of importance is decided in advance by the central headquarters. After watching the chair try to extract itself from the confusion caused by a trilingual ballot on which the French text said exactly the opposite of the English and German ones, an AP staffer from Britain remarked that the parliamentary procedures of the W.C.C. could at best be described as "feeble." The procedures were not really at fault, nor—with occasional lapses—were the presiding officers. Lack of time was the crucial limiting factor and the haste it demanded was fatal to calm discussion and deliberation.

It may seem uncharitable to emphasize the operational difficulties inherent in the attempt of any multi-lingual assembly of over 700 delegates to write and approve reports on a broad spectrum of issues within the space of so few days. Yet it is clearly possible—even probable—that the haste, bustle, and actual railroading tactics of the business meetings raise considerable doubt whether any vote really represents the informed opinion of the delegates. Fatigue and confusion (e.g., in the case of the tri-lingual ballot mentioned earlier, which was for the election of one of the W.C.C.'s six presidents) often appeared to dominate over deliberation and understanding. The AP man felt that four-fifths of the delegates did not know what they were voting for. Even allowing for exaggeration, the confusion was such that it is necessary to caution the reader against accepting any W.C.C. vote as representing the sincere and informed opinion of the delegates. Unfortunately, this holds true not only of what was said on politics and economics, but also of what was said on matters of faith and even of what was prayed.

This dichotomy and ultimately this chaos result from a fundamental confusion in the minds of most ecumenists and of many ordinary Christians between *the unity of Christians* and *the reunification of the churches*. If there is any substance to the biblical message at all, there already is a real and important unity *between* Christian believers, which was not destroyed by the Reformation or any other new departure and which therefore cannot be recreated. This observation needs to be reiterated time and again to overcome the widespread impression that Christian unity is to be obtained by organizational means.

2. *The Real Unity of the Church*

There can be no doubt that—organizationally speaking—Christendom is in great disarray. Yet through the Christian centuries, even when ruptures were being actively promoted, Christians have professed a belief in *one* church. In the Apostles' Creed, the most nearly universal confession of Christians, we say, "I believe in the holy, catholic church." Luther put it a bit differently, "ich glaube an eine allgemeine christliche Kirche,"—in a universal Christian church— but these words also affirm that unity is there. All the ancient Christians, the Fathers and Doctors of the Church, feuding Greeks and Latins, Roman Catholics, Lutherans, and Reformed Protestants have said this Creed, and we continue to say it right up to the present day. Were they so blind that they did not see the fact that the church was in fact divided? Surely after the Reformation had begun, this formal, organizational division was obvious. It had to be obvious to the Reformers, who were themselves *responsible* for it. How could Luther say "eine allgemeine christliche Kirche" after he began the Reformation? Evidently he and the others were talking about something other than formal, structural unity.

The fact that so many centuries of Christians have said this Creed is something that we should take seriously, for it attests *the reality of the unity of the invisible church* despite structural divisions. This unity was not destroyed in Luther's eyes, or in Calvin's, by the divisions within the visible church. Are we to say that such a unity, which the church has confessed since its earliest days, is meaningless? We may want to say that it is not perfect, i.e. not complete: perhaps full structural and organizational unity would be better. We can even admit that it is far short of ideal. But we must proclaim and confess that it is *real*, for otherwise we cut ourselves off from the community of those who have confessed this apostolic Creed down the centuries. We cannot say that it is trivial and without meaning, as some of our ecumenists would have us think, without saying that for centuries the church has been confessing its faith in a triviality.

What does the Bible itself say about the unity of Christians? The classical text is in St. John's Gospel, chapter 17, especially verses 21-23. This text was the watchword of the Faith and Order meetings in Lausanne in 1927, and is the "mandate" of the W.C.C. We have already pointed out in the preceding chapter that there is something inconsistent about our trying to fulfill Jesus' prayer to his Father for unity while disregarding his clear command to us to "make disciples of all nations" (Matthew 28:19). The unity which he means cannot be separated from obedience to the will of the Father. Obedience is not a question of the organization of individuals or of the amalgamation of organizations. These are not irrelevant, but they can never be primary.

That individuals, not organizations, are of primary importance to Jesus in John 17 is quite clear from what he says, for he is praying for his disciples, and to those "who will come to believe in me through their word" (v. 20). He is speaking of those who will come to share the apostolic faith through the witness of the Apostles; he is praying that *they* may be one. But who are those who come to believe in him through the Apostles' teaching? Do all baptized

Roman Catholics fit this definition? Does Jesus' expression apply to all the members of the Swedish Lutheran Church? Have they all come to faith in him through the Apostles' teaching? Have all the members of the Congregational churches (Reformed)? If we unify, for example, the Roman Catholic, the Lutheran, and the Reformed churches, together with all their members, are we making one those who have come to faith in Jesus through the apostolic teaching? Or are we doing quite a different thing?

It is necessary to ask whether this prayer is a command for us. Or can we believe that God has in fact answered it by making unity real, not among churches, but among believers, among those "who will come to believe in me through their word"? It is part of the great High-Priestly Prayer uttered by Jesus before his crucifixion. Did he mean for *us* to answer it? The New Testament teaches in stead that the Father *has fulfilled* the request of his Son. Christ himself dwells in the heart of each one who believes in him (cf. Ephesians 3:17). If Christ dwells in the heart of every believer, is there not already a very significant unity between them all? Is Christ divided (I Corinthians 1:13)? Is the New Testament wrong about his indwelling the believer? Or is this indwelling insignificant?

According to the New Testament, then, there already *is* a reality of unity among believers. We shall not claim that the unity of believers in Christ is perfect, nor that we could not or should not improve it by better outward forms of unity, but we must hold fast to the fact that it is real. Otherwise we deny an important central teaching of the New Testament. Unfortunately, as we have seen, the World Council, in John Stott's words, uses the Bible for support and not for illumination. As a result it should not surprise us if the fate of the Council will be to harm the church of Christ, as has happened before when men have tried to impose a rigidly unified structure upon the people of the New Testament.

3. The Sad History of Apparent Unity

A glance at the New Testament shows that the word for church, *ekklesía*, is used in two ways: first, to mean the individual congregation (by analogy with a secular assembly); second, to mean the universal church. The concept of the church as a structured organization was not yet clearly developed when the New Testament was written. We cannot say that because the idea is not explicitly developed in the New Testament, therefore the church ought not to have a structured organization, but we can doubt that this concept of the church, as an organized, structural unity, was a goal of primary importance. In fact, historical conditions made it unthinkable at first.

Constantine the Great

The Christians were not able to develop a unified functioning organizational structure until the Roman persecutions ceased with the accession to power of the Emperor Constantine. He immediately gave the church an impetus to promote unity, permitting it to use the Imperial Post; he it was who convened the great Council of Nicaea, which we call the First Ecumenical Council.

What kind of a man was the Emperor Constantine? The Greek church called him *Isoapóstolos,* the Equal of the Apostles. This enigmatic Roman emperor, who gave European civilization its nominally Christian stamp (Cf. Chapter 5, above) was also a fervent proponent of church unity. Many people have doubted that he was truly a Christian. It is likely that Constantine was genuinely converted, but in any case, this much is clear: he had largely political motives for trying to give the church unity. He wanted harmony and unity in his Empire.

Regardless of whether he was a Christian, Constantine I was a tyrant and a shrewd one. He saw the need of unifying the institution which he wanted to provide the moral foundation for his empire. This was not necessarily a wrong or immoral motivation on Constantine's part, but it was a dangerous one for Christianity, as subsequent history has amply shown. In setting the church to serve the Emperor as well as God, he established a pattern which has often seriously impaired its integrity and its credibility.

In the Middle Ages, the motto of those trying to give substance to the re-established Empire (the so-called Holy Roman Empire) was "Ein Gott, ein Reich, ein Kaiser!" (One God, one empire, one emperor!). It was echoed in secular terms by Hitler: "Ein Volk, ein Reich, ein Führer!" Reformation and Counter-Reformation political leaders, with varying degrees of personal sincerity, promoted the Protestant or Catholic unity of their realms as the best means to preserve their political unity and their own authority.

In our own day we see an even clearer example of non-Christian motives for promting church unity in the religious policies of the Soviet Union. The Soviet government has intervened in church affairs not to "divide and conquer," but to bring about the amalgamation of many different churches. The so-called Uniate churches in Communist countries, i.e. Greek- or Slavic-speaking churches obedient to Rome, have been forced to break with Rome and to join the Orthodox churches. Smaller Protestant churches have also been put under pressure to unite into larger bodies. A similar trend is promoted even in the United States of America. Of course, there is no suggestion of any actual government compulsion in America, but even here the government, as it gives financial assistance and other concessions to church agencies, prefers to deal with a few big church groups, not with many little ones. Consequently there is a government-stimulated drift towards centralization.

The state thus frequently prefers a *united* church. Because the state desires it, it is not necessarily bad. Even Hitler built the *autobahn*. But we must recognize that the desire for unity can have quite a non-Christian motive behind it. If we take the call for the unity of the church seriously, we must also take the history of the church seriously. Throughout its history there has been too much ambiguity in the motivation for organizational church unity. Is the ecumenical movement free from such ambiguity today?

"Unity" and the Christian Witness

From Constantine onward, then, the church was unified and the civil authorities allowed it to exercise its authority with their approval and cooperation. We can ignore the real elements of disunity that were still present after the Council of Nicea in 325—the Arians, Monophysites, and the great East-West schism of 1054, for example —because in spite of them, church unity of a substantial kind did exist before the Reformation? But if a major reason for Christian unity is "that the world may believe," we have to admit that the history of the united church before the Reformation is not altogether encouraging.

The unitedly "Christian Europe" of the Middle Ages was not good at evangelizing the non-Christians. Its real "missions" were the Crusades, which undoubtedly sent a good many Moslems to meet their Maker sooner than they would otherwise have gone, but which hardly won them to faith in Christ. Other "missionary" endeavors included the "evangelization" of the Lithuanians by the Teutonic Knights, which was a religious failure, although a partial military success. The most significant genuinely missionary spirit of the Middle Ages was that manifested by St. Francis of Assisi and his followers, who promoted both "inner missions" among the professing Christians of Europe and foreign missions among the Moslems of North Africa. But it was precisely the Franciscans who were at daggers drawn with the church's administrative hierarchy. The most intense group of Francis's followers, the so-called spiritual Franciscans, influenced by the ideas of abbot Joachim of Floris (d. about 1202), became constantly more outspoken in their opposition to the papacy; the more moderate Franciscans were "domesticated" by Popes Gregory IX and Nicholas III and soon lost their original enthusiasm. The Dominican order showed a great deal of interest in winning back the heretical Albigenses, but also became prominent in the work of the Inquisition. Aside from the peoples of Northern and Eastern Europe, barbarians who accepted Christianity as they entered the orbit of European civilization, the missionary record of the united medieval church is not good.

The Arab and Turkish conquests of formerly Christian lands did not stimulate missionary expansion, but the loss of Northern Europe to the Reformation did provoke a surge of Roman Catholic missionary activity. While the followers of Luther and Calvin were wresting Northern Europe away from papal jurisdiction, the counter-reforming Jesuit order, established by Ignatius Loyola, was sending missionaries to India, China and Japan. What Rome lost through the revolt of the evangelicals, it recouped through the conversion of the South and Central American Indians in the wake of Spanish

and Portugese discovery and conquest. Within the Protestant countries a kind of religious unity on a territorial basis prevailed, according to the principle, *cujus regio, ejus religio,** but this unity led
to neither a vital inner nor outward missionary thrust. The real
flowering of Protestant missions came after national Protestantism
had been fragmented by new movements, such as pietism and
Methodism. The reunion of individual Protestant churches has reduced rather than increased missionary efforts, as many students
have pointed out.[4] When Sir Henry Lunn's efforts to bring about
a reunion of Methodist churches in Britain were crowned with success, he wryly commented to his son Arnold, "My dear boy, there
was a great deal more life in Methodism when the primitive Methodists doubted the salvation of all other Methodists than there is
today."[5]

The World Council of Churches has achieved a measure of apparent unity, but it has had to make two great sacrifices in order
to do so: it has had to abandon its mandate both for prophetic and
for evangelistic witness. The W.C.C.—as its Fourth Assembly has
shown—can criticize a secular power only if the criticism is spear-
headed by the representatives of that power with the W.C.C. Thus
the Uppsala meeting could condemn the United States on Vietnam,
but not the U.S.S.R. on Czechoslovakia nor even Nigeria on Biafra.
In other words, the "unified" church is in no stronger a position to
witness to the powers that be concerning their wrongdoing than the
divided church. Everything depends on the liberty of expression
which particular governments grant their citizens and upon each
individual's civic courage. Perhaps witnessing in this sense has become *passé* since the Orthodox Church of the Soviet Union has
joined the World Council; perhaps a judiciously closed eye to persecution in and by the Soviet Union is the price that the W.C.C.
must pay for the presence of the Russian brethren. But is it the sign
of new strength for the church to adulterate and weaken its prophetic social witness in such a way? St. John Chrysostom (died
407) denounced his Roman rulers, who could and did punish him
for it; he is remembered and they are not. His spirit is strangely

*"Whose the rule, his the religion."

lacking among the polished diplomats of the ecumenical movement, for all their talk of prophetic witness, challenge, and protest. They challenge the bourgeois democracies, who will do no more than beat their own breasts in reply; they are very careful about the real tyrants.

The Reverend Richard Wurmbrand, a Rumanian pastor who has suffered extensively at Communist hands, was present at Uppsala, but as an uninvited guest. It is a curious kind of Christian witness to invite an anti-Christian demagogue, James Baldwin, to address a plenary session, and to restrict a man who has suffered imprisonment and torture for Christ's sake, Pastor Wurmbrand, to passing out leaflets on the sidewalk. Of course, American churchmen like to be affronted and told how rotten they are. In a sense it is a credit to them that they will listen to Baldwin's reproaches, even though he is hardly a spokesman for their professed Lord. And of course well-fed Soviet delegates do not like to be told that Communist jails hold countless Christians whose record of cooperation with their governments is not as good as that of the Uppsala delegates. In both these things the World Council's daring goes just far enough to tell each country what its own delegates want it to hear. Is that prophetic witnessing?

The situation with witness in the sense of *evangelism* is if anything even bleaker. We have spoken of the "ecumenical imperative" of John 17. We are not sure that these words properly apply to the organized ecumenical movement, but in any case the movement's zeal to be obedient to a divine imperative is commendable. But what about ambiguity? In the Great Commission in Matthew 28:19-20, Jesus told his disciples, "Go out, therefore, and make disciples of all the nations . . . teaching them to observe everything that I have enjoined upon you." It is precisely in this area that the ecumenical movement embodied in the World Council of Churches—and also that embodied in the Second Vatican Council, we might add—is failing abjectly. The W.C.C. has absorbed the International Missionary Council, claiming that it too has missions and evangelism as one of its major goals. But today missions which seek conversions are being rapidly abandoned in favor of "dialogue." The World Council stands for many things, but certainly not for evangelism, any more than for martyrdom.

A Wrong Road

Of course there were positive aspects to the W.C.C. Assembly. The delegates themselves often displayed strong and vigorous theological, evangelistic, and moral conviction and sentiment. Unfortunately, it is all too clear that while these convictions may act as a brake on the movement's progress towards secularization, they cannot change its direction. A correspondent for the *Rhein-Main Zeitung*, Dr. Klaus Bockmühl, pointed out that the Fourth Assembly could not be easily manipulated like a smaller conference and thus did not produce the desired "revolutionary" statements like the "by invitation only" W.C.C. Conference on Church and Society held in Geneva in 1966. But is this a reason for optimism? Is it enough to be able to say merely that the ecumenical troops refuse to retreat from theology, evangelism, and Christian personal morality as fast as their ecumenical generals would like?

The real area of failure for the W.C.C. does not lie in the fact that, hamstrung by its political liabilities, it can speak out on Vietnam but not Czechoslovakia. It does not even lie in the fact that its sociologically-tinted spectacles allow it to see the moral and spiritual danger of racism, but not of sexual libertinism. Its deepest failure lies in the fact that it is evading its responsibilities to give clear answers to one central question on which the Christian church ought still to be competent: What can I believe? Today the powerful Chinese and the pitiable Albanian Communists join in expressing their confidence that the power of Marxism-Leninism will enable them to resist the Russian army. What power does the World Council proclaim? Not the power of Christ, but "new styles of living."

Are man's most essential needs today for improving social conditions, better distribution of this world's wealth, more effective economic and agricultural methods? If these were man's deepest needs, there would be no fighting in Biafra or Vietnam, no bitter disillusionment in Czechoslovakia. If they were man's deepest needs, would it be the church which should deal with them? The competent— or successful—social, economic, and political leaders are in politics, business, and education, not in church jobs. They do not need the churches to tell them *how* to produce, or even *that* wealth should be shared, *that* political power should be used responsibly. What they need is to be convinced *why* these things are necessary. They know well enough that "Man does not live by bread alone." The hungry masses may think so, but their well-fed, powerful rulers, both political and economic, know better. "Red Danny"—Daniel Cohn-Bendit—could shout to the rioting French students in May, 1968, "Man does not live by bread alone!" But it took a courageous French pastor to climb up on his platform and finish the sentence, "but by every word which comes from the mouth of God" (Deuteronomy 8:3).

No man has to be told that he should eat when he is hungry. Hunger is a basic and easily recognized human need. The distinctive message of the church is not that hungry men ought to be fed, but that there is a famine more terrible than the famine for bread: that "of hearing the words of the Lord" (Amos 8:11). The scientists, technologists, agricultural experts and economic planners may succeed in filling the emptiness in men's stomachs. It is their job, they know it, and they work on it—often with a compassion more genuine than that of professional ecclesiastics. But they cannot fill the emptiness in men's hearts with their agricultural and industrial products. They cannot even fill their own hearts. That emptiness must be filled by faith—but, as St. Paul tells us, "Faith comes from hearing, and hearing from the word of Christ" (Romans 10:17). As Anglican John R. W. Stott charged from the Uppsala platform, the World Council offers very little food for the spiritual hunger of men. It is by failing to fill men's hearts with the answers God himself gives to the riddle of existence, not by failing to revamp social and economic life, that the churches will merit the just condemnation of Christ and the deserved contempt of disillusioned men.

This dereliction of the church's deepest duty, to communicate to men the divine word by which alone they can have true life, its down-grading in favor of social solutions, is not confined to members of the World Council. Even the monolithic Roman Catholic Church, whose teachings Protestants have always found *clear* (although sometimes clearly *wrong*), is caught in the current. Instead of offering clear answers (as the Pope seemed to do in his 1968

Confession and in *Humanae vitae*), the Vatican, as recently as
October 1, 1968, has launched the dubious project of uniting all
"believers" (Christians, Moslems, and Jews) in order to "establish
a dialogue with those who do not believe in God." Jesus did not
come to bring belief in God: He spoke to chiefly *believing* Jews.
Even St. Paul in Athens found his hearers to be "very religious in
all respects" (Acts 17:22, NASB). Christ did not commission his
disciples to proclaim theism or religion, but the whole Gospel. Any
church or association of churches which contents itself with doing
less than this—other than very briefly, to meet a very specific situa-
tional need—is not serving Christ but dishonoring him. To attempt,
without qualifications, authority, or practical power, to direct the
rulers of men in their efforts to reform social and economic structures while neglecting to give either men in general or their rulers
the only Word which is a lamp for their feet, and a light for their
path (Psalm 119:105), is to commit the sin with which Jesus
charged the Pharisees: "You shut off the kingdom of heaven from
men, for you do not enter in yourselves, nor do you allow those
who are entering to go in" (Matthew 23:13); it is to tithe the spices
and neglect the weightier matters: judgment, mercy, and faith
(23:23). No one can blame the churches for not knowing all the
social, political, and economic answers: but they can—and will—be
blamed for failure to know, or to proclaim—the necessary spiritual
answers. The churches should not evade social issues, for the message of Christ is for the *whole* man. But by evading the central
issues of faith, by remaining silent in the face of the crying *spiritual*
questions of our day, the churches deny that man is the unity as
which God made him—a unity of soul and body, who *cannot* live
by bread alone. Thus they deny the true nature of man, and they
deny the God who made him in his image. This—not Czechoslovakia, Biafra, or Vietnam—is the true and tragic evasion of Uppsala.

Notes

[1]Cf. David Hedegård, *Ecumenism and the Bible* (London: Banner of Truth, 1964), for an accurate if unfriendly history of the W.C.C.

[2]*The Church of England Newspaper*, August 23, 1968, p. 6.

[3]The major difference between Arianism and the orthodox Christianity of Athanasius was the Arian belief that the Son of God came into being *after* the Father. They accepted the divinity of Christ in every respect except that of the Son's consubstantiality with the Father: the Son was *homoiousios* (of similar nature) with the Father, but not *homoosios* (of the same nature). The *homoiousios* Son of Arian theology, however, did atone for our sins on the cross, rise from the dead, and is coming again to judge the living and the dead. In consequence we can say that Arius, despite the dangerous implications of his teaching, retained far more of the Christian message than does a man like Bishop Robinson. The Monophysites held that Christ had only one nature, a divine nature, his humanity having been absorbed into his divinity. This teaching, while seriously deficient inasmuch as it removes Christ farther from us, at least has the merit that it does not reduce his stature, like liberal modern theology.

[4]Hedegård, *Ecumenism*, pp. 90ff.

[5]Cited in Arnold Lunn and Garth Lean, *The New Morality*, revised edition (London: Blandford, 1967), p. 188.

[6]Associated Press report, *Gazette de Lausanne*, Wednesday, October 2, 1968, p. 12.

· CONCLUDING
UNSCIENTIFIC POSTSCRIPT ·

For I am not ashamed of the Gospel of Christ.

ROMANS 1:16

The conservative, evangelical Protestant often vacillates between shamefacedness and self-satisfaction. Faced with the fact that liberal, "modern," secular, even anti-Christian nominal Protestants dominate in the universities and theological faculties, he is inclined to embarrassment and self-pity. The domination of the news media by the most unrepresentative religious radicals—unrepresentative of true Christianity, that is—fills him with chagrin, sometimes even with jealousy. Harvey Cox can get more attention from newspapers throughout the nation for addressing one hundred religious cranks than Billy Graham does when he preaches to one hundred thousand people. A real statement of the teaching of the Bible about itself, about Christ, about sin, forgiveness, and punishment, about sexual morality or capital punishment, brings cries of horror, shock, and ridicule. No one likes to be thought of as out of date, reactionary, and inflexible. The words which are or were designations of virtues in Christian language have become bad names, suggestive of arrogance, harshness, or mental derangement: loyalty, purity, fidelity, chastity, obedience. All these things work together to embarrass the conservative Protestant—unless he is a man with rhinoceros skin and a backbone to match. The Christian who is ashamed on these counts has less than he should have and is less than he ought to be. He should not be ashamed of the Gospel of Christ any more than

St. Paul was, for in it he really does have "the power of God for salvation."

The Gospel does indeed give access to power—real power, the most real in the universe. Therefore it is not surprising that it sometimes produces a certain smugness and self-satisfaction. It is spiritual power, not physical. It cannot be measured in kilovolts or in army divisions, but it is real enough to be accompanied at times by what Senator Fulbright calls the arrogance of power. The Christian knows that he ultimately stands on the winning side. If the adherents of the opposite side, flushed with pride in their momentary triumph, seem to gloat, it is only natural for him to want to cast back at them, "You'll get yours soon enough!" And it is true. Theoretically, of course, a man can repent and turn to Christ at any time in a long life, no matter how full it has been of sin and rebellion. He can. The difficulty is that the practice of rebellion and contempt for God changes a man, and makes it progressively harder for him to repent in reality. The unrepentant will pay a heavy penalty for their wickedness. No one made this clearer than Christ, who gave his life to save those who believe. But this punishment, inevitable apart from Christ, should not be a reason for *self*-satisfaction for the Christian. It should be a reason for sorrow for him as much as it is for his Lord. Because man, even conservative, evangelical, Protestant man, is what he is, it will not surprise us that Christians can and often do take a kind of unworthy comfort in contemplating the destiny awaiting the enemies of Christ. The feeling is wrong, and unworthy of a disciple of Christ, but this does not change the facts. The Christian side ultimately *will* triumph, and the enemies who refuse to be won to Christ must be judged by him.

Both this embarrassment and this smugness are false: no Christian should be ashamed of holding fast to the truth, though others laugh at him; it is something of which to be proud. No Christian should take satisfaction in contemplating the destiny awaiting his persecutors unless they repent; it should grieve him, as it grieves Christ. But there is a more legitimate reason for the conservative, evangelical Protestant to be ashamed—and a more legitimate one for his pride. This book has included much that is *confession* in an old and valid Christian sense. It is confession in the sense in which we would often say *pro*fession today: speaking out about and on behalf of what one

deeply believes. Such confession is necessary, because we really believing Christians are isolated from one another by a haze of confusion, uncertainty, and diffidence. We must speak out and identify
ourselves even at the risk of probably drawing much enemy fire, so
that we can find each other and strengthen and encourage one another. But there is also need for confession in the other sense—admission of sin and shortcomings.

1. An Evangelical Confession

The Greek New Testament word for sin is *hamartia*. It means
"missing the mark" and has a strong connotation of incompleteness,
inadequacy or imperfection. Often it is falsely assumed that because
hamartia means inadequacy, missing the target, rather than transgres-
sion/rebellion, sin is not such a deeply serious matter. Suffice it to
say that if one has only one shot with which to stop a charging lion,
missing the mark will be fatal. Likewise, if one is trying to leap across
a chasm, a slight inadequacy is more than enough to take care of him
for good. We must remember that the purpose of God for man is
perfection—completeness—and missing the mark, however close one
comes, spoils this perfection. (The Greek word *teleosis,* perfection,
we recall, does not mean an abstract summing up of all virtues, but
rather the fulfillment of one's truest potential; it is in this sense that
Jesus is speaking when he says, "Be ye perfect," in Matthew 5:48.)
The difference between the Christian and the non-Christian does not
lie in the Christian's greater success in hitting the mark of perfection,
but in his union by faith with Christ, the One who is perfect and
who can perfect us. *Hamartia* remains a problem for the Christian,
and it is subject-matter for confession.

(a) *Evangelical Sin in Society.* All segments of the church are now
agreed, it seems, that it has a duty to society. Evangelicals sharply
criticize liberals and modernists for abandoning the church's God-
appointed task, to save men, in order to try to reshape society. This
criticism is serious and legitimate. But we evangelicals are stained by
the sin of our relative indifference to society's problems. In part we
may excuse this by saying that we were putting first things first: con-

centrating on true doctrine—and that *is* essential. But true *Christian* doctrine must lead to Christian lives. Evangelicals have failed society both where we are *weak* and where we are *strong*.

We are weak in dealing with the structures and ills of society—with government, education, race, poverty, and the like. This is not a new thing for Christians. The early church, for example, did nothing about slavery. And evangelicals, like the early Christians, have often been a despised minority without much real hope of changing the structures of society. But where evangelicals have been strong—as for example in the American South—they have been as slow to deal with prejudice as the ancient church was to deal with slavery—and even more reluctant. There is no other word for this lethargy in obedience than *sin*. It is ultimately probably less serious than some sins committed by other alleged or actual Christians, but that cannot conceal the fact of its wrongness. This weakness on our part is a guilty weakness. It places us in a difficult position. The pressure by apostate elements within the organization of many churches to turn them into instruments of social revolution must be resisted—but it must not be resisted by turning our back on social problems. Simply to reject every form of social involvement because there is pressure upon us to engage in the wrong forms would be like giving up marriage because there are inducements to adultery. Evangelicals must not dance to the tune of non-Christian social revolutionaries. We have clearly said that this profanes the Gospel. But we must learn to write our own music: a program of social action in harmony with God's Word and with the ring of honesty to those it is supposed to help. We must cultivate anew a Christian social conscience. This too is part of the biblical message. Emphasis on individual salvation is necessary if the church is to exist. But society is also involved in God's plan. Therefore conservative Christians must be willing to take its structures seriously. But—if it is true that Christian faith makes us new creatures and gives us a radically different standpoint—it stands to reason that Christians must bring something unique to the task of reshaping social structures. They cannot merely parrot liberal, much less Marxist, reformers. Not to be concerned with structures, where evangelicals feel weak and insecure, is to fail our fellow men. That alone is bad enough, but we also fail them where we are *strong*, or should be: in the area of the transmission of moral values.

The evangelical Christian has often come close to exemplifying what God promised in Jeremiah 31:33, namely, that he would write his law in human hearts. Like a certain kind of pious Jew, the ideal evangelical Christian has acted in obedience to the law written in his heart, and not by compulsion from outside. (We should note that this is *not* a subjective, individualistic law in Jeremiah 31:33. The prophet is referring to the Law of the Old Testament, the law already written down. What is individualistic about this promise of a new covenant is the inward, personal comprehension and appropriation of God's unchanging law.) This characteristic of the pious, committed orthodox Christian has been noted by many sociological studies, which describe such a man as inner-directed. In our contemporary society we are often encouraged to look upon this as a kind of weakness or even mental illness, so that the "true believer" easily becomes an "authoritarian personality" in the eyes of the critic, because his law is written in his heart and therefore he does not sway with every wind of fashion. Whatever success this widespread denigration of the man who holds tenaciously to his principles may have among the uncommitted, today it is more evident than it ever was before what a tremendous strength a clearly-understood and firmly-believed Christian moral code gives to a man. This strength is something needed by society itself, not just by individual Christians. A great failure of Christians in our generation has been that they have kept their moral strength to themselves.

We are all familiar with the stereotyped figure of the blue-nosed Puritan who always functions as a wet blanket, dampening spirits, repressing fun, replacing gaiety with solemnity. Of course such Puritans exist, and they can be disagreeable. But today we live in a society where *all* moral influences are being effectively banished or neutralized. Nothing could illustrate the chaotic crisis of a pretended absolute freedom better than the crimes of violence which produced what *Newsweek* called a "crisis in hippiedom." When there were enough active, inner-directed people around who were willing to speak out for their moral convictions, such crises did not arise. The only practical alternatives today are either a return to the active expression by Christians of their moral convictions to the non- and post-Christian society, or else a progressive chaos which will eventually call forth a new tyranny for the sake of order.

Convinced Christians have all too often deprived their fellow-citizens of a necessary, vital help by keeping their moral convictions to themselves. "I have my principles," they would say, refusing to participate in an immoral course of action, but allowing the society of non-Christians and merely nominal Christians to go its merry, suicidal way. This course of action is easier than appearing to be a Puritan, an authoritarian, or a "true believer," but it is a violation of God's sovereign will. The moral law of God is for the welfare and happiness of all men, and is beneficial for all men, not merely for Christians. If Christians have the welfare of their fellow-men at stake, they *must* stand up for legislation in accordance with Christian moral standards. If the other members of society cannot be persuaded, if they insist on purging every possible remnant of biblical morality from their civil laws, then the Christian may withdraw and say, "I have my principles." But even *then* he cannot fail to demonstrate clearly, by *words* as well as by actions, that God's moral law is good and worthy of obedience, for all men and not merely for Christians. He must *communicate the content* of God's law, not merely appear to follow his own code.

The liberal church is committing a terrible sin in attempting to make itself more attractive to modern man by abandoning the moral principles to which theological liberals of a previous generation still largely adhered. Evangelicals usually do not give the principles up, but often feel it better to keep quiet about them, lest prospective converts be frightened. "After they've signed up there will be time enough to spring the hard bits on them." That seems to be the motto. Quite apart from the fact that this violates God's law, in a sick society moral health is attractive to many people. It is these people whom Christians cheat if they do not bear audible testimony to the Law of God as well as to the Gospel.

The social failure of evangelical Protestantism is something we must confess with shame—not that others may not have been worse, but that God expects his church to be better. We must confess this failure and seek to remedy it in the area of social responsibility, to meet men's physical needs, and also in the area of moral exhortation and persuasion, to meet men's moral need for a law that is in harmony with the truth of the universe.

2. An Evangelical Profession

The evangelical must confess, to his shame, having missed the mark by an inadequate witness to the love and sovereignty of God in the social sphere. In the area of doctrine, he has been less reticent. But there too he must be alert, so as not to be pushed into a defensive posture: "Christian doctrine? That's only for committed Christians." Christian doctrine, to the extent that it is soundly built on God's self-revelation, is the truth of the universe. It is not just for the Christian, any more than the sun is just for the Christian. Man is made in the image of God—every man. Every man has need of a framework which he can accept as true to give meaning to his life.

Philosophy today is a junk-yard of rejected systems. Many formerly attractive possibilities have been demolished, whether by scientific progress as in the case of philosophical materialism, by history as in the case of faith in progress, or by being tried as in the case of Marxism. Orthodox Christianity cannot be destroyed by true science, for it is based on the self-disclosure of the God who makes science possible. Scientific progress in recent years has tended more to destroy objections to Christianity and to strengthen the case for the historic faith. History will not destroy Christianity, for it puts its final hope in God's decisive intervention with the return of Jesus Christ, not in human progress. Therefore it cannot be threatened by human failures. And being tried does not destroy its credibility, as has been the case with Marxism, but it confirms it. "O taste and see," says the Psalmist, "that the Lord is good. Happy is the man who takes refuge in Him!" (34:8). The Christian faith is not afraid of the honest experiment of obedience. If God is real, he *can* give happiness to the man who takes refuge in him. Obedience is not proved in a day, nor is Christian faith established by a single fanciful brush with Christian commitment. We must be careful of giving the impression that we mean, "Try it for a day." Or for a week, or a month or a year. The experiment of obedience must be genuine, and without safety-valves and mental reservations which would render it a deception. But God, unlike modern theologians, does not demand blind obedience to I know not what. The message of the Bible stands or falls with the truth of the Psalmist's song of praise. "Those who seek the Lord lack no good thing" (34:10).

We must be careful to understand what is being said in Psalm 34, and in the many other similar promises. They are not the simple *Do ut des* formula of natural religion: "I give, that You may give." The Psalmist spoke out of the context of a life in which he had known sin, suffering, and treachery. The Psalm's heading says that David composed it during his exile, when he feigned insanity in the court of Abimelech. These affirmations must be taken in the light of a whole life, and in recognition that God rules beyond the grave as well. Yet they *must* authenticate themselves, or the Gospel is false and unworthy of belief.

Arthur Koestler and other disillusioned ex-Communists wrote *The God That Failed* to tell the story of their disenchantment. There are many ex-Christians too who have written such books, and we cannot pretend that they do not exist. But when we ask the question concerning the God of the Christians, "Does he fail?" we receive a million-fold answer from twenty centuries of history, and from the present. Saints, apostles, prophets, martyrs, all answer, "No!" The Bible's teachings work in individual lives. Of this we can be certain. And they also represent the truth of the universe. They give us authoritative knowledge of the God who really is there, who created the universe—the God of power. And they tell us that he is also the God of love, and that in faith in his Son, who became one of us, we can call him Father. And all this is not philosophy or speculation, not legend or allegory. It is truth, and it will stand investigation. It is worthy of our belief and allegiance, of our commitment and trust. It is something we can tell to the oppressed and downtrodden, and can hurl in the teeth of the oppressor. We have no need, we have no right to be ashamed of the Gospel, for it is the power of God.